PAINTINGS
of the BRITISH
SOCIAL SCENE
from Hogarth to Sickert

PAINTINGS

of the BRITISH SOCIAL SCENE

from Hogarth to Sickert

E. D. H. Johnson

WEIDENFELD AND NICOLSON

LONDON

Photographic Acknowledgments

Bridgeman Art Library figs 8, 35, 143, 192,
194, 197
A.C. Cooper figs 13, 66, 135, 138
Courtauld Institute of Art figs 22, 146, 203
Fine Art Society Ltd figs 206, 212
Christopher Hurst fig. 69
Paul Mellon Centre for Studies in British Art
figs 7, 32, 33, 37, 38, 44, 45, 65, 136, 164, 173
National Gallery of Scotland figs 93, 101
National Portrait Gallery fig. 32
Otto E. Nelson fig. 169
Royal Academy of Arts figs 116, 158
Sotheby's fig. 207
Rodney Wright-Watson fig. 201

Frontispiece: Joseph Wright, *A Blacksmith's Shop*, 1771
Front endpaper: Johan Zoffany, *John, 3rd Duke of Atholl and his Family*, 1765–7
Back endpaper: Sir Hubert von Herkomer, *Hard Times*, 1885

The Franklin Jasper Walls Lectures

Franklin Jasper Walls, who died in 1963, bequeathed his residuary estate to The Pierpont Morgan Library to establish a lecture series in the fine arts, iconography, and archaeology, with the provision that the lectures be ultimately published in book form.

Throughout his life, Mr Walls was interested in the fine arts and in the study of art history. When the Association of Fellows of The Pierpont Morgan Library was organized in 1949, he became one of the founding members. He was particularly concerned with the Library's lecture program, and served on the Association's Lecture Committee. Without ever revealing his testamentary plans, he followed with keen attention the design and construction of the Library's new Lecture Hall, completed a few months before his death.

Professor Johnson's lectures, here printed in revised and expanded form, are the eighth series of the Franklin Jasper Walls Lectures to be published.

CONTENTS

PREFACE

THE SUBSTANCE OF THIS VOLUME was first presented in the autumn of 1979 at The Pierpont Morgan Library as the tenth in the series of Franklin Jasper Walls Lectures. My gratitude to the Library, and especially to its Director, Charles Ryskamp, is twofold, not only for the initial invitation to address my subject through oral delivery to an audience, but also for the continuing very generous support which has enabled me to recast these talks into book form with accompanying illustrations.

I am happy, as well, to acknowledge grants from the National Endowment for the Humanities in 1973–4 and from the Guggenheim Foundation in 1977–8, which made possible prolonged periods of research in museums and art galleries throughout the United Kingdom. In all of these places I met with an unfailingly kind reception, I would like in particular to express thanks to John Sunderland, Librarian of the Witt Library of the Courtauld Institute of Art, and to Brian Allen, Assistant Director and Librarian of the Paul Mellon Centre for Studies in British Art, for placing at my disposal the photographic archives over which they preside. The library of the Victoria and Albert Museum was equally responsive to my requests for rare exhibition and sales catalogues.

The two centres for British art historical studies in the United States are the Henry E. Huntington Library and Art Gallery in San Marino, California, and the Yale Center for British Art in New Haven, Connecticut. It is a pleasure to record my thanks to Dr Robert R. Wark, Curator of Art Collections in the former, and to Malcolm Cormack, Curator of Paintings in the latter, for their guidance in exploring the riches of their respective collections. Extensive examination of primary source material for this book and most of its writing were carried on in the splendid Marquand Art Library of Princeton University; and special thanks are due to Mary Schmidt, its librarian, and her staff for their constant readiness, indeed eagerness, to answer my calls for assistance.

Anyone undertaking to write about British painting must take into grateful account those pioneering works which have in recent years done so much to promote a more just appreciation of the accomplishments of this school. The list of distinguished scholars whose contributions to the study of its various aspects have influenced in their formative stage my own ideas about subject-painting includes the following: Frederick Antal, Mary Bennett, Joseph Burke, Ralph Edwards, Judy Egerton, Dennis Farr, William Gaunt, E. H. Gombrich, Lawrence Gowing, John Hayes, John Ingamells, Jeremy Maas, Sir Oliver Millar, Benedict Nicolson, Richard Ormond, Ronald Paulson, David Piper, Mario Praz, Robert Raines, Graham Reynolds, Sacheverell Sitwell, Denys Sutton, Basil Taylor, Sir Ellis Waterhouse, Mary Webster and Edgar Wind.

Robert L. Patten and Peyton Skipwith read my manuscript in its entirety at a period prior to its completion, with suggestions for its improvement which I have been glad to heed. It is impossible to list all of the friends and acquaintances with whom I have discussed my ideas over the two decades during which the work has been in progress; but, in addition to many of the names cited above, I recall the encouragement I have derived from the critical responses of the following: Alisdair A. Auld, Sir Ivor Batchelor, the late Sir Arthur and Lady Elton, Henry Ford, Catherine Gordon, Richard Green, Francis Greenacre, Simon Houfe, Lionel Lambourne, George Landow, Lady Mander, Hamish Miles, the late J. N. Naimaster, Ronald Parkinson, David Robertson, David Rodgers, Sir David and Lady Scott, Dudley Snelgrove, Julian Spalding, Julian Treuherz and Rosemary Treble.

The kind sponsorship of my work by Eugène Braun-Munk inaugurated a happy relationship with its publishers. To the book's design Simon Bell has brought a rare combination of originality and insight into the author's intentions. Barbara Mellor has filled the demanding role of editor in a most exemplary manner; no problem has proved so vexing as to ruffle her equanimity and good judgement. For all of the welcome help which I have thus received my gratitude is deep and lasting.

A final word of appreciation goes to Mrs Jennifer Martin for her expeditious and accurate preparation of the final typescript from my manuscript.

E. D. H. Johnson

LIST OF ILLUSTRATIONS

and [?] his Sister Frances, 1769
$39\frac{3}{8} \times 49\frac{3}{4}$ in (100.2 × 126.6 cm) National Gallery of Art, Washington; Gift of Mrs Charles S. Carstairs in memory of her husband
42 George Stubbs, *John and Sophia Musters riding out at Colwick Hall*, 1777
$38 \times 50\frac{1}{2}$ in (96.5 × 128 cm) Private Collection
43 Francis Wheatley, *George and Mary Browne with their Five Elder Children*, *c*1779
$27\frac{3}{4} \times 35$ in (70.5 × 89 cm) Yale Center for British Art, New Haven
44 Joseph Wright, *Mr and Mrs Thomas Coltman*, *c*1771–2
50 × 40 in (127 × 101.5 cm) Derby Art Gallery
45 Joseph Wright, *The Rev. d'Ewes Coke, his Wife Hannah and Daniel Parker Coke*, MP, *c*1780–2
60 × 70 in (152.4 × 177.8 cm) Derby Art Gallery
46 Joseph Wright, *A Philosopher giving a Lecture on the Orrery*, *c*1764–6
58 × 80 in (147.3 × 203.2 cm) Derby Art Gallery
47 Joseph Wright, *An Experiment on a Bird in the Air Pump*, *c*1767–8
72 × 96 in (182.9 × 243.8 cm) Tate Gallery, London
48 Francis Hayman, *The Milkmaid's Garland, or the Humours of May Day*, *c*1740
$54\frac{1}{2} \times 94\frac{1}{2}$ in (138.4 × 240 cm) By courtesy of the Board of Trustees of the Victoria and Albert Museum, London
49 Francis Wheatley, *Four Times of the Day: Morning*, 1799
$17\frac{1}{2} \times 21\frac{1}{2}$ in (44.5 × 54.5 cm) Yale Center for British Art, New Haven
50 Francis Wheatley, *Four Times of the Day: Noon*, 1799
$17\frac{1}{2} \times 21\frac{1}{2}$ in (44.5 × 54.5 cm) Yale Center for British Art, New Haven
51 Francis Wheatley, *Four Times of the Day: Evening*, 1799
$17\frac{1}{2} \times 21\frac{1}{2}$ in (44.5 × 54.5 cm) Yale Center for British Art, New Haven
52 Francis Wheatley, *Four Times of the Day: Night*, 1799
$17\frac{1}{2} \times 21\frac{1}{2}$ in (44.5 × 54.5 cm) Yale Center for British Art, New Haven
53 Francis Wheatley, *Scene from a Camp with an Officer buying Chickens (The Encampment at Brighton)*, 1788
40 × 50 in (101.5 × 127 cm) The Royal Pavilion, Art Gallery and Museums, Brighton
54 Francis Wheatley, *Scene from a Camp with an Officer buying Ribbons (The Departure from Brighton)*, 1788
40 × 50 in (101.5 × 127 cm) Yale Center for British Art, New Haven
55 George Morland, *St James's Park*, *c*1790
16 × 19 in (40.5 × 48.3 cm) Paul Mellon Collection, Upperville, Virginia
56 George Morland, *The Tea Garden*, *c*1790
$16 \times 19\frac{7}{8}$ in (40.5 × 50 cm) Tate Gallery, London
57 George Morland, *The Miseries of Idleness*, 1790
$12\frac{1}{4} \times 14\frac{1}{2}$ in (31.2 × 36.9 cm) National Gallery of Scotland, Edinburgh
58 George Morland, *The Comforts of Industry*, 1790
$12\frac{1}{4} \times 14\frac{1}{2}$ in (31.2 × 36.9 cm) National Gallery of Scotland, Edinburgh
59 Edward Penny, *The Profligate punished by Neglect and Contempt*, 1774
$48\frac{1}{2} \times 39$ in (123 × 99 cm) Yale Center for British Art, New Haven
60 Edward Penny, *The Virtuous comforted by Sympathy and Attention*, 1774
$48\frac{1}{2} \times 39$ in (123 × 99 cm) Yale Center for British Art, New Haven
61 William Redmore Bigg, *The Rapacious Steward, or the Unfortunate Tenant*, 1801
$40\frac{1}{2} \times 50\frac{1}{8}$ in (102.2 × 127.3 cm) Yale Center for British Art, New Haven
62 William Redmore Bigg, *The Benevolent Heir, or the Tenant restored to his Family*, 1797
$40\frac{1}{2} \times 50\frac{1}{4}$ in (102.2 × 127.6 cm) Yale Center for British Art, New Haven
63 William Ward, *The Sailor's Orphans, or the Young Ladies' Subscription*, mezzotint after painting by W. R. Bigg, 1799
$19 \times 23\frac{1}{2}$ in (48.5 × 60.3 cm) Fitzwilliam Museum, Cambridge
64 Edward Penny, *The Marquess of Granby aiding a Sick Soldier*, 1765
$17 \times 22\frac{1}{2}$ in (43 × 57 cm) National Army Museum, London
65 Francis Wheatley, *John Howard visiting and relieving the Miseries of a Prison*, 1787
41 × 51 in (104.1 × 129.5 cm) Private Collection
66 George Morland, *A Visit to the Child at Nurse*, *c*1788
$25\frac{1}{4} \times 29\frac{3}{4}$ in (64.1 × 75.3 cm) Courtesy of Christie's
67 George Morland, *A Visit to the Boarding School*, *c*1789
$25\frac{1}{4} \times 29\frac{3}{4}$ in (64.1 × 75.3 cm) By permission of the Trustees of the Wallace Collection, London
68 James Ward, *The Rocking Horse*, engraving, 1793
$18 \times 21\frac{7}{8}$ in (45.7 × 55.6 cm) Courtauld Institute of Art, London
69 Philip Mercier, *The Oyster Girl (The Fair Oysterinda)*, *c*1745–50
36 × 28 in (91.5 × 71.1 cm) Private Collection
70 Henry Walton, *Girl plucking a Turkey*, *c*1776
$28\frac{1}{2} \times 24$ in (72 × 61 cm) Tate Gallery, London
71 Francis Wheatley, *The Seller of Primroses*, engraving, 1893
$16\frac{1}{2} \times 13$ in (41.9 × 33 cm) British Museum, London
72 Sir Joshua Reynolds, *The Cottagers*, 1788
95 × 71 in (241.3 × 180.3 cm) Detroit Institute of Arts; Gift of Mrs K. T. Keller
73 George Romney, *The Spinstress*, 1787
68 × 50 in (172.7 × 127 cm) The Greater London Council as Trustees of the Iveagh Bequest, Kenwood
74 Joseph Francis Nollekens, *Two Children playing with a Top and Playing Cards*, 1745
$14\frac{1}{8} \times 12\frac{1}{4}$ in (36 × 21 cm) Yale Center for British Art, New Haven
75 George Morland, *Blind Man's Buff*, 1787–8
$27\frac{1}{2} \times 35\frac{1}{2}$ in (69.8 × 90 cm) Detroit Institute of Arts; Gift of Elizabeth K. McMillan in memory of her sisters Mary Isabella McMillan and Anne McMillan
76 Sir Joshua Reynolds, *Lady Caroline Scott as 'Winter'*, 1777
$56\frac{1}{4} \times 45$ in (141 × 112 cm) From the collection of the Duke of Buccleuch and Queensberry, K.T., at Bowhill, Selkirk, Scotland
77 Joseph Wright, *Sir Brooke Boothby*, 1780–1
$58\frac{1}{4} \times 81\frac{1}{4}$ in (148 × 206.4 cm) Tate Gallery, London
78 Thomas Gainsborough, *Cottage Door with Girl and Pigs*, 1786
$38\frac{3}{4} \times 48\frac{3}{4}$ in (98.4 × 123.8 cm) By courtesy of the Board of Trustees of the Victoria and Albert Museum, London
79 Thomas Gainsborough, *The Cottage Door*, 1780
58 × 47 in (147.3 × 119.4 cm) Henry E. Huntington Art Gallery, San Marino
80 Thomas Gainsborough, *Cottage Girl with Dog and Pitcher*, 1785
$68\frac{1}{2} \times 49$ in (173.9 × 124.4 cm) The Beit Collection, Russborough, Blessington, County Wicklow, Ireland and the Medici Society, London
81 Thomas Gainsborough, *The Woodman*, engraving by P. Simon, 1787
Courtauld Institute of Art, London
82 George Lambert, *A Hilly Landscape with a Cornfield*, 1733
$35\frac{3}{4} \times 72\frac{1}{2}$ in (91 × 184 cm) Tate Gallery, London
83 Edward Haytley, *An Extensive View from the Terraces of Sandleford Priory*, 1744
$35\frac{1}{4} \times 60$ in (89.5 × 152 cm) Leger Galleries Ltd, London
84 George Stubbs, *Labourers: Lord Torrington's Bricklayers at Southill 1767*, 1767
24 × 42 in (61 × 106.6 cm) Philadelphia Museum of Art: John H. McFadden Collection
85 George Stubbs, *Reapers*, 1784
$35\frac{1}{4} \times 53\frac{1}{4}$ in (89.5 × 135.3 cm) Tate Gallery, London
86 George Stubbs, *Haymakers*, 1785
$35\frac{1}{4} \times 53\frac{1}{4}$ in (89.5 × 135.3 cm) Tate Gallery, London
87 Joseph Wright, *A Blacksmith's Shop*, 1771
$50\frac{1}{2} \times 41$ in (128.25 × 104 cm) Yale Center for British Art, New Haven
88 Samuel Scott, *A Quay on the Thames at London*, *c*1756
$62\frac{7}{8} \times 53\frac{1}{4}$ in (159.7 × 135.2 cm) By courtesy of the Board of Trustees of the Victoria and Albert Museum, London
89 George Morland, *Inside of a Stable*, 1791
$58\frac{1}{2} \times 80\frac{1}{4}$ in (148.6 × 203.8 cm) Tate Gallery, London
90 George Morland, *Morning: Higglers preparing for Market*, 1791
$27\frac{1}{2} \times 35\frac{1}{2}$ in (64.8 × 90.2 cm) Tate Gallery, London
91 George Morland, *Door of a Village Inn*, 1793
$41\frac{1}{8} \times 49\frac{3}{4}$ in (104.4 × 126.4 cm) Tate Gallery, London
92 George Morland, *The Reckoning* (undated)
29 × 39 in (73.7 × 99 cm) By courtesy of the Board of Trustees of the Victoria and Albert Museum, London
93 David Allan, *The Penny Wedding*, watercolour, 1795
$13 \times 17\frac{3}{8}$ in (33 × 44.1 cm) Private Collection.
94 Sir David Wilkie, *Pitlessie Fair*, 1804
23 × 42 in (58.5 × 106.7 cm) National Gallery of Scotland, Edinburgh
95 Sir David Wilkie, *The Blind Fiddler*, 1806
$22\frac{3}{4} \times 31\frac{1}{4}$ in (57.8 × 79.4 cm) Tate Gallery, London
96 Sir David Wilkie, *The Letter of Introduction*, 1813
$24 \times 19\frac{3}{4}$ in (61 × 50.2 cm) National Gallery of Scotland, Edinburgh
97 Gerard Terborch, *Officer writing a Letter (The Despatch)* 1658–9

INTRODUCTION

IN AUGUST 1748, at the time of the armistice ending the War of the Austrian Succession, William Hogarth visited France in company with artist friends, including Francis Hayman. On his return journey he was arrested at Calais as a suspected spy while he was engaged in sketching the drawbridge and gate of the ancient English fortifications. His sketchbook established his innocence; but the Governor remanded him to his lodgings under orders to take passage for England on the first available boat. The artist's sense of outrage over this treatment, inflaming pre-existent francophobia, was voiced as follows in his *Autobiographical Notes*:

> The first time any one goes from hence to france by way of Calais he cannot avoid being struck by the Extreem different face things appear with at so little a distance as from Dover a farcical pomp of war, parade of riligion and Bustle with little very little bussiness in short poverty slavery and Insolence (with an affectation of politeness) give even here the first specimen of the whole country ...

Soon after arriving home Hogarth began a painting entitled *O the Roast Beef of Old England, or The Gate of Calais (1748, fig. 1)*, its name taken from a song by the novelist, Henry Fielding, contrasting the hearty fare enjoyed by Englishmen to the scanty rations of their neighbours across the Channel. The succulent sirloin of beef at the centre of the picture, addressed to Madame Grandsire, proprietress of a hostelry catering to travelling Britishers, is thus emblematic of their country's prosperity and well-being. It draws the gluttonous looks of two ragged French soldiers holding bowls of *soupe maigre*, as well as of a friar, the only well-fed figure in the composition, who appears to be blessing the meat in order to suck the fat from his fingers. Supporting details are marshalled further to discredit French ways of life. The disgruntled individual in the right-hand corner beside his onion and oatcake is a Scottish Highlander, a veteran of Bonnie Prince Charlie's rebellion of 1745, who has fled to France for refuge and become a soldier in the French army, as the white cockade in his hat denotes. The group of old crones on the other side, displaying the crosses of their religious faith, includes a pair of farm women and a fishwife. The latter points derisively at the face of a large skate, unaware that its grotesque expression is duplicated in the countenances of the onlookers. Behind them another soldier in a tattered uniform (his trousers are held up by a wooden skewer) seems to dangle puppet-like from the chain of the drawbridge. The gate in the background, its portal like a gaping mouth with serrated teeth, presents a threatening aspect to all who would pass through. It frames a religious procession, with priests bearing the Host, which is passing beneath a tavern sign showing a dove in satirical reference to the Holy Spirit. And the artist has introduced himself at the far left, sketching the whole spectacle, his head menaced by a pike and an arresting hand laid on his shoulder.

Hogarth's self-portrait in this painting might equally well be a representation of John Bull, that effigy of quintessential Englishness invented earlier in the century by John Arbuthnot; for the picture embodies a full measure of the insular prejudices which bolstered his country's nationalist pride. More than this, however, through scenes of this sort the artist was inaugurating a native tradition of genre painting which retained its popularity for nearly two centuries and which is without parallel in other countries. Just as the English novel sprang full-blown from the genius of his friend, Henry Fielding, so Hogarth gave his subject-pictures most of the characteristics which were henceforth to distinguish the mode. Indeed, the novel of manners and paintings of the contemporary social scene have much in common: richness of narrative texture, full-blooded characterization and a sharp eye for local detail.

Like prose fiction again, genre painting is by its very nature a plebeian form of art. Its emergence in England accompanied the rise of the commercial middle class to a dominant position in the social hierarchy. In Protestant Britain, with its parliamentary government, the kind of official history painting in the grand style sponsored by the Catholic monarchies of Continental Europe never took root; and while the reins of patronage remained in the hands of the aristocracy throughout the eighteenth century, their support of living painters was largely confined to the commissioning of family portraits. The spread of the print trade, however, was nurturing a demand for more popular forms of artistic expression. The middle-class audience to which it was primarily addressed was similar in many respects to that which had come into being in the Netherlands during the preceding century. And as was the case with their predecessors among the Dutch and Flemish burghers of that time, eighteenth-century British merchants looked to art not for exalted subjects inspiring noble thoughts and a spirit of emulation, but rather for truthful reflections of their earthbound values and ways of life.

Hogarth, who always distrusted the fickle favours of his aristocratic clientele, was the first English painter deliberately to court this new public, not only in his paintings, but through the practice he fathered of making them widely available in engraved versions. It was not, however, until the early years of the nineteenth century that the home-grown school of painting fostered by him gained sufficient standing to lead to the formation of collections devoted primarily to British art. And another fifty years were to pass before the Exposition Universelle des Beaux-Arts of 1855 in Paris accorded international recognition to the existence of such a school. Only works by living artists were shown in this exhibition; and in the British section it was the preponderance of domestic genre, wholly devoid of foreign influence, which excited the attention of critics. As Théophile Gautier wrote: 'Les caractères distinctifs de

Fig. 1
William Hogarth
O the Roast Beef of Old England, or The Gate of Calais (with details)
1748

l'Angleterre sont une originalité franche, une forte saveur locale; elle ne doit rien aux autres écoles.'

The continuity of an artistic tradition is in large part dependent on its responsiveness to the culture of which it is a product. To this principle the unfolding pageant of contemporary life revealed in the work of generation after generation of British genre painters bears witness. The sense imparted by their work of providing access to the worlds which they so intimately reflect resulted in large part from two factors. British artists, unlike their European contemporaries, were as a general rule trained at home; and no entrenched system of state and church patronage intervened between them and the general public, with whose tastes they were so closely attuned. But to see these pictures solely in the perspective of social history, however informative and fascinating that may be, is to deny their claim to be considered also on their artistic merits and to blur the grounds for critical discrimination. For there is no necessary correlation between the documentary interest of a painting and its quality as a work of art. Indeed, the very literalness of the lesser painter's approach to his subject is likely to result in a closer semblance of reality than a more imaginative handling of the same material. It should come as no surprise that the rise of photography spelled the demise of genre painting.

No artistic tradition is self-sustaining. Its vitality, on which of course its survival is also contingent, results from a process of constant renewal through the agency of new talent. It must be able to attract the best efforts of original artists, steeped, to be sure, in a sense of their artistic heritage, but alert as well to all the forces making for change in society.

The uniqueness of British painting from the outset resided in its extreme versatility, its capacity to appropriate to its own ends the expressive potential of other styles. Thus, in such a picture as *The March to Finchley (fig. 13)* Hogarth converted history painting, shorn of its heroic trappings, into a humorous commentary on human fallibility in times of crisis. By the same token, formal portraiture deriving from Van Dyck became domesticated by such artists as Devis and Zoffany into the conversation piece, that matchlessly urbane depiction of home life among the privileged classes. And Gainsborough and Stubbs, among others, replaced the Arcadian visions of Claude and Poussin with a pastoralism rooted deep in British soil. By the opening of the nineteenth century genre had become so firmly established as the representative mode of British painting that there was no longer any need to draw on borrowed conventions. Painters were to find in the protean nature of the style a medium supremely adaptable to their continuing exploration of fresh fields of subject-matter, in furtherance of the artist's inherited role as chronicler of his times.

This study thus proposes two goals in tracing the central theme of reportage in British art. In its historical aspect it records the rise and progress of a school of painting devoted with uniform consistency to portrayals of the contemporary social scene. Secondly, in a field where there has been little effort to develop standards of judgement, it undertakes to suggest criteria for assessing the contributions of those artists who have been largely responsible for maintaining the ascendancy of this school, while at the same time providing its most lasting achievements.

Chapter One

HOGARTH AND GEORGIAN LONDON

IN EARLY EIGHTEENTH-CENTURY ENGLAND a school of painting mirroring contemporary life emerged which was the direct outgrowth of the political settlement of 1689 and the consequent rise of the commercial middle class to a dominant role in society. Under the Stuart dynasty canons of artistic taste had remained rigidly subservient to the prescriptions of historical painting in the grand manner, endorsed in theory and practice in post-Renaissance Italy and France. So pure an example of genre painting as the village gathering portrayed in *The Tichborne Dole* (*c*1670) by the Flemish Gillis van Tilborch is virtually unique in the age.[1] Such slight reflections of daily life as occur in English paintings of the seventeenth century creep casually into works concerned with other subject-matter. Thus, topographical artists often included figures engaged in various activities to animate their architectural compositions, as in the London scenes of Wenceslas Hollar (1607–77), or in portraits of country houses and their environs by Jan Siberechts (1627–*c*1700). In similar ways the sporting painters Jan Wyck (1652–?1700) and Peter Tillemans (1684–1734) individualized their scenes with passages of local colour. Towards the end of the century a number of Netherlandish artists, settling in England for longer or shorter periods, sought to render local scenes in the manner of their native genre traditions. Of these the most notable was Egbert van Heemskerk (1634/5–1704), best represented by *An Oxford Election* (1687) and by his satirical depictions of Quaker meetings. His reputation is thus recorded by the historian of the contemporary art world, George Vertue: 'He became very eminent for Painting Drolls after the Manner of Brower. His Gross & Comical Genius succeeded for a long while among us, In most of his Conversations, as he calld them, you may see the Picture, & read the Manners of the Man at the same time . . . His Drunken-Drolls, his Wakes, his Quakers-Meetings & some lewd Pices have been in vogue among waggish Collectors, & the lower Rank of Virtuosi.' Among other more immediate precursors of Hogarth may be cited the elder Marcellus Laroon (?1653–1702) whose uncompromisingly realistic *The Cryes of the City of London Drawne after the Life* was published in numerous editions from 1687, and Pieter Angillis (1685–1734), of French extraction though Flemish-trained, who after his arrival in 1712 painted a number of closely observed views of Covent Garden market.

It cannot be said, however, that any of these foreign-born artists exercised any significant influence over the development of genre painting in England. Hogarth knew their work, of course, and, through engravings, that of their greater countrymen, Brouwer, Ostade, Steen, Teniers. But the moral rectitude which fuelled his satiric impulse was so deeply ingrained that he could never condone the bawdy vulgarity of Dutch pictures of low life; and he would doubtless have agreed with Horace Walpole's dismissal of them as 'drudging Mimicks of Nature's most uncomely coarsenesses . . .'

Born in 1697, Hogarth was from his earliest years caught up by the exuberant vitality and boundless pride in the fact of being English that characterized the national temper of mind in the early decades of the eighteenth century. The prevailing spirit of optimism had its sources in the newly gained political stability provided by parliamentary rule, in the economic well-being resulting from expanding trade, and in the ethical principles of Puritanism supporting freedom of conscience and individual enterprise. The intellectual ferment of the times gave birth to a burst of cultural activity, primarily literary, in which humanitarian zeal was tempered by an unshakable faith in man's rational faculties. The great age of Augustan writing was not without its antecedents, but there were no models to inspire a similar flowering in painting. Hogarth's supreme achievement was to create, virtually unaided, for the readers of the satires of Pope and Swift, the familiar essays of Addison and Steele, the novels of Defoe and Fielding, and the plays of Gay and Lillo, a body of painting which would match in graphic terms the appeal of their work.

Hogarth's youthful apprenticeship to an engraver on silver plate and subsequent brief exposure to the academic routine of the St Martin's Lane Academy inspired an enduring antipathy to the accepted copy-book procedures of artistic training. Accustomed from his earliest years to store up in memory his daily impressions of life about him, he would write in his *Autobiographical Notes*: 'by this Idle way of proceeding I grew so profane as to admire Nature beyond Pictures . . .'[2] For Hogarth 'Nature' or 'Life' could only mean the teeming spectacle of the great metropolis at the heart of which he had been born, in Bartholomew Close, and of which he has left a record unparalleled in vitality, variety and veracity.

No aspect of the life of Georgian London escaped the artist's inquiring eye. His *oeuvre* captures in all their riotous excess the ways of its inhabitants – their eating, drinking, brawling, gaming, whoring, haggling, thieving, play-going, church-going, electioneering. We are conducted from a whore's miserable crib in Drury Lane to the garret which shelters a destitute poet and his family; from the religious hysteria of the Methodist Chapel to the brutal mêlée of the cockpit; from a mad scene in Bedlam Hospital to a hanging at Tyburn. On first view Hogarth's canvases may seem unduly crowded with a bewildering array of discrepant incidents. Closer examination reveals how precisely calculated was the artist's choice of details and how cunningly they are disposed to deliver the overall message of the scene he is depicting. So attentive was he to topographical accuracy that it is nearly always possible to determine the exact place in which an episode occurs, while he also provided, wherever relevant, clues to the dating of occurrences, the time of day, and other matters which have contextual bearing. A brief résumé of the events portrayed in the series entitled *The Four Times of the Day* (1738, *figs 2–5*) will illustrate the rich rewards which the social historian may reap from the artist's scenes of contemporary street-life.

Sequences depicting the times of the day which exhibit a fusion of mythological with genre elements are common in Netherlandish genre painting of the sixteenth and seventeenth centuries. The theme had then been taken over by late Baroque artists for decorative purposes, as, for example, in the ceiling of the ballroom at Wanstead House, painted by William Kent, Hogarth's *bête noire*, in his most flamboyant Italianate style. Hogarth visited Colen Campbell's first neo-Palladian mansion to paint his conversation piece, *An Assembly at Wanstead House* (1729–31), and the setting of the picture gives some indication of what Horace Walpole called 'the ceilings of Kent in his worst'. By the date of Hogarth's sequence, the times of day had become a favourite subject with French rococo painters. Lancret, for example, rendered it as a series of *conversations galantes*, and Boucher used it to trace a day in the life of a woman of fashion. Viewed against this background of conventionalized contemporary treatments of the subject-matter, the originality of Hogarth's fresh and bitingly realistic recreation of the diurnal turbulence of the London streets appears all the more remarkable.[3]

Morning (fig. 2) is set in Covent Garden on a dark, forbidding winter's day. An ageing dame is crossing the snow-covered square on her way to St Paul's Church, built by Inigo Jones, the clock on the pediment of which gives the hour as five minutes to eight. Erect and stiff in her starched finery, she is the very effigy of prudish spinsterhood (Fielding was to take her as the model for Bridget Allworthy in *Tom Jones*). Despite her scanty attire the old maid seems impervious to the cold, in contrast to her page who shiveringly trails behind, prayer-book clutched to his side. In parody of Baroque painting, the composition is built on a number of bold oppositions. Below the portico of St Paul's is Tom King's Coffee House, an infamous den of debauchery, open from midnight to dawn, which Hogarth moved from its actual place across the square for the sake of dramatic effect. Spilling out from the fracas within the tavern, two drunken gallants have accosted a pair of market-girls on whom they thrust their attentions. From her frozen gaze and way of holding her fan, one may infer that the prude's disapproval of this display is not unalloyed with prurient curiosity. On the other side of the picture two school-bound urchins are loitering by a woman who supports on her head a huge basket of produce. Beyond them a crowd has gathered around a vendor whose placard advertises Dr Rock's panacea for venereal disease. He was a notorious quack of the time whose ointment Hogarth also satirized in *The March to Finchley* and *Marriage A-la-Mode*.

In *Noon (fig. 3)* the scene shifts to Hog Lane facing the Church of St Giles-in-the-Fields, on which the clock now reads twelve-thirty. A gutter divides the groups into opposing camps. On one side the congregation is issuing from a chapel which was the gathering place of French Huguenots who inhabited this quarter of London. Their presence gave Hogarth an opportunity to vent his spleen against all things French, which is displayed more venomously in *O the Roast Beef of Old England, or The Gate of Calais (fig. 1)*. The over-dressed couple in front with the even more preposterously got-up boy express through their mannerisms as well as their garb the foppish affectations which for the artist characterized Gallic behaviour, and which he further ridicules in the hideous old women embracing each other at the extreme left. The

facing scene with its unabashed licence comments sardonically on the self-conscious antics of the church-goers. Beneath the sign of the Baptist's Head eating establishment a blackamoor fondles a serving-girl. Just as this pair mocks the posturing couple opposite, so the conceited little prig is played off against the distress of the baker's boy sobbing over his broken plate, and unaware that his loss is the gain of the greedy girl kneeling below. Among other Hogarthian details are the kite dangling from the chapel roof, a satirical glancer at the limpness of faith within, and the dead cat lying in the gutter. The weeping boy gains a certain derisive dignity from the fact that his pose was modelled on a figure in the centre foreground of Poussin's *Rape of the Sabines.*

Evening (fig. 4) takes place late on a sultry summer afternoon, the time indicated by the milking of the cow. The inscription on the building at the left shows that the place is Sadler's Wells, a pleasure resort for London 'cits' in Islington. An artisan's family is wearily trudging homeward after a day's outing. The hen-pecked husband (his blue-stained hands in the second state of the engraving mark him as a dyer) resignedly struggles along under the burden of his youngest child, while the buxom wife carries his hat and gloves. The showiness of her apparel, with a fan depicting *Venus detaining Adonis from the Chase*, hardly accords with her pregnant state until one notices the cow's horns which seem to adorn the husband's brow, mute emblem of cuckoldry. The reversal of sexual roles is duplicated in the two children in the rear, as the girl tries to bully her sobbing brother into surrendering his gingerbread man. As the sign indicates, Sir Hugh Middleton, a seventeenth-century civic benefactor who channelled fresh water into London, has given his name to the inn in the background where holiday-makers, ostensibly seeking to escape the confines of the city, have nevertheless immured themselves in a smoke-filled room. The pastoral landscape stretching away in the background stands in ironic contrast to the human disarray marring its harmony.

Le Sueur's statue of Charles I, erected in 1675, places the events of *Night (fig. 5)* in a brothel-lined street near Charing Cross, lighted by fires of varying origin. The oak leaves that decorate the barber's pole and the hats of two individuals commemorate the anniversary of Charles II's escape after his defeat at the battle of Worcester on 3 September 1651 by hiding in a hollow oak.[4] The drink-sodden man whose bloody head is being cooled by the contents of a chamber-pot, and who carries the Masonic insignia of a carpenter's square about his neck, is supposed to have been Sir Thomas De Veil, a Bow Street magistrate whose public denunciations of drunkenness were at odds with the profligacy of his private life. He is being guided homeward by the porter of his Lodge who has taken charge of his sword to avert further violence. The Salisbury Flying Coach has been overturned, as the horses took fright from a burning link or faggot flung by the boy in the lower left-hand corner, who is preparing another charge. He kneels by an improvised shelter in which some derelicts are sleeping. The open window above shows a drunken barber-surgeon about to combine his two offices of shaving and blood-letting on a reluctant customer. The cups by the window-sill hold blood from previous patients. Down the street a pipe-smoking drayman seems to be watering down a hog's head of beer, while further along a loaded van carries the belongings of a family which has defaulted on rent and is making its getaway under cover of darkness. One notices that this night scene is more luridly illuminated than any of the preceding daylight ones, and that the various episodes suggest a degree of frenzied uproar calculated to banish any hope of sleep for the populace. Although the artist's mordant perception of the irreconcilable oppositions at the heart of all appearances plays over the entire series, there is little hint of moral reproof such as informs his other paintings, patently satiric in purpose. Rather, the ever-diverse spectacle of the London streets in all seasons and at all times is here viewed, unlike such street scenes as *Gin Lane* or *The Four Stages of Cruelty*, with a humorously tolerant eye, alert to the full spectrum of human absurdity.[5]

While the present discussion is primarily concerned with Hogarth's paintings, it should be born in mind that most of these were designed for translation into engravings, through the sale of which he could free himself from the artist's traditional reliance on aristocratic patronage and at the same time address a genuinely popular audience. Furthermore, by his practice of retaining the rights to these prints and advertising their sale through private subscription, he was able to remain independent of the control of printsellers. As a result of these revolutionary procedures Hogarth asserted for British painters a degree of autonomy which they had never before enjoyed. Of his first great success, *A Harlot's Progress* (1731), Vertue wrote, 'he proposing to Engrave in six plates to print at, one guinea each sett. he had daily Subscriptions came in, in fifty or a hundred pounds in a Week – there being no day but persons of fashion and Artists came to see these pictures ...'; and the same writer further states that 'between 14 *or fifteen*' hundred subscriptions had been disposed of before the plates were completed.

The popularity of *A Harlot's Progress* spawned a motley progeny of imitations in prose and verse, as well as ballad-operas and pantomimes; and its scenes were reproduced on all sorts of domestic objects, including cups and saucers, snuff-boxes and box-lids. Incensed by the widespread pirating of the prints, Hogarth originated and successfully guided through Parliament the Engraver's Copyright Act of 1735, which for the first time protected the rights of graphic artists and guaranteed to them the proceeds from the sale of their handiwork. To reap its benefits Hogarth withheld the engravings of his second series, *A Rake's Progress* (1735), until the passage of the bill, which greatly stimulated the traffic in prints in England.

In most cases the engraved versions of Hogarth's pictures adhere quite closely to the canvases from which they derive, but the artist was prepared on occasion to sacrifice the painterly qualities of the originals in the interest of greater explicitness of meaning for the sake of a less sophisticated audience. In some cases this resulted in the contrivance of new details, the most notable example occurring in the fourth scene of *A Rake's Progress*. To make it clear that the rake is being arrested for gambling debts, Hogarth added in the right-hand corner the group of card-playing and dice-throwing street-urchins, as well as the jagged streak of lightning pointing to White's, a gambling establishment at the lower end of St James's Street.

Hogarth was fully aware of the extent to which class distinctions were reflected in the tastes of his public. Thus, for his third series, *Marriage A-la-Mode* (1743–5, *figs 10–12*), which in contrast to its predecessors was designed to present 'a variety of modern occurrences in high-life', he commissioned French engravers to make the plates, conscious that his own hand lacked the delicate skill of the Parisian masters. On the other hand, with two later sequences, *Industry and Idleness* (1747) and *The Four Stages of Cruelty* (1750–1), the artist not only dispensed with preparatory paintings, but coarsened the engraving style to lower the price of the prints to a shilling each, while at the same time adapting their lesson to a lower-class public whose literary fare was chap-books and broadside sheets. Of his humanitarian intent and its matching method in the latter series, he wrote in the *Autobiographical Notes*:

> The four stages of cruelty, were done in hopes of preventing in some degree that cruel treatment of poor Animals which makes the streets of London more disagreeable to the human mind, than any thing what ever. . . . The circumstances of this set . . . were made so obvious . . . that neither great correctness of drawing or fine Engraving were at all necessary but on the contrary would set the price of them . . . out of the reach of those for whome they were cheifly intended.

Through the agency of engravings Hogarth's fame spread across the Channel, making him the first British artist to enjoy a European reputation. Of the reception in France of *A Rake's Progress*, the Abbé Jean-Bernard LeBlanc wrote in his *Letters on the English and French Nations* (1747): 'They have made the graver's fortune who sells them; and the whole nation has been infected by them, as one of the most happy productions of the age. I have not seen a house of note without these moral prints . . .' The concern exhibited by Hogarth that his work be properly understood in foreign countries tells much about his sense of mission. He empowered the Swiss engraver, Jean-André Rouquet, to prepare an explanatory text to accompany the export of his engravings; it appeared under the title *Lettres de Monsieur ** à un de ses Amis à Paris, Pour lui expliquer les Estampes de Monsieur Hogarth* (1746). With regard to this commission Hogarth wrote, 'I was struck with the use such an Explanation in French might be to such abroad as purchased my prints and were unacquainted with our characters and manners.' In providing his own gloss for some of his pictures in the *Autobiographical Notes*, furthermore, the artist showed foresight of his future fame as a social historian. His explanations, he hopes, 'may be Instructive and amusing in future times when the customs manners fasheons Characters and Humours of the present age in this country may possibly be changed or lost to Posterity . . .'

So endlessly fascinating is the documentary aspect of Hogarth's work that writing about the artist tends to be largely descriptive. To limit attention to the subject content of his pictures, however, is to relegate them exclusively to the category of social chronicles and to reduce the artist to the status of an unusually observant recorder of the passing show. Hogarth's greatness is inseparable from the imaginative use which he made of his subjects, from the transforming vision with which he viewed them, and from the array of techniques embodying that vision. The province in painting to which he laid claim was comedy, and he was the first British artist to do so. His well-known late self-portrait (*c*1758) seated before an easel on which he has outlined Thalia, the muse of comedy, crystallizes the role which he had chosen for himself. Like Fielding, who conceived the comic novel in epic terms, Hogarth aspired to elevate the hitherto despised genre of comic realism to the stature of history painting. His purpose is by inference explained as follows in the *Autobiographical Notes*: 'Painters and writers speak and writers never mention, in the historical way of any intermediate species of subjects for painting between the sublime and the grotesque. We will therefore compare subject[s] for painting with those of the stage.' By the 'sublime' Hogarth, of course, meant the so-called Grand Style, hallowed by the authority of the French Academy, and accepted throughout Europe as the proper mode for all painting with serious pretensions to greatness, embodying heroic themes derived from classical antiquity or Scripture.[6] The 'grotesque,' in contrast, may be represented by those portrayals of everyday life of the middling and lower classes in its ignobler aspects which were a staple of Netherlandish genre painting in the seventeenth century. In defining his goals, Hogarth had in mind Fielding's distinction between burlesque, as an inferior form of humour, and true comedy, which he had made in the Preface to *Joseph Andrews*, where he cites the artist's work as exemplifying the latter. Hogarth's own terminology, appearing in the inscriptions to two engravings, *Characters and Caricaturas* (1743) and *The Bench* (1758; he was still making changes in this plate on the day before his death), draws a line of demarcation between *Character*, which renders nature with absolute fidelity, and *Caricatura*, whose effect depends on the distortion of appearances.

Hogarth was essentially a man of his time in his espousal of the pragmatic belief that it is the function of art both to divert and to instruct. 'Subject[s] of most consequence', he wrote, 'are those that most entertain and Improve the mind and are of public utility ...' He was convinced, furthermore, that 'true comedy in painting stands first as it is most capable of all these perfection[s].' For Hogarth incongruity was the wellspring of the comic spirit. Laughter, as he stated in his theoretical treatise, *The Analysis of Beauty*, results from the 'joining of opposite ideas', or, more specifically: 'When improper, or *incompatible* excesses meet, they always excite laughter ...'

The manifestations of the comic spirit to which Hogarth most readily responded from his early years were the various theatrical spectacles which he encountered in his wanderings about London. Of his inclinations in this respect, he wrote, 'I had naturally a good eye shews of all sort gave me uncommon pleasure when an Infant and mimickry common to all children was remarkable in me.' So, it is not surprising that the subjects of his pictures presented themselves to him in dramatic guise. In confessing his tendency to 'compare subject[s] for painting with those of the stage,' he declared: 'my picture was my Stage and men and women my actors who were by Mean[s] of certain Actions and express[ions] to Exhibit a dumb shew.' The sequential form of the progresses and the significant similarities in subject-matter and treatment between them and the contemporary novel have led to the notion that prose fiction was the principal non-artistic influence on the formation of Hogarth's manner; but this association is somewhat misleading. It takes insufficient account of Fielding's early addiction to the drama, a fact attested by the unmistakable 'scenic' quality of the most memorable passages of his novels, reliant as they are on narration through dialogue. By the same token, the epistolary form used by Richardson in *Pamela* and *Clarissa Harlowe* and by Smollett in *Humphry Clinker* stresses the dramatic impact of episodes described immediately after the events by participants in the action. The drama, indeed, invariably provided the analogy resorted to by critics of the age when seeking to define the distinguishing characteristics of Hogarth's painting. Reynolds grudgingly allowed that he 'had invented a new species of dramatick painting'; and, in a eulogy which has never been bettered for sympathetic insight, Horace Walpole wrote:

If catching the manners and follies of an age *living as they rise*, if general satire on vices and ridicules, familiarized by strokes of nature, and heightened by wit, and the

Fig. 6
William Hogarth
The Beggar's Opera, Act III,
Scene XI
1729

Fig. 7
William Hogarth
A Scene from 'The Indian Emperor'
(*or 'The Conquest of Mexico'*)
1731–2

whole animated by proper and just expressions of the passions, be comedy, Hogarth composed comedies as much as Molière: in his *Marriage A-la-Mode* there is even an intrigue carried on throughout the piece. He is more true to character than Congreve; each personage is distinct from the rest, acts in his sphere, and cannot be confounded with any other of the dramatis personae.

Not surprisingly, Hogarth made a number of pictures of theatrical subjects. These included *Falstaff examining his Recruits* (c1728) and *Scene from 'The Tempest'* (c1730–5), the first paintings of actual Shakespearian productions ever undertaken and, as such, the progenitors of an increasingly popular genre in the later years of the eighteenth century. His portrait of *David Garrick in the Character of Richard III* (1745) admirably captures the natural style of acting which that great actor introduced to the English stage. The play which first elicited the artist's full imaginative response, however, was John Gay's comic masterpiece, *The Beggar's Opera (fig. 6)*. This 'Newgate pastoral', as Swift called it, in the form of a burlesque of the popular Italian opera, enjoyed phenomenal success when it opened in 1728, being in Pope's words, 'a piece of satire which hit all tastes and degrees of men, from those of the highest quality to the very rabble.' Hogarth painted six versions (the finest in 1729 for the operetta's producer, John Rich) of the climactic scene in which the mock-hero, the highwayman Macheath, stands trial for his life, while his two mistresses, each of whom thinks she is his wife, intercede for clemency with their respective fathers, the jailer and the thief-taker. The picture is clearly transcribed from an actual performance; and many of the actors and spectators are identifiable. 'Occular demo[n]stration,' Hogarth contended, 'will convince ... sooner than ten thousand Vols ... let figure[s] be consider[ed] as Actors dressd for the sublime genteel comedy or same in high or low life.'

Macheath, arrogantly disdainful of his shackles, holds the centre of the stage, with his two doxies kneeling on either side, Lucy Lockit to the left and Polly Peachum to the right. The composition plays on the manifold ironies implicit in the situation through a two-fold interchange involving not only the tensions between the actors, but also their relations with the aristocratic audience. For Polly's glance, apparently directed at her father, the informer who has apprehended Macheath, reaches beyond him to include the nobleman at the extreme right wearing the star of the Order of the Garter. The part of Polly was played by the comic actress, Lavinia Fenton, who was to become the mistress and later the wife of this grandee, Charles, third Duke of Bolton. The effigy of the satyr leering down at the peer from the wall above underscores Hogarth's theme that the play mirrors life, in which the declared rascals are no worse than their pretended betters; or, in Gay's own cynical comment, 'All professions berogue one another.'

The give-and-take between make-believe and reality is projected with deepening insight in *Scene from 'The Indian Emperor'* (1731–2, *fig. 7*), which depicts in the form of a conversation piece a group of aristocratic children acting out a scene from Dryden's play before a private audience in the home of John Conduitt, Master of the Mint under George I, who produced the play and whose daughter was one of the players. The spectators were equally aristocratic, including three younger members of the royal family seated in an improvised box before the fireplace. By giving them as prominent roles as the actors, the artist created a variety of ironic oppositions between

Fig. 8
William Hogarth
Southwark Fair
1733

the children on stage, who stiffly simulate the behaviour of grown-ups, and an audience made up of adults and children whose responses convey with uninhibited naturalness the differing degrees of their involvement in the performance, from rapt absorption to careless inattention. The scene from the fourth act of the play exactly parallels the situation in Hogarth's picture of *The Beggar's Opera*. The hero Cortez, imprisoned and in irons, stands between Almeria and Cydaria, who are rivals for his love.

The Brueghelesque *Southwark Fair* (1733, *fig. 8*) carries still farther Hogarth's exploitation of the analogies between the stage and life, and the ways in which they may be made to reflect on each other. Southwark Fair took place annually in early September near St George's Church, Southwark, and rivalled the more famous St Barthomolew's Fair in disorderliness, which led to its suppression in 1762. In

Hogarth's treatment the upper part of the composition is given over to show-cloths advertising the different theatrical offerings, a number of which have a common theme, the fall or descent from good fortune to calamity. Thus, the large placard in the centre background gives notice of Elkanah Settle's *The Siege of Troy*. The top part of the advertisement to its immediate left shows the fall of Adam and Eve from the biblical puppet-show, *The Old Creation of the World*, while the lower portion depicts Punch pushing his wife Joan in a wheelbarrow toward the jaws of Hell. On the right, where a lantern announces Theophilus Cibber and William Bullock in *The Fall of Bajazet*, the dramatic metaphor has materialized into unscheduled melodrama with the collapse of the platform, precipitating the actors and with them the viewer's eye into the mêlée which takes up the lower part of the painting.[7] Amidst the bewildering array of episodes, the motif of reversal in fortune keeps recurring. To the left a procurer is enticing a pair of country girls to their ruin; at the right an altercation has

Fig. 9
William Hogarth
Strolling Actresses dressing in a Barn
1738, engraving

broken out between a farmer and a crone who has cozened him in a dice-game; and at the centre a player in Roman garb from the company of the drummer girl is being arrested for debt by bailiffs. To the extreme left a battered professional fighter, sword upraised, waits to knock down any adversary who challenges him.

The subtlest and most enjoyable of all Hogarth's theatrical subjects in which play-acting merges imperceptibly with life and vice versa is *Strolling Actresses dressing in a Barn* (1738, *fig. 9*), which survives only in engraved form, since the original canvas was destroyed by fire in 1874. Horace Walpole thought that, 'For wit and imagination without any other end', this was 'the best of all his works.' As the playbill on the cot at the left proclaims, we are in the presence of a provincial company getting ready to present *The Devil to Pay in Heaven*. The scene is a makeshift dressing-room at the George Inn. This may well be the troupe's last performance, since also on view is a copy of the Licensing Act of 21 June 1737 which made it illegal to stage plays without licence, and, in effect, banned all performances outside the royal theatres in London. On the other hand, the fact that the company consists entirely of women and children may indicate an effort to circumvent this act, which applied only to male actors.

Within its setting of a tumbledown barn Hogarth's composition is a ludicrous parody of Baroque ostentation. If the tawdry finery of the costumes emphasizes by contrast the precarious livelihood of those who don them, the insouciance with which they are worn marks in turn the sham of the corresponding parts. This incommensurateness of the role with the conditions environing it provided the artist with a comic theme on which to embroider brilliantly imaginative variations. Starting from the lower left and moving in a clockwise direction we observe: a mother clad as the Jovian eagle feeding her squalling babe; a girl in the male attire of Ganymede afflicted with a toothache, for the relief of which she accepts a dram of gin proffered by a player dressed as a Siren; Cupid mounted on a ladder reaching for a pair of stockings under the supervision of Apollo with his sun-crown; Flora dressing her hair with a tallow candle and flour-shaker; Diana in undress practising postures by a sacrificial altar on which repose her beer mug and tobacco pipe; a ghostly dame drawing blood from a cat's tail for some supernatural bit of stage business; and, finally, Juno rehearsing her part, while the Goddess of Night darns the stocking on her outstretched leg. Here and there about the scene animals contribute to the puncturing of pretence: chickens roost on props that simulate ocean waves, a monkey relieves himself into an imperial helmet, and kittens frolic with a lyre and the orb of kingship. The onlooker peering through the hole in the roof at the upper right is a voyeuristic device common in Dutch genre painting of the seventeenth century, and a surrogate for the viewer of the painting. He may well be enthralled by what he sees below; the actual performance could not conceivably match the fascination of these back-stage preliminaries, the real-life stuff from which illusion is spun. In presenting his players caught, as it were, between two worlds, the interaction of which makes for high comedy, the artist has at the same time compelled sympathy with the essential humanity of the spectacle. Comic awareness is tempered by the accompanying recognition of all that is admirable in the lives of these bohemians – unquenchable vitality, devotion to each other, love of calling and the toughness to make the best of its vicissitudes. Hogarth's methods of displaying emblematic devices in *Strolling Actresses* might well have been the cue for Reynolds' statement in his *Third Discourse*:

Fig. 10
William Hogarth
*Marriage A-la-Mode: The
Marriage Contract*
1743-5

'. . . it is not the eye, it is the mind, which the painter of genius desires to address' in achieving 'his great design of speaking to the heart.'

The full scope of Hogarth's artistic resources is best displayed in the so-called Moral Progresses to which he first turned in the 1730s on finding portrait painting insufficiently remunerative. According to his own account, he then directed his thoughts 'to a still more new way of proceeding, viz painting and Engraving moder[n] moral Subject[s] a Field unbroke up in any Country or any age.' Although various sources, of which the most likely was the growing vogue for book illustration,[8] have been proposed, there seems no reason not to accept the artist's claim for the originality of these productions. Indeed, as Vertue informs us, the first of the series, *A Harlot's Progress*, had sprung from a single painting:

> he began a small picture of a common harlot, supposd to dwell in drewry lane. just riseing about noon out of bed. and at breakfast. a bunter waiting on her. – this whore's desabillé careless and a pretty Countenance & air. – this thought pleasd many. some advsd him to make another. to it as a pair. which he did. then other thoughts encreas'd, & multiplyd by his fruitfull invention. till he made six. different subjects which he painted so naturally. the thoughts, & strikeing the expressions that it drew every body to see them . . .

Taken together, these progresses provide a comprehensive view of the Georgian social scene. *A Harlot's Progress* surveys the lower, *A Rake's Progress* the middling, and *Marriage A-la-Mode (figs 10–12)* the upper-class levels. Yet, within this hierarchy remarkable fluidity prevails. The one constant is the artist's point of view, based solidly on the middle-class morality of which his painting was an early vindication. For the same vices, subversive of the Protestant ethic of temperance, industry, and charity, haunt all reaches of the social fabric – lechery, drunkenness, gambling, laziness, spendthrift love of display, bad faith and hardness of heart. Of these 'Pictur'd Morals', as David Garrick called them, Fielding declared: 'I almost dare affirm that [they] . . . are calculated more to serve the Cause of Virtue and the Preservation of Mankind than all the *Folios* of Morality which have been ever written . . .'

In considering Hogarth's artistic procedures in his cycles, the theatrical analogy is again helpful. It is its dramatic quality which most clearly sets Hogarth's work apart from seventeenth-century Netherlandish genre, which is almost wholly devoid of the kind of emotional intensity which the English artist generates. The action of each cycle, virtually the artist's own creation, adheres to the classic stage pattern of unmasking; the protagonist is the architect of his own undoing by invoking misfortunes which strip him of his pretences and affectations. Each episode in his downfall is presented through a scene taking place at a pivotal moment, dramatic in itself and to which all that has gone before leads up and from which ensuing events naturally flow. The eight episodes in *A Rake's Progress* trace the inevitability of the stages through which the viewer follows Rakewell's descending path: from foolish exhilaration over coming into his inheritance, to the first flush of vulgar display, to the great scene of debauchery at the Rose Tavern, to arrest for debt, to contrived marriage with a rich old woman, to total ruin in a gambling hell, to pauperdom in Fleet Prison, and finally to confinement under duress as a raving maniac in Bedlam Hospital.

Every scene in the three progresses takes place within the enclosed space of a room, one wall of which is open to the spectator so that he views the action as if through a proscenium arch giving onto the stage where the actors are performing their parts. The sense of observing a stage performance is further sustained by the skill with which Hogarth disposes his characters and the business he contrives for each of them, so that the world of the picture is wholly self-contained. The first picture of *Marriage A-la-Mode (fig. 10)* brilliantly illustrates the artist's directorial finesse. Parents and children form opposing groups, with the merchant's clerk and the earl's lawyer making a third in each case. Even as the two fathers complacently conclude the terms of the marriage settlement, the victims of this mercenary transaction forecast through their behaviour its calamitous outcome. The foppish viscount is far too much taken up with his reflection in the mirror to notice the attention which the lawyer is paying to his bored fiancée, as she carelessly toys with her engagement ring. Her curving back and the slovenly droop of her shoulders duplicate the bourgeois mien of her parent, while the nobleman and his son affect identical poses of languid elegance in their lolling postures with legs spread apart and gesturing hands. By a kind of inversion of the dramatic proprieties, the actor bent on making his performance as lifelike as possible has been replaced by the character from real life who ostentatiously acts out the role in which he has cast himself.

Pictures of the type of Hogarth's moral progresses are called in France *drames muets*; and the artist displayed extraordinary ingenuity in adapting the non-verbal resources of the theatre to his pictorial purposes. Samuel Johnson's proposed epitaph for Hogarth, contained in a letter to David Garrick, concludes with the lines:

> Here Death has clos'd the curious eyes
> That saw the manners in the Face;

and all subsequent critics have dwelt on the expressive qualities of his pictures, that talent for catching 'momentary actions and expressions' which was the direct result of early cultivation of his visual powers. In the caption to *The Bench* he wrote: 'It has ever been allow'd that, when a CHARACTER is strongly mark'd in the living Face, it may be consider'd an Index of the mind, to express which with any degree of justness in a Painting, requires the utmost Efforts of a great Master.' The study of physiognomy was held to be an essential article in the training of the history painter, since his primary means of rendering character was through the emotions reflected in the human face.[9] The acknowledged authority on the subject was Charles Le Brun, Louis XIV's court painter, whose *Conférences... sur l'expression générale et particulière* with illustrative engravings by B. Picart (1698) was translated into English in 1701 and again in 1734. In *The Analysis of Beauty* Hogarth referred to this treatise as 'the common drawing-book... for the use of learners; where you may have a compendious view of all the common expressions at once.' Le Brun, however, was concerned only with presenting the stereotypes of passions appropriate to the exalted themes of painters in the grand manner, such as joy, grief, anger, fear, pity, scorn or jealousy. Hogarth's concern for peopling his canvases with individualized figures (in contrast to the generalized types of history painting, and Dutch and Flemish genre) displayed in comic everyday situations led him enormously to expand the standard vocabulary of facial expression. Le Brun, furthermore, confined his attention almost exclusively to physiognomy; but Hogarth would also have been familiar with Gerard de Lairesse's *Het Groot Schilderboek* (1707), translated into English in 1738 under the title, *The Art of Painting in all its Branches*, in which the author explored the language of bodily gesture; and he would also have known one of the many editions of Cesare Ripa's *Iconologia* with its numerous explanatory plates.[10] Again, however, these popular works sought to provide only a very general catalogue of the external signs through which character stands revealed, with little or no attention to the particularized characterization which is so unique an aspect of Hogarth's art.

Yet, as his contemporaries were quick to note, it was only rarely that the painter included identifiable figures in his imaginative works, such as the portraits of the notorious rake, Colonel Francis Charteris, and the harlot-hunting magistrate, Sir John Gonson, in the first and third plates of *A Harlot's Progress*. At its finest, as in the cycle of *Marriage A-la-Mode*, Hogarth's skill in so delineating character that the individual is never lost in the type (of which he is nevertheless the epitome) rivals that of the supreme masters of the novel and drama. The second painting of this series (*fig. 11*) superbly exemplifies his success in the graphic projection of the subtlest psychological gradations of thought and feeling. By the fireplace is seated the young couple of the preceding picture, now wedded and sharing a home. Their postures mutely declare the reversal in relationship that has taken place. For the wife has now acquired the pertness of demeanour which the fop originally exhibited, while he has inherited her initial lassitude. It is late morning, following a night's dissipation for both, but with contrasting after-effects. The disorder of the adjoining room indicates that she has been entertaining at a card-party. While she smiles complacently as if luxuriating in the memory of some secret conquest, her sly gaze misses no detail of her husband's bedraggled condition after a night on the town – the sword broken in a scuffle, the woman's cap hanging from his pocket at which the lap-dog sniffs. His vacant stare, on the other hand, denotes how little satisfaction he derives from sour reflections on the night's escapades. Bodily postures bear out the contrasts in facial expression, she stretching lazily in a gesture instinct with impudent vitality, he slumped down with legs listlessly outstretched in abandonment to apathy and dejection. And the hypocritical stance of the Methodist steward (from whose pocket a tract labelled *Regeneration* protrudes), hands raised in mock piety, supplies a devastatingly witty foil to both husband and wife as he stumps off with his tally of unpaid bills. The fourth painting, of the Countess's levée (*fig. 12*), shows that by this time Hogarth was equally master of the crowded scene. For each of the figures assembled in the boudoir is a fully realized individual, distinguishable from the others, whether it be the self-infatuated Italian singer (perhaps a portrait of the castrato mezzo-soprano, Francesco Bernardi, known as Senesino, who was the current operatic idol) carolling in the left foreground, the lovelorn dame who swoons towards him, the country squire snoring behind, or the two black servants whose smirking detachment provides a kind of sardonic commentary on the proceedings.

Equally arresting in their originality are the differing uses to which Hogarth put the stage-like settings within which the stories of the progresses unfold. In *The Analysis of Beauty* he is unusually explicit in giving directions for the proper viewing of his pictures. He requires nothing less than the ardent collaboration of the viewer, that 'imaginary work', in Charles Lamb's phrase, 'where the spectator must meet the artist

Fig. 11
William Hogarth
Marriage A-la-Mode: Shortly after the Marriage
1743–5

Fig. 12
William Hogarth
Marriage A-la-Mode: The Countess's Morning Levée
1743–5

in his conceptions half way ...' The artist based this demand on the psychology of audience response, as exhibited among theatre-goers or novel-readers. 'It is a pleasing labour of the mind', he wrote, 'to solve the most difficult problems; allegories and riddles, trifling as they are, afford the mind amusement: and with what delight does it follow the well-connected thread of a play, or novel, which ever increases as the plot thickens, and ends most pleas'd, when that is most distinctly unravell'd.' On such grounds Hogarth justified the formal complexity of his compositions: 'Intricacy in form, therefore, I shall define to be that peculiarity in the lines, which compose it, that *leads the eye a wanton kind of chace*, and from pleasure that gives the mind, intitles it to the name of beautiful ...'

Hogarth here suggests the proper context for regarding his art as an English version of the rococo style. His more intricate compositions rarely provide a focal point of entry; rather the eye is invited to arrive at a total impression by a cumulative process in which it is led from one suggestive detail to another. Yet it does not wander at random, since its progress is controlled by the serpentining lines, which for Hogarth were the ultimate principle of beauty, as well as by the exquisite control over tonal harmonies which he had learned from Watteau and his followers. The artist's phrase for the unity within diversity at which his paintings aim was a 'composed variety', achieved, as Horace Walpole recognized, through 'a multiplicity of little incidents ... always heightening the principal action.'

Hogarth's elaboration of his *mise-en-scènes* was of such a nature that every object could assume the role of an inanimate actor. Lamb remarked on the painter's 'dumb rhetoric of the scenery'; and Walpole observed: 'It was reserved to Hogarth to write a scene of furniture. The rake's levée-room, the nobleman's dining-room, the apartments of the husband and wife in *Marriage A-la-Mode*, the alderman's parlour, the poet's bedchamber, and many others, are the history of the manners of the age.' Any scene in *Marriage A-la-Mode* illustrates the manifold functions performed by apparently trivial details, which may concurrently serve more than one purpose.

Often an object supplies a narrative link, giving essential information about events that have occurred in the time elapsing since the previous scene. Thus, the coronets above the dressing table and bed in the wife's boudoir indicate that the old earl has died and that she is now a countess, while the coral teething-ring suspended from her chair tells us that she has also become a mother, although the sickly child will not appear until the final painting. By the same token, a detail may forecast what lies in the future. The masquerade tickets which Counsellor Silvertongue holds out to the Countess and his calling attention to the scene on the screen behind, which depicts a masquerade of the kind which he is proposing that they attend, prepare for the tragic denouement, in which the husband surprises the guilty couple in the house of assignation to which they have gone from the masked ball.

Hogarth also used stage properties as a means of characterization, supplementary to the language of facial expression and gesture. The invitations strewn on the floor to the left in the scene of the Countess's levée attest to the giddiness of her social life; the gathering of grotesque trash set forth in the opposite corner, the yield of a recent auction, bespeaks the undiscriminating bourgeois taste which she has never shed; and the copy of Crébillon's licentious novel, *Le Sopha*, on the settee by the lawyer indicates the kind of reading in which she finds diversion.

With his unfailing sensitivity to the nuances of Hogarth's style, Walpole observed that if the artist 'had an emblematic thought, he expressed it with wit, rather than by a symbol.' Research in recent years into the iconography of seventeenth-century Netherlandish genre and still-life painting has revealed the full extent to which these artists invested realistic details with emblematic significance to expand the thematic implications of their scenes of everyday life. Hogarth was the inheritor of this tradition,[11] but with an important difference. Whereas Lowland painters directed the covert message of their pictures outwards in illustration of some commonly accepted proposition, a proverb or popular saw, Hogarth's emblems operate centripetally to intensify the meanings inherent in the situation which he is depicting. Thus, the two dogs yoked together in the foreground of the first picture of *Marriage A-la-Mode* directly reflect the state of the young couple whose marriage is being arranged, the alert bitch forecasting the dominance of the wife-to-be, while the male, supine at her feet, is the counterpart of the effete viscount. Similarly, the sculpture of Actaeon to which the Negro page points in the fourth episode signifies that the husband has been cuckolded.

A further refinement of Hogarth's incorporation of explicatory motifs in his settings is provided by the wall decorations. In each of the six scenes of *Marriage A-la-Mode*, these pictures, in addition to their narrative and characterizing functions, serve a choral purpose, in that they convey the artist's own ironic commentary on the scene. They are thus a graphic counterpart to the device of authorial commentary with which Fielding enriched the texture of his novels. In the fourth picture, for example, the portrait of Counsellor Silvertongue testifies to the privileged position which he now enjoys in the Countess's household. The subjects of the other paintings not only travesty the works of Old Masters, but relate to the dispositions of the individuals above whose heads they hang. Just as Correggio's *Rape of Ganymede* glances mordantly at the ambiguous sexual proclivities of the fop in curl papers, so the same artist's representation of Jupiter possessing Io and the companion piece of Lot's seduction by his daughters mirror the Countess's wanton nature, to which further reference is made by the platter in the basket on the floor, with its depiction of Leda and the swan.

Hogarth's paintings in the later stages of his career evince a notable strengthening of the satiric impulse; and this development went hand in hand with the search for subject-matter appropriate to his increasing seriousness of purpose. Fielding had called the artist 'a Comic History-Painter' in the Preface to *Joseph Andrews*; and in advertising the sale of the six paintings of *Marriage A-la-Mode* in 1751, Hogarth categorized this cycle, along with *A Harlot's Progress* and *A Rake's Progress*, as belonging to the 'historical or humorous kind'. It is clear that by the 1740s he was committed to demonstrating that the comic mode could accommodate themes which by tradition had been reserved for history painting. None of his works better embodies this theory than *The March to Finchley* (1749–50, *fig. 13*).

The scene takes place in September 1745, the year in which the Young Pretender Bonnie Prince Charlie invaded England, only to be disastrously overthrown at Culloden in April 1746 by George II's forces under the command of the Duke of Cumberland. Here we see the King's Guards, freshly recalled from the Low Countries, setting out from London along Tottenham Court Turnpike to form a

OVERLEAF

Fig. 13
William Hogarth
The March to Finchley
1749–50

secondary line of defence at Finchley. In the distance the vanguard is proceeding in orderly ranks; but in the foreground total confusion prevails. As in *Southwark Fair (fig. 8)* and many of Hogarth's outdoor compositions, the setting at the intersection of the Hampstead and Euston Roads is stage-like, framed on the left by the Adam and Eve Inn (the sign representing the moment of temptation), and on the right by the King's Head public house with a portrait of Charles II. He was popularly celebrated as the patron of brothels; and, indeed, this establishment has been converted to that purpose, as is apparent from the girls filling every window to bid farewell to the troops. The fat woman with hands clasped in the lower right window was the proprietress, a notorious bawd known as Mother Douglas. Her tearfulness is a typically Hogarthian touch; for she had recently become a convert to Methodism, and the viewer is left to surmise whether her prayer for the safe return of her clients is prompted more by mercenary or pious considerations.

Although every detail in this thronged composition merits attention, the three groupings forming a kind of triptych in the immediate foreground especially stand out. At the centre is a soldier whose doleful countenance expresses the dilemma posed by the two women who are tugging him in opposite directions. The girl to the left is a seller of loyalist ballads; one exposed to view reads 'God Save our Noble King'. Indisputably pregnant, she anxiously seeks to draw her lover towards the path of virtue and duty. The harridan on the right is his wife, who tries to restrain him from joining his companions in arms. The cross on her mantle betokening Roman Catholicism and the insurrectionary news-sheets, the *Jacobite Journal* and the *Remembrancer*, protruding from her pouch bear witness to her treasonous sympathies.

The groups to left and right support the theme of a choice between alternative courses of action. In the former a tearful wife and her brat are trying to detain the drummer whose rat-a-tat-tat, supported by fife music, sounds forth as much to drown out their supplications as to muster the soldiers. In the right lower corner a drunken officer rejects the offered canteen of water and instead reaches for the noggin of gin his woman is pouring out, a potation which her baby seeks to share.

The March to Finchley reveals on the artist's part a twofold purpose: to expose with the uncompromising realism of an Ostade or Steen the parade of human folly, but to do so with an artistry that elevates the scene above conventional genre depictions of such scenes from low life. Hogarth's principal means for accomplishing the latter goal was the mock-heroic divesting of commonly accepted attitudes and norms of behaviour. As with the actresses dressing in a barn, the soldiers through their unruly conduct on the eve of conflict belie the patriotic roles for which their uniforms cast them. Played off against the long tradition of paintings in the grand manner idealizing warfare, *The March to Finchley* asserts an anti-heroic and intensely bourgeois view of history, almost Brechtian in its disenchantment. Hogarth's full daring in thus flouting established attitudes is well illustrated by an anecdote, which may or may not be true, accounting for why he dedicated the engraving of *The March to Finchley* to the King of Prussia instead of to George II, as he had originally intended. According to legend, the British sovereign, on being shown the plate, demanded, 'Does this fellow mean to laugh at my guards?' Assured that an element of mockery was certainly present, the King stormed in his thick Germanic accent, 'What a *bainter* burlesque a soldier? He deserves to be picketed for his insolence!'

In amplifying the contextual scope of *The March to Finchley*, the artist further resorted to a device which he had previously employed, but was henceforth to use with increasing wit. This was the borrowing for parodic ends of artistic motifs from the Old Masters. The soldier in the central group is ludicrously acting out the so-called 'Choice of Hercules', a familiar theme most memorably depicted in Rubens' *Hercules between Virtue and Vice*.[12] By the same token, the drunken officer and his fellow at the right evoke with savage jocularity the story of the Good Samaritan, which the artist had previously treated with full stylistic gravity in his painting at St Bartholomew's Hospital.

The March to Finchley, with its adoption of the mock-heroic mode, marks a significant expansion in Hogarth's vision as a social satirist. In each of the great earlier progresses, the protagonist may be said in large measure to have brought his downfall on himself. The moral judgement which George Meredith voiced in *Modern Love*, a Victorian poetic version of *Marriage A-la-Mode*, might with equal justice be applied to Hogarth's cycles:

> Passions spin the plot
> We are betrayed by what is false within.

In the ensuing works the artist's target tends to shift from individuals (however much they may reflect their environments) to society at large. The broader focus is accompanied by a darkening of tone, most apparent in a number of subjects which appeared only in engraved form. One thinks of the ferocious onslaughts on drunkenness in *Gin Lane* (1750–1), on reckless gambling in *The Cockpit* (1759), and on religious mania in *Credulity, Superstition and Fanaticism* (1762). The growing social awareness reflected in *The March to Finchley* was accompanied by a commensurate increase in technical mastery, apparent in the new ease and confidence with which the crowd scene is handled. The somewhat indiscriminate clutter of earlier compositions has been replaced by a subtle counterpointing of discrete groups whose activities, arresting in themselves, play supporting roles in building up the dramatic effect of the scene as a whole.

For his final and greatest series, *An Election* (1753–4, *figs 14–17*), Hogarth chose a subject that provided grounds for the comic anatomization of the entire body politic. Although his initial inspiration was the grossly corrupt Oxfordshire election of 1754, the artist employed his theme to satirize every venal aspect attendant on the electoral procedures of a country whose proudest boast was parliamentary government. The dimensions of the canvases, 40 × 50 inches, were significantly greater than in any of the preceding sequences, allowing room for the portrayal of a very large number of figures representative of every class of society, and given over to every variety of excess to which graft and bribery can lead. There is no single leading character to establish continuity as in the other progresses; instead, each picture focuses on a critical stage in the bitterly contested political campaign, as the rival parties seek by whatever unscrupulous means to coerce votes for their candidates. Taken together, the four scenes thus present a panoramic view of an evolving sequence of events affecting the lives of the local populace. The format is that of *The Four Times of the Day*, but with the temporal progression now fortified by a historical dimension. Just as each scene is a microcosm of the overall phenomenon, so each of the many and various episodes

Fig. 14
William Hogarth
An Election: An Election Entertainment
*c*1754

Fig. 15
William Hogarth
An Election: Canvassing for Votes
*c*1754

Fig. 16
William Hogarth
An Election: The Polling
*c*1754

within the scenes has its compositional function, both contributory to and symptomatic of the swelling theme of political anarchy.

Since both parties shamelessly resort to the same nefarious practices and since human nature is exhibited as uniformly prone to corruption, Hogarth takes no sides. His mockery, all-encompassing and even-handed, is here devoid of reforming zeal. Moral opprobrium is quenched by the transcendence of the comic spirit with its detached perception of human fallibility. For Hogarth the release into full play of that spirit depended increasingly on the witty conversion of stark, even brutal actualities of life into mock-heroic approximations of a more ideal order; and in the *Election* series he brought to perfection the technique of implanting in the overt subject-matter of his pictures allusions, primarily artistic in reference, which would dignify scenes of pure genre without falsifying their factual truth.

As iconographic studies of *An Election* have pointed out, each of the four paintings draws on the reservoir of traditional themes made familiar by painters of the Renaissance and Baroque periods. The composition of the first, *An Election Entertainment (fig. 14)*, derives unmistakably from presentations of *The Last Supper*. Hogarth had already daringly utilized this design for the drunken orgy in *A Midnight Modern Conversation* (*c*1731); and he was to invoke it again in the riotous scene of *The Cockpit*. Here its application is especially appropriate to the exposure of the many forms of treachery taking place under the mask of good fellowship and party loyalty. It will be seen that despite the tumultuous swarm of figures crowding around, exactly thirteen persons are seated at the table. The trio standing at the extreme right, in which a bribe is being offered to the Methodist tailor, who has adopted a saintly pose, evokes Judas's betrayal; and this episode is balanced by the electoral candidate seated with his two toadies at the left end of the table in a configuration that travesties Judas, Peter and John in Leonardo's famous painting.

The scandalous prevalence of bribery in the electioneering process provides the keynote to the second painting, *Canvassing for Votes (fig. 15)*. As in *The March to Finchley*, the composition follows a triangular pattern, with a central group and two flanking ones in the foreground. The crafty farmer at the centre is being solicited by Tory (to the left) and Whig innkeepers who are acting as agents for their respective parties. Like the guardsman in *The March to Finchley* (as well as Macheath in *The Beggar's Opera*), he re-enacts *The Choice of Hercules*, although in a comically inverted version, since there is here no question of choosing between virtue and vice, but rather of capitalizing on both invitations to accept bribes, by playing one off against the other.

The third canvas (*fig. 16*) represents with scathing ridicule the mustering to the polling booth of voters recruited from the ranks of the maimed, the feeble-minded and the moribund, with the chariot of state shown breaking up in the background. The use of the platform as the setting for confrontation parodies in a general way the temple steps that appear in Renaissance ceremonial scenes, such as Titian's *Presentation of the Virgin* and *Christ before Pilate*. Hogarth had adopted a similar compositional format in two of his serious history paintings, *Moses brought to Pharaoh's Daughter* and *Paul before Felix* (of which he also made a burlesque version).

In the concluding picture, *Chairing the Member (fig. 17)*, the election has taken place and the two victorious candidates (one shown only in shadow on the wall

Fig. 17
William Hogarth
An Election: Chairing the Member
*c*1754

at the back) are being carried in triumph through the streets. The threatened disorder in previous scenes has broken all bounds, degenerating into open violence. Here the parodic content is twofold, secular and religious. On the one hand, the artist makes fun of the fat candidate toppling to his fall by placing the incident in the perspective of a military triumph, specifically either Pietro da Cortona's *The Victory of Alexander over Darius at the Battle of Arbela*, or Charles Le Brun's version of the same event. Both paintings portray the imperial eagle that was said to have flown above the head of Alexander in token of victory; in Hogarth's painting it is replaced by a white goose, an emblem of the inane cackling which will be the new member's contribution to parliamentary debate. But, as Joseph Burke has proposed, the street procession also parodies Renaissance renderings of the *sacra conversazione*, in which the enthroned Virgin is traditionally represented surrounded by adoring saints and music-making angels, here replaced by club-wielding ruffians, performing animals, and a demented fiddler. The sow with her litter plunging into the sewer may recall the Gadarene swine; and the shadow of the second candidate suggests a Catholic pontiff bestowing blessings.

Like the Homeric similes, epic epithets and other mock-heroic apparatus in Pope's satires and Fielding's novels, Hogarth's appropriation of thematic and stylistic motifs from the Old Masters imposes significant form on the incongruities of mundane existence. To his matchless skill in arresting aspects of the passing show is added by this means a number of associations which endow seeming trivialities with timeless relevance. If the wand of the comic spirit in Hogarth's hands promotes disenchantment with the inconsequent nature of all appearances, it at the same time purges misanthropy and releases the floodgates of laughter over man's mixed nature and incorrigible capacity for self-delusion.

In summarizing Hogarth's achievement, Charles Lamb remarked:

> It is the force of these kindly admixtures, which assimilates the scenes of Hogarth and of Shakespeare to the drama of real life, where no such thing as pure tragedy is to be found; but merriment and infelicity, ponderous crime and feather-light vanity, like twiformed births, disagreeing complexions of one intertexture, perpetually unite to shew forth motley spectacles to the world.

In its consummate picturing of the lights and shadows, the embodied humours and perpetual contrarieties of the *comédie humaine*, Hogarth's *oeuvre*, as Frederick Antal observed, is perhaps rivalled only by Goya and Daumier.

Chapter Two

DOMESTIC PORTRAITURE

THE DOMINANT PLACE accorded to portraiture in Tudor times carried on throughout the eighteenth century, with the eventual emergence of a recognizable native school. Previously, beginning with the establishment of Holbein as court painter to Henry VIII, portrait styles had been set by a succession of Continental artists whose practice conformed to Renaissance and Baroque models. Foremost among these was Van Dyck, the court painter of Charles I, whose example inspired in turn Lely and Kneller in a courtly tradition that survived virtually unchallenged into the reign of George I. It was Van Dyck's towering achievement to establish a mode of state portraiture which projected an ideal version of absolute monarchy. In his portraits, not only the sovereign and members of the royal family, but also the entourage of statesmen, soldiers, poets and scholars assembled round the throne emerge as embodiments of all the qualities of nobility, grandeur and elegance gracing a divinely ordained hierarchical order. Swathed in the emblems of rank, the distinguishing characteristics of individuality were subsumed in the public roles accorded by birth and privilege. As a result, portraits were conceived not only to immortalize the originals, but also, as was the case with history painting, to present for emulation patterns of noble behaviour. In the words of Gerard de Lairesse, 'pictures should create an ardour for virtue'; or, as Jonathan Richardson wrote with regard to portraits of great men in *An Essay on the Theory of Painting* (1715): 'Men are excited to imitate the Good Actions, and persuaded to shun the Vices of those whose Examples are thus set before them.'

While the portraits of Van Dyck and his followers tell us much about the ideals of the social order which they portrayed, they reveal little of what their sitters were like as individuals or of the reality of their daily lives.[1] And for the members of the new mercantile middle class emerging on the Georgian scene with their democratic Puritan antecedents and regard for power based on self-aggrandizement rather than hereditary privilege, such images of aristocratic refinement were not only inappropriate, but also unacceptable. Of this class, as we have seen, Hogarth was one of the earliest articulate spokesmen; and his contempt for contemporary history painting on Continental models carried over to the equally derivative school of portraiture. His bold assertion of a new type of portrait, in opposition to the academic procedures which he scornfully called 'phizmongering' (best exemplified in the work of the visiting French artist, Jean-Baptiste Vanloo, then much in demand among noble patrons),[2] is brilliantly exemplified in the portrait of *Captain Thomas Coram* (1740, *fig. 18*). To suggest the eminence of the sitter he endowed the scene with Baroque trappings. Coram's pose is modelled on that of the French financier, Samuel Bernard, in a portrait by Hyacinthe Rigaud; and the setting retains the conventional backdrop of classical column and falling drapery, with a seascape opening to the left to indicate the source of the sitter's wealth. Other emblems of authority are the seal in his hand attached to the Royal Charter of the Foundling Hospital on the table, and the globe at his feet turned to show the Atlantic Ocean.

In all other respects, however, the portrait breaks radically with the precedent, since the artist designed it specifically to reflect credit on the virtues of the type to which the sitter belonged, that of philanthropic merchants. Apprenticed to a shipwright in the 1680s, Coram had gone to Boston in 1697, where he made a fortune in shipping before returning to England, henceforth to devote his energies to social welfare. His most notable accomplishment was the establishment in 1739 of the Foundling Hospital to provide a home for abandoned waifs from the London streets. Hogarth was one of the circle associated with the originator of this enterprise; and he donated the portrait, as well as *The March to Finchley*, to the Foundling Hospital. He was instrumental as well in persuading other artists, including the youthful Gainsborough, to contribute examples of their work, with the result that the Foundling Hospital became the first gallery in England where paintings were on public display.

In Hogarth's handling, the man who so solidly occupies his stately setting is immediately recognizable for what he was. Bluff, hearty, down-to-earth in the genial ease with which he confronts the viewer, he is the very image of the self-made benefactor. Notable are the alert posture of the sturdy figure, the firm grip of the sinewy hands, the short legs hardly reaching to the ground, yet restless in repose. He is dressed not in the ceremonial robes customarily prescribed for formal portraits, but in good serviceable broadcloth of everyday wear; and the absence of a wig bespeaks his disregard for social usage. Nevertheless, the good Captain's composed demeanour shows that he is fully aware of the authoritative position to which he has risen and perfectly confident of his credentials to occupy it.[3]

The more intimate and sympathetic relationship between artist and subject implied by such lifelike portraits as that of Captain Coram was something new in English painting, and profoundly affected the practice of subsequent painters in the great century of English portraiture. The example was not, for instance, lost on the supreme master of the art, Sir Joshua Reynolds. By replacing the Baroque swagger, the pomp and circumstance of the Van Dyckian manner with a new concept of classical realism, Reynolds was able to endow his portraits with the dignity of history painting. In so doing, he capitalized on all that he had learned from his long study of the Old Masters, including the use of 'borrowed attitudes' and other ennobling allusions, to cast his subjects in heroic roles. Yet his portraits, such as the magnificent *Lord Heathfield* (1788), are never devoid of elements which suggest the unique personality of the sitter.

Revealing as the formal portraits of the eighteenth century often are, their value as

Fig. 18
William Hogarth
Captain Thomas Coram
1740

Painted and given by Wm Hogarth 1740.

an index to contemporary life and manners cannot match that of another type of portraiture which rose to prominence in Georgian England and in which the social climate of that age is preserved perhaps more faithfully than in any other artistic genre. Portraits in this mode acquired the name of 'conversation pieces'. Their distinguishing characteristics were defined by George Vertue in some remarks about the pictures of the short-lived Gawen Hamilton (*c*1697–1737), a Scottish follower of Hogarth. He described them in his racy idiom as 'family peeces – small figures from the life in their habits and dress of the Times. well disposd gracefull and natural easy actions suteable to the characters of the persons and their portraitures well toucht to the likenes and Air, a free pencill good Colouring and ornamented or decorated in a handsom grand manner every way Suteable to people of distinction . . .'

The term 'conversation' is akin in meaning to the Italian *conversazione*. According to the *New English Dictionary* it referred in the eighteenth century to 'The action of living and having one's being *in* a place or *among* persons'; 'The action of consorting or having dealings with others'; 'Circle of acquaintance, company, society'; 'An "At Home".' The conversation piece is first and foremost a group portrayal of two or more persons, based on certain assumptions about the make-up of polite society. The sitters, whether relations or close associates, are presented in a familiar setting, demonstrating their shared interests and activities. In contrast to formal portraiture, the emphasis is less on the being as an individualized and self-directing personality than on his presence within the social order of which he is a representative. As with genre painting, there is often a muted narrative element present, since conversations present their sitters engaged in communal pursuits and interacting with each other. The occasion may be a musical assembly, a card party or other game, a tea party, a drinking bout (such as Hogarth's satirically entitled *A Midnight Modern Conversation*), or any other festivity which brings men and women together in circumstances that display them at ease and enjoying favourite diversions. Conversations, however, are distinguishable from pure genre, since they present identifiable people rather than types, and record the genteel pursuits of the middle and upper classes rather than low life. The keynote of the type is the immediacy and informality with which the scenes arrest the passing moment. In Vertue's words again: 'You may see the Pictures, & read the Manners of the Man at the same time.' In this respect the painter's perspective is analogous to today's candid camera shot. And, again as in photography, the subjects are usually presented very much smaller than life-size, twelve to eighteen inches in height, although this practice was by no means uniform.

The vision of society emerging from the conversation piece is of a singularly placid and carefree world, in which the main business of life was the cultivation of its amenities. There is hardly a hint of the material concerns and cares of daily existence; rather, these pictures are almost exclusively devoted to portraying the uses which the privileged classes made of the leisure conferred by their wealth.

The origin of the mode has been traced far back in the annals of painting. Jan van Eyck's fifteenth-century masterpiece, the *Arnolfini Wedding*, the iconography of which has been so brilliantly spelled out by Erwin Panofsky, is often cited as the most conspicuous early example. Holbein's portrait of *Sir Thomas More and his Family* (*c*1527), which survives only in the drawing, conforms to the type and is perhaps the earliest English progenitor. Informal group portraiture enjoyed its Continental heyday in the Low Countries during the seventeenth century, when, with the establishment of peace, a burgher class assumed the dominant role in society, implanting a culture which in many respects anticipated that which accompanied the rise of the middle class in Hanoverian England fifty years later. The spread of wealth coincided with an artistic awakening, as shown by the great school of Netherlandish genre painters, including such masters as Dou, Terborch, Metsu, Coques and Netscher. Their skills were admirably suited to the demands placed on them by their bourgeois patrons, eager to see themselves displayed with members of their families in scenes commemorating their domestic happiness amidst the possessions they took such pride in amassing.

Despite the presence of a number of artists from the Low Countries around 1700, however, the formative impetus for the conversation piece in England came from France, where Watteau had invested the relatively stiff and formalized Flemish manner with the aristocratic grace and fancifulness of the rococo style. His versions took the forms of *assemblées galantes*, largely imaginary groups of courtly figures disposed in idyllic pastoral settings. Watteau's work became known when on the verge of death he visited London in 1719 to consult Dr Richard Mead, who combined medical practice with artistic interests, and whose collection contained two original pictures by the French artist.[4] In Watteau's wake followed a band of Parisian draughtsmen and engravers, foremost among whom was Hubert Gravelot (1699–1773), who was to have an important impact on English artists through his teaching at the St Martin's Lane Academy in the time of Hogarth's proprietorship, as well as through his scintillating book illustrations.

Two widely travelled artists foreign by birth, Marcellus Laroon the Younger (1679–1774) and Philip Mercier (1689–1760), both of whom settled in England, were the first to modify Watteau's manner in conformity with the changing temper of a society no longer at home with the stale traditions of court painting passed down from Lely and Kneller. As is apparent from their practice, no clear line of demarcation can be drawn at this early stage between imaginary gatherings, strongly marked with genre attributes, and group portraits. Indeed, the term 'conversation' was often applied to pure genre. Its first appearance in English, in Bainbrigg Buckeridge's *Essay towards an English School* (1706), occurs in a reference to Marcellus Laroon the Elder as 'fam'd for Pictures in little, commonly call'd Conversation-Pieces.' This Laroon, who was of Dutch-French descent, after coming to England carried on the manner of Brouwer and Ostade.[5] The hybrid style of the younger Laroon reflects in its realistic and satiric qualities the father's influence, but is strongly infused with more fanciful elements derived from Watteau's *scènes galantes*; and at least two of his pictures, *A Musical Assembly* (1715–20) and *A Dinner Party* (1725), conform closely enough to the conversation piece to entitle them to be regarded among its earliest examples in England.

A more significant figure was Philip Mercier, born in Germany of French Huguenot stock, who studied in Berlin under Antoine Pesne and spent a considerable time in France before arriving in London about 1716. His early manner was strongly influenced by Watteau, whom he both copied and imitated; and this association is reflected in the lightness and gaiety of tone he imparted to the small number of group portraits he painted before taking up work in a different vein. Mercier's pioneer

contribution to the art of the conversation is well exemplified in *Viscount Tyrconnel with his Family* (1725–6, *fig. 19*). Each individual in this vivacious open-air gathering is an identifiable portrait. John Brownlow, Viscount Tyrconnel, wearing the ribbon and star of the order of the Bath, stands at the left, with the family seat, Belton House, in the background. His wife is seated at the centre and the young woman perched on the swing is her cousin, Miss Dayrell, while another relation, Savile Cockayne Cust, holds the controlling string. In the left corner sits the artist. Despite a certain stiffness in composition, Mercier has clearly sought to capture the atmosphere of Watteau's pastorals by placing the figures in a grove shadowed by feathery trees, and by the inclusion of such details as the swing and the artist at his drawing-board.

Fig. 19
Philip Mercier
Viscount Tyrconnel with his Family
1725–6

Fig. 20
Bartholomew Dandridge
The Price Family
*c*1728

The adaptability of rococo elegance and grace to domestic portraiture is more fully apparent in the style of one of the earliest English-born practitioners of the mode, Bartholomew Dandridge (1691–after 1754), the son of a liveryman of the Painter Stainers' Company. Vertue greatly admired Dandridge, whose conversation pieces he called: 'really a degree higher than any body in that way', the figures being 'gracefully designed with great Variety & much fine invention.' These qualities are delightfully manifested in Dandridge's *The Price Family* (*c*1728, *fig. 20*), a picture formerly ascribed to Hogarth. The setting was the celebrated garden of the Prices at Foxley in Herefordshire, presented so as unmistakably to recall Watteau's *Embarkation for Cythera*. Uvedale Tomkyns Price, shown to right of centre helping his wife from the punt, bequeathed his property to the distinguished landscape architect of the same name, author of *An Essay on the Picturesque* (1794). A son, Robert, sits at the left, stroking a dog, and the other individuals were members of the Greville and Rodd families. Their elegant mannerisms derive, as Vertue tells us, from the artist's habit of making little models of his figures, 'each single figure placed upon a plane, whereby he coud see to dispose the groopes. & lights & shades to very great advantage.'[6] Yet there is no mistaking that these beings so gracefully distributed on the terrace by the lake were real individuals united by close family ties and dressed in the fashions of the day.

Dandridge's group exudes an air of refinement and good breeding; but although in its earliest and Frenchified phase, during the 1720s and 1730s, the conversation piece was in vogue among aristocratic patrons, the genre was particularly suited to the tastes of the new middle class, and it was among such people that it enjoyed the greatest popularity in the middle years of the century, especially in the provinces. Only with the shift towards a more homely tone in domestic observances, instilled by the example of George III on his accession in 1760, did it regain popularity among the upper circles of society. There were many reasons why the conservative country gentry, as well as the mercantile and professional families who were seeking to join its ranks through becoming landowners, should have preferred this type of portraiture to perpetuate their images. The relatively small size of the conversation suited the modest dimensions of rooms in the houses they were erecting, in contrast to the stately residences of the hereditary nobility; and the informality of treatment accorded with their unostentatious habits and dislike of display better than the more flamboyant style of individual portraiture practised by such reigning masters as Reynolds, which incidentally commanded much higher prices. Perhaps an equally weighty consideration was the harmonious relationship which can be demonstrated to have existed between these patrons of more modest station and artists who, sharing the values of those who commissioned their services, were content to record, without the grandiose inflation of a Reynolds or the implicit irony of a Hogarth, the quiet gratifications of the stable and ordered way of life mirrored in these pictures.

Yet, it was Hogarth who during the early stages of his career, while he was embarking on his 'Pictur'd Morals', also exploited the new fashion for the conversation piece and set the trajectory for its future development. In this, as in so many other respects, he was the first to sense an artistic tendency inherent in the temper of the age, awaiting only the imprimatur of his genius. As early as 1729 Vertue wrote: 'The daily success of Mr Hogarth in painting small family peices & Conversations with so much Air & agreeableness Causes him to be much followd, & esteemd. whereby he has much imployment & [is] like to be a master of great reputation in that way.'

A Family Party (*c*1730–2, *fig. 21*) already exhibits virtually every feature of the conversation piece. Although in this case their identities remain undetermined, the portraits are clearly of real individuals, engaged in activities which typify their social standing and customary way of life. Hogarth's theatrical sense is apparent not only in the disposition of the figures as on a stage, but also in the business which keeps them engaged with one another to the exclusion of the viewer. The lady at the left is at work on an embroidery-frame, while her companion looks on admiringly. The pair is related to the couple taking tea both by the gesture of the man standing between them and by the fact that his head provides the apex of the triangular configuration unifying the two groups, a compositional device often employed by Hogarth. The bored isolation of the boy at the right is accentuated by his fondling of the household pet which has climbed into his lap, and the kitten frolicking by the overturned work-basket in the foreground adds an additional note of amusing animation to the scene.

Hogarth was equally at home with the other leading category of the conversation piece, set in the open air. A delightful example from his hand is *Lord Hervey and his Friends* (*c*1738–9, *fig. 22*), the dimensions of which are somewhat larger than *A Family*

Fig. 21
William Hogarth
A Family Party
*c*1730–2

Fig. 22
William Hogarth
Lord Hervey and his Friends
*c*1738–9

Party. The central figure and commissioner of the painting was John, Lord Hervey, wearing the gold key of office as Vice-Chamberlain of the Queen. A notoriously time-serving courtier, he was the original of Pope's searing portrait of Sporus in 'Epistle to Dr Arbuthnot'. Hervey is shown surrounded by his cronies on the terrace at Maddington, the shooting-box of the Fox brothers on Salisbury Plain near Stonehenge. The individual at the left with whom he appears to be discussing an architectural drawing is Henry Fox, later Lord Holland, whose brother Stephen, later Lord Ilchester, is placed at the table where a collation is spread. At the right sits Charles, third Duke of Marlborough with Thomas Winnington MP beside him. Hogarth's irrepressible iconoclasm emerges in the treatment of the figure at the extreme left, a portrait of a French cleric, the Rev. Peter Louis Willemin. Having climbed on a chair to level his spy-glass at the church on the distant hill, he has lost his balance and is about to topple over. Willemin's ludicrous posture betrays his eagerness to feather his nest, since the living of the church, Eisey, near Cricklade, was in the gift of Stephen Fox (he was in fact made Vicar of Eisey on 20 October 1737). That the other occupants of the scene are so oblivious of their companion's imminent downfall heightens the humour of the situation, while the solidly based statue of Minerva on the right seems to mock the cleric's pretensions.

The prominence of children in conversation pieces confirms the importance of this mode as a reflection of domestic life.[7] And once again it was Hogarth who took the lead in giving imaginative expression to this deeply characteristic side of contemporary society. An early (1730) and charming pair of pictures, entitled *The House of Cards* and *A Children's Party*, shows children at play. In each the games, cards, make-believe warfare, etc., are invested with emblematic meaning, illustrative of the *vanitas* theme of life's uncertainty, so prevalent in Netherlandish genre painting. This theme recurred more impressively a decade later in Hogarth's two masterpieces of child portraiture, *The Graham Children* (1742, *fig. 23*) and *The MacKinnon Children* (*c*1742). The sitters in the former were significantly of relatively lowly origin, having for their father Daniel Graham, apothecary at the Royal Hospital, Chelsea. This incomparably vivacious depiction of four handsomely dressed children at play includes, nevertheless, motifs at variance with its apparent light-heartedness. The boy at the right is making music on a hand-organ of a kind known as a serinette because it imitates birdsong. On the side of the instrument is shown Orpheus, whose lute charmed all animals into docility, as the present performance has enthralled the little girls. Contravening this legendary evocation from the Golden Age is the cat scrambling over the back of the chair, his fierce gaze fixed on the goldfinch in the cage above. At the left stands a clock surmounted by the image of the infant Cupid who has discarded his traditional bow for a scythe, the attribute of Old Father Time. In his selection of incidental detail the artist thus fosters the sombre speculation that the radiant happiness of these children is evanescent in a world of rapacious cruelty, where time remorselessly wastes away the fair dreams of youth.

The artist's treatment of *The Graham Children* was derived with extensive modification from Van Dyck's portrait of *The Five Eldest Children of Charles I* (1637, *fig. 24*), which is almost the same size. This association suggests that for Hogarth the conversation piece had come to assume an importance rivalling formal portraiture. Van Dyck's children are touched with the melancholy which the artist prophetically

Fig. 23
William Hogarth
The Graham Children
1742

Fig. 24
Sir Anthony Van Dyck
The Five Eldest Children of Charles I
1637

Fig. 25
William Hogarth
*Captain Lord George Graham
in his Cabin*
*c*1742

lent to all his portraits of the ill-fated Stuart line. Yet there could hardly be a more graphic way of illustrating the radical shift in artistic taste which ushered in the eighteenth century than to oppose his marvellous projection of royal children in a ceremonial setting to Hogarth's ambiguous evocation of the make-believe world of the offspring of well-to-do bourgeois parents, a century later. The artist's replacement of the markedly placid great guard-dog in the earlier picture with a bloodthirsty cat in itself epitomizes the domestication of the court tradition in the conversation piece.

Captain Lord George Graham in his Cabin (*c*1742, *fig. 25*) is the culminating example of Hogarth's inventiveness in extending the range of informal group portraiture. The principal figure, who was the youngest son of the Duke of Montrose, is discovered smoking his pipe and very much at ease in his quarters aboard the *Nottingham*, a 60-gun frigate to the command of which he had been promoted in reward for a successful naval engagement against French privateers off Ostend in June 1745. Graham is handsomely but carelessly dressed, with fur-lined cape thrown back and bonnet askew, uniforms not being prescribed for wear in the navy until 1748. The captain's chaplain is seated at the table as his guest. While the two await their repast, entertainment is supplied by a singer to the accompaniment of pipe and tabor, played by the blackamoor at the right. This performance to an attentive audience within the carefully defined space of the cabin emphasizes the scene's theatrical quality, which is further enhanced by passages of high comedy. The grinning servant at the left, as if made self-conscious by the presence of the viewer whose gaze he seems to return, is spilling gravy from a roast duck over the chaplain's back. On the opposite side Hogarth has introduced his pug Trump as a kind of signature. Adorned with a wig and reared on its haunches as it pretends to join the chorus from the song-sheet propped in front, the animal's ludicrously pompous appearance sets off by contrast the atmosphere of jovial relaxation that prevails throughout the scene. Although so far removed in handling from the splendidly imposing portraits of military heroes which were soon to be painted by Reynolds, Gainsborough, and Raeburn, Hogarth's *Captain Graham* moves the conversation piece into the realm of history painting beside his great narrative pictures, such as *The March to Finchley (fig. 13)*.

Other early painters of conversations subject to the same influences which helped mould Hogarth's manner, and not least to his own example, included Gawen Hamilton, Joseph Francis Nollekens (1702–48), Charles Philips (1708–47), Francis Hayman (1708–76) and Joseph Highmore (1692–1780).

The most notable achievement of the latter, who was the son of a coal merchant and who studied under Kneller, was the series of twelve pictures which he painted to illustrate Richardson's *Pamela*. Although indebted to the French in their rococo delicacy, these works rival the Hogarthian moral progress in the graphic handling of episodes forming a narrative sequence.[8] During the 1720s and 1730s Highmore enjoyed a large portrait practice among members of the upper-middle and aristocratic classes. Like Hogarth, whose senior he was by five years, he developed an original style, combining the lightness of touch and suave colouring of Watteau and his followers with the directness and forthright honesty demanded by British sitters. A good deal of the warmth and intimacy of mood irradiating *Captain Graham* is present in Highmore's masterpiece of the same period, *Mr Oldham and his Guests* (*c*1740–50,

Fig. 26
Joseph Highmore
Mr Oldham and his Guests
*c*1740–50

fig. 26), a painting which because of its realistic handling was long thought to be by Hogarth.

Nathaniel Oldham was a sporting country squire with artistic tastes, residing at Ealing. According to a plausible anecdote (recounted by J.T.Smith in *Nollekens and his Times*), he had invited friends to his house and, arriving late, had found them very much at home over a bowl of punch. Taken with the scene, he forthwith commissioned Highmore to paint it. The somewhat bellicose, bewigged figure at the right was the village schoolmaster. The portly man opposite, pipe in one hand, glass in the other, who gazes out so complacently at the viewer, was a neighbouring farmer. The artist himself, in a red cap, leans between the pair, smiling quizzically, while their host standing at the left looks on in enjoyment of the pleasant atmosphere created by his hospitality. The individuality of the sitters is admirably realized through highlighting, each being presented from a slightly different angle, from profile to full face, to emphasize some dominant trait of character. Furthermore, seen at three-quarters length against a plain backdrop, the group is tightly knit by the strong diagonal and vertical thrusts of their postures, in such a way as to suggest the bond of fellowship prevailing among them. This scene might have been lifted from *Tom Jones*; redolent of all that is most ingratiating in that novel, it could, one feels, only have been set down at one time and in one place to commemorate the convivial ways of English country life in the eighteenth century.

As has been remarked, the initial vogue for the conversation piece among aristocratic patrons soon died down, with the result that during the middle years of the century this type of portraiture was principally sponsored by members of the landed gentry, such as Oldham. And the artist who best answered the requirements of these patrons was one of their own kind, Arthur Devis (1711–87), from Preston in Lancashire. His clientele, even after he moved to London in 1842, was largely made up of Tory squires, forming a class without court connections and deeply conservative in its attachment to traditional ways of life. A regard for family continuity based on the hereditary transmission of property was especially strong among these provincial landowners. This concern carried with it a firmly lodged regard for the rights of proprietorship, reflected in the pride which owners took in the improvement of their land and the adornment of their houses. Devis' conversation pieces constitute a unique record of the manners and tastes of this class.

Several of Devis' most engaging pictures portray married couples posed in the drawing-rooms of their homes. An excellent example is *William Atherton and his Wife, Lucy* (*c*1743–4, *fig. 27*). Atherton, a friend of the artist's father, had served as mayor of Preston and then as alderman. Although the likenesses of the sitters are convincing, the portrait exhibits little of the animation that characterizes the work of Hogarth and other artists subject to French influence. Nor, spaced stiffly apart and gazing impassively out at the viewer, do Atherton and his wife give much impression of the intimacy of shared lives. In their detachment and solemn bearing they recall the Tudor miniatures of Nicholas Hilliard (1547–1619) and Isaac Oliver (*c*1556–1617) which undoubtedly influenced Devis and which help to account for the somewhat primitive style in which he worked. The couple are characterized exclusively by external details, their richly fashionable garb, the dignity and self-possession of their postures, and the spare but handsome and tastefully arranged furnishings and

Fig. 27
Arthur Devis
William Atherton and his Wife, Lucy
*c*1743–4

decorations of the room which they occupy. These last, especially, seem to provide objective confirmation of the decorous and well-regulated lives led by their owners. Such details, furthermore, reflect the sense of security and material well-being emanating from the sitters, an impression traceable to their confident acceptance of and immersion in their prescribed roles within the social hierarchy.

More evocative of the occupants' way of life is the setting of Devis' portrait of *John Bacon and his Family* (*c*1742–3, *fig. 28*). Bacon, the scion of a Northumberland landowning family, is shown with his wife and children in their London house, surrounded by the scientific paraphernalia of the pursuits to which he devoted himself. He was a member of both the Royal Society and the Society of Antiquaries. Among the instruments on view are a transit quadrant by the window, in front of it a reflecting telescope on a wall-bracket, and in the back room an air-pump. The grisaille medallion portraits on the facing wall represent, along with Milton and Pope, Newton and Sir Francis Bacon (apparently not a forebear of the present Bacon). Five of the six figures look out of the picture plane towards the viewer, and their constrained and self-conscious poses bring to mind early photographic portraits. The artist has introduced a slight anecdotal element in the two children building a house of cards on the table at the right. This motif, as has been said, is common in Dutch genre, where it is an emblem for the vagaries of fortune; with Devis, however, its function is merely to add a playful domestic note to the scene. Characteristic of the artist's practice is the wide spacing of the sitters in a line, which on first sight seems the result of compositional ineptitude, but which in reality is a device for conveying the harmonious accommodation between figures and setting viewed as an extension of their social presence.

Devis had studied with Peter Tillemans, from whom he learned much about the placing of houses in country settings. This is apparent in the conversation piece entitled *Robert Gwillym and his Family* (*c*1749, *fig.* 29). The Gwillyms were a substantial Lancashire family related by marriage to the Athertons. Robert is the second figure from the left, facing his wife and four children, while his father, also named Robert, and one of his brothers stand to left and right respectively. In the distance is Atherton Hall, which Mrs Gwillym had inherited unfinished and which her husband had completed at the cost of £63,000 shortly before commissioning this picture. No work could illustrate more clearly the proprietary pride which the country gentry took in their estates. The two groups of individuals are widely separated, as if they had drawn to either side to open a clear view of their imposing new residence, to which its owner is pointing. The servant approaching in the middle distance, perhaps with a message for his master, not only leads the eye in the same direction, but also serves as a reminder of family affluence.

Devis' most ambitious canvas was *Sir Joshua Vanneck and his Family* (1752, *fig.* 30). Vanneck, a financier of Dutch ancestry, had become a baronet in the year before the conversation was commissioned. He stands at the extreme left, his dominant position supported by the overshadowing tree. The party, made up of members of his family, including the husbands of two older daughters, is gathered on the lawn of Sir Joshua's rural retreat, Roehampton House, described by Horace Walpole as a 'beautiful terrace on the Thames with forty acres of ground'. The bridge and church identify the locality as Putney. Devis, however, made no attempt to integrate the figures with the scenery before which they are posed. And although these individuals form a semicircle enclosed by two benches, the artist was equally unconcerned with establishing among them any interplay suggestive of their relationships. The young woman in pink gestures towards the river, to be sure, as if calling attention to some happening, but only her sister by the telescope and the husband behind pay attention; the remaining seven gaze unconcernedly at the viewer. Their similarly rendered features show consanguinity; but in their total lack of expression these figures might be gorgeously dressed mannequins. The individuality of each is submerged in the social type. Thus, Sir Joshua's cross-legged stance, which appears in innumerable Georgian portraits, was the customary posture adopted by gentlemen of breeding when standing at ease; and its precise duplication in the young heir by the table attests to the father's dynastic pretensions. In the same way, the gestures of the daughters, whether intuitive or calculated, can be matched in contemporary manuals of decorum, which showed with the help of illustrations a whole repertory of models for polite behaviour in every kind of social situation.[9] The

Fig. 28
Arthur Devis
John Bacon and his Family
*c*1742–3

Fig. 29
Arthur Devis
Robert Gwillym of Atherton and his Family
*c*1749

Fig. 30
Arthur Devis
Sir Joshua Vanneck and his Family
1752

loving attention which Devis devoted to dress, furthermore, reveals nothing about personal style or taste, but rather aims at setting a norm of fashionable elegance to which each sitter conforms. The impression which emerges from the painting is one of shared assumptions expressed through a code of manners that merges the individual in the entity of the family, as the family in turn forms an intrinsic part of a yet larger entity, the class of which it is representative.

The arrival of Johan Zoffany (1733–1810) in England coincided with George III's coming to the throne in 1760; and the stage was thus set for the heyday of the conversation piece. Zoffany had grown up at the court of Prince von Thurn und Taxis in Regensburg, where his father was official cabinet-maker and architect; and he continued his studies under fashionable portrait painters in Italy. With the adaptability which was a product of his foreign background and eclectic training, he sensed the bourgeois temper of the new reign and soon won the patronage of Queen Charlotte. Zoffany's artistic skills were as various as his point of view was flexible; and although in no sense an innovator, he took from his predecessors and perfected every feature of the conversation piece. Perhaps the quality which most distinguishes his

OPPOSITE ABOVE

Fig. 31
Johan Zoffany
Queen Charlotte with her Two Eldest Sons
1764

OPPOSITE BELOW

Fig. 32
Johan Zoffany
Mr and Mrs Garrick by the Shakespeare Temple at Hampton (detail)
1762

work is its *intimacy*, the heartwarming way that he exposes his sitters in the felicity of their private lives.

Zoffany's portrait groups of children illustrate his ability to penetrate behind the public façade of his subjects; none more so than *Queen Charlotte with her Two Eldest Sons* (1764, *fig. 31*), which was among the first of the artist's court commissions. The Queen, splendidly garbed, sits before the dressing-table in her recently decorated boudoir, overlooking the garden of Buckingham House. She faces the viewer, but the adjoining mirror shows her in profile. Gathered about her are her two sons and a household pet. To show how profound a shift in artistic taste had occurred, this picture, like Hogarth's *Graham Children* (*fig. 23*), should be compared with Van Dyck's *The Five Eldest Children of Charles I* (*fig. 24*), which George III was to acquire for the royal collection in the following year. The stately world of the Stuarts, obsessed with divine prerogative, has been replaced by the withdrawn and unpretentious domestic circle of 'Farmer George'. Far from being decked out in robes of state, the two youths, George, Prince of Wales, at the right in fancy dress as a Roman warrior, and Frederick, later Duke of York, dressed as a Turk, are play-acting solely for their own and their mother's diversion.

David Garrick was Zoffany's first patron in England. As the great portraits of Hogarth and Reynolds testify, the actor was at all times concerned about his public image. Through his popularity and friendship with many of the leading figures in the intellectual and artistic life of the day, he achieved for his profession a social standing never before accorded to players. The kind of image which he sought to project is in part reflected in the four conversations he commissioned from Zoffany while the painter was his guest in 1762. These, the first examples of the type painted by Zoffany, show Garrick not as an actor, but rather as a cultivated gentleman of leisure enjoying the company of family and friends in his suburban retreat at Hampton. In the picture illustrated (*fig. 32*) Garrick stands in the familiar cross-legged pose beside his wife, a Viennese dancer, before the portico of the Shakespeare Temple, designed by Adam to adorn the garden. He points to the Thames, and a waterman is approaching. A servant brings tea around the other side of the octagon. The sprightly child playing among the columns has been identified as Garrick's nephew, Carrington Garrick; and the large dog, a familiar adjunct of the conversation, was his St Bernard, Dragon, to which Hannah More dedicated an ode. Barely visible within the temple is Roubiliac's bust of Shakespeare, placed there in 1758.

Thanks in no small part to Garrick's domination of the stage, this was a period when the public attended the theatre to see an actor performing a favourite role rather than the production of a play. Hogarth, as well as Hayman, had already painted portraits of actors on stage, thus producing a variety of theatrical conversation which Zoffany was to make peculiarly his own during the latter half of the eighteenth century. His initial excursion in the mode, and the picture which launched his career in his adopted homeland, was *David Garrick in 'The Farmer's Return'* (1762, *fig. 33*), an interlude written by the actor himself and first performed at Drury Lane in March 1762. The farmer's wife, standing at the right, was played by Mary Bradshaw. Zoffany has arrested the action at the climactic moment when the farmer, just returned from the coronation of George III, is narrating his encounter with the Cock Lane ghost, whose manifestations were the sensation of the season until they were shown up as a

Fig. 33
Johan Zoffany
David Garrick in 'The Farmer's Return'
1762

hoax. The artist's rendering of the set, lighted by a window at the side and opening on an inner chamber, is unmistakably modelled on Dutch genre interiors. In contrast to the static quality of Devis's scenes, however, the most remarkable feature is the lifelike appearance of the figures. Calling the picture 'a most accurate representation on canvas of that scene as performed at Drury', a contemporary newspaper account continues: 'The painter absolutely transports us in imagination back again to the theatre. We see our favourite Garrick in the act of saying, *for* yes *she knocked* once – and *for* no *she knocked* twice. And we see the wife and children – as we saw them on stage – in terror and amazement; such strong likenesses has the painter exhibited of the several performers that played the characters.'[10]

The meticulous attention to detail combined with high finish which Zoffany had inherited from Netherlandish genre painting made him an unrivalled recorder of the treasured possessions among which his patrons lived, and which were emblematic

alike of their taste and wealth. Many of the objects appearing in his pictures are traceable down to the present day. For example, the French long-case clock in the portrait of Queen Charlotte with her sons is still at Windsor Castle; the silver tea-urn in the conversation of *John, 14th Lord de Broke and his Family* (*c*1771–2) remains in use by descendants; and the gold-headed walking-stick on which the elderly gentleman leans in *The Drummond Family* (*c*1765–9) is preserved in a glass case at Drummond's Bank, of which the sitter was founder. As testimony to the age's zeal for collecting, no picture by Zoffany is more revealing than *Sir Lawrence Dundas and his Grandson* (1769–70, *fig. 34*). The son of an Edinburgh wool-draper, Dundas amassed a vast fortune by shrewd dealing between 1748 and 1759, when he served as commissary-general and paymaster of the army in Scotland, Flanders, and Germany, while at the same time speculating on the Stock Exchange. A discriminating connoisseur as well, he devoted his wealth to furnishing his several residences with collections of art. Here he is shown with his grandson (whose eventual ennoblement as first Earl of Zetland compensated for Dundas's futile manoeuvres to secure a title for himself) in the library or pillar room of his house at 19 Arlington Street, London, which had recently been remodelled by Robert Adam. The artist compliments his sitter by surrounding him with more examples of his holdings than were ever assembled in a single chamber. So faithfully are these presented that it has been possible to draw up an accurate inventory of every picture, piece of furniture and *objet d'art* on view. The painting above the mantelpiece, for instance, is Jan van de Cappelle's *Shipping Becalmed*, now at the Zetland residence at Aske. The documentary interest which Zoffany's conversations hold for the student of eighteenth-century social history is illustrated by the bell-pulls hanging on either side of the fireplace, thought to be the first depiction of this domestic contrivance.

The neo-classical revival which so markedly influenced the arts in the later eighteenth century is strikingly documented in Zoffany's conversation piece of Charles Towneley, the great collector of antique statuary, seated among his marbles in the library of his London residence in Park Street (*fig. 35*). This work, completed in 1783, now hangs in the gallery at Towneley Hall, Burnley. If the portrait of Dundas principally shows pride of ownership, that of Towneley conveys a more intimate and loving relationship with objects with which the collector seems to be engaged in mute discourse, quite as much as with his guests. Most of the pieces, which are readily identifiable, have found a permanent home in the British Museum.[11] Seated opposite Towneley is Pierre Hugues, known as d'Hancarville, a French entrepreneur and antiquary, who was cataloguing the collection. The other individuals are Charles Greville, who kept Emma Hart, the future Lady Hamilton, from 1782 to 1786, discoursing on *Clytie*, Towneley's most treasured bust, to another antiquary, Thomas Astle. Nor should the dog at Towneley's feet be overlooked (it was named Kam, after Kamchatka, for its mother had served as one of the sled-dogs on Captain Cook's expedition to the peninsula of that name).

A different aspect of the intellectual curiosity which contributed so materially to the cultural breadth of social life in Georgian England is illustrated in Zoffany's *John Cuff and an Assistant* (1772, *fig. 36*). George III and Queen Charlotte, who commissioned the work, shared the contemporary enthusiasm for scientific inquiry and technological inventions. Cuff, who had been Master of the Spectacle Makers' Company in 1748, made notable improvements in the design of microscopes, examples of which he provided to the King and Queen. Here he appears with his assistant, both in their working clothes, in his shop at the Sign of the Reflecting Microscope, Fleet Street, surrounded by the instruments of his trade which are depicted with Dutch amplitude of detail. The expressions and postures of the two men are painted with the liveliness that characterized Zoffany's theatrical conversations, and admirably communicate the zeal of dedicated craftsmen.

Zoffany was at his happiest with that most typical form of the conversation, the 'family piece', as it continued to be called throughout the eighteenth century. With considerably more vivacity than Devis in the treatment of facial expression, as well as in the grouping of figures, Zoffany combined a pleasant anecdotal element, almost absent in Devis, which greatly heightens the feeling of informality imparted by his pictures. Such is the case with *John, 3rd Duke of Atholl and his Family* (1765–7, *fig. 37*), commissioned as an overmantel for the drawing-room at Blair Castle, where it still hangs. With the Duke standing at the left, the family is gathered by the river Tay in the grounds of the estate at Dunkeld. The scene's Arcadian mood and details such as the swans suggest Zoffany's conceptual debt to Dandridge's *The Price Family (fig. 20)*. As head of a great territorial family, who took his wealth and position for granted, the Duke exhibits none of the self-consciously proprietary manner so conspicuous in Devis's conversations, but rather genial participation in the holiday mood of his wife and children. John, Marquess of Tullibardine, the eldest son, proudly exhibits a fish that has just been caught. On the opposite side a younger brother, Lord James, has climbed the tree to play with a household pet, a raccoon named Tom, brought back from the West Indies by another relation, Admiral James Murray, to join the menagerie at Blair Castle. The artist's precision in noting fine distinctions is indicated by the two boys to the right of the seated Duchess. The younger, Lord William, who flourishes a branch, is still dressed in an infant's 'coat', while his brother, Lord George, who keeps watch over the hats of the male members of the family, has graduated to a suit. Family groups of this complexity, while challenging the resources of the painter, carried commensurate rewards, for Zoffany received twenty pounds for each of the nine figures represented.

In 1772 Zoffany went to Italy for a prolonged stay,[12] commissioned by Queen Charlotte to paint his most ambitious work, a rendering of the Tribuna in the Uffizi (1772–7/8), crowded with portraits of English *cognoscenti* examining the masterpieces. While in Italy, Zoffany also painted the musical conversation of *Lord Cowper and the Gore Family* (1775, *fig. 38*). The setting, overlooking the Tuscan countryside, is the Villa Palmieri near Florence, purchased in 1776 by George, third Earl Cowper, who commissioned the painting. He is the figure standing at the centre, his gaze fixed on the girl at the left, Hannah Anne Gore, whom he married in June of the same year. In the manner of Hogarth, the marriage is given emblematic significance by the painting on the wall, an allegorical representation of a Roman wedding ceremony. The gentleman playing the violoncello was Charles Gore of Horkstow, Lincolnshire, said to be the original of the 'travelled Englishman' in Goethe's *Wilhelm Meister*. Another daughter accompanies him on the square piano, while Mrs Gore, book in hand, and a third daughter listen to the concert. Zoffany had an informed love of music, and his portraits of performers are unfailingly accurate in detail. Here the musical motif,

OPPOSITE ABOVE

Fig. 37
Johan Zoffany
John, 3rd Duke of Atholl and his Family
1765–7

OPPOSITE BELOW

Fig. 38
Johan Zoffany
Lord Cowper and the Gore Family
1775

OVERLEAF

Fig. 40
Thomas Gainsborough
Robert Andrews and his Wife Frances
c1748–9

abetted by the warmth of colouring, seems by suggestion to flood the composition with its harmonizing power, so that the impression made by the picture is the graphic equivalent of an epithalamium.

Among the most successful artists in portraying the large families of the age was David Allan (1744–96), known as the Scottish Hogarth because of his robust works of pure genre. A letter written to Lord Buchan in December 1780, on Allan's return from Italy, gives his reason for taking up the conversation mode of portraiture: 'I woud bend toward the small Domestic and conversational style, as it tends most to improvement & [is] the most useful as it is the means of everlastingly joining friends together on the canvace . . .' Like Zoffany, though without his expressive qualities, Allan introduced entertaining narrative passages into his group portraits, which unify them by implying communal ties among the sitters. *The Cathcart Family Group* (1784) celebrates the first cricket match to be played north of the Tweed. *The Erskine Family Group* (1783, *fig. 39*) is even richer in anecdotal content. The aloof nobleman seated at the left, John Francis Erskine, was the great nephew of the sixth Earl of Mar, who forfeited his title and was exiled for support of the Old Pretender in the uprising

Fig. 39
David Allan
The Erskine Family Group
1783

of 1715. Three of the children portrayed here are said to have been blind, a fact considered prophetic of the reversal of the attainder and consequent restoration of the title. This event did in fact occur in 1824, allowing the father depicted here to become the seventh earl. The original painting showed the eldest son and heir, John Thomas, perched in the branches of the tree on the right. His portrait was subsequently obliterated when he fell into disfavour with his father, and replaced by the tall hat at which another son aims his arrow. In the background is Alloa House, the family seat, destroyed by fire in 1800.

Portraiture necessarily took precedence over other considerations in the conversation piece; and although the painters, as we have seen, usually portrayed their sitters in surroundings typifying their ways of life, the setting was treated primarily as a backdrop in front of which the figures struck poses as in a photograph. This was especially the case with outdoor scenes, which were invariably painted in the studio, and often more in imaginative terms than from first-hand knowledge of the places ostensibly represented.[13] It took an artist who was also a countryman at heart to make a natural setting a truly operative element in the outdoor conversations which were so much in demand from members of the landed gentry. The artistic inclinations and talents of Thomas Gainsborough (1727–88) were ideally suited to attract the patronage of this class. He was by preference a landscape painter, who throughout life remained nostalgic for his blissful early years in the Suffolk countryside. And during his first period as a portraitist, after he returned from London to Sudbury in 1748 and before his departure for Bath in 1759, he painted a series of exquisite small portraits in which for the first time setting is of equal importance with the figures. These included such works as *The Gravenor Family* (c1747), *Heneage Lloyd and his Sister* (early 1750s), the self-portrait with his wife and elder daughter (c1751–2), and *Mr and Mrs John Browne and Child* (1754–5).

Gainsborough had studied with Gravelot at the St Martin's Lane Academy; but while French fancifulness and delicacy of touch linger in his uniting of figure with landscape, the lighting and atmospheric effects unmistakably belong to the Suffolk scene. Most remarkable of these intimate portraits is *Robert Andrews and his Wife Frances* (c1748–9, *fig. 40*). The sporting country squire and his young wife (just sixteen years of age) are portrayed at Auberies, the former's estate near Sudbury. The sun-drenched prospect opens over a scene familiar to Gainsborough from childhood, as it was to Constable to whom this picture looks forward. The couple had been married in November 1748 at All Saints, Sudbury, the tower of which shows through the distant trees; and since wheat sheaves traditionally symbolize fertility, it has been plausibly proposed that this work was commissioned as a wedding portrait. The postures of the pair, he in the familiar cross-legged pose with gun at rest, she seated primly erect at his side, suggest a restrained intimacy from which the viewer is excluded by the remote gaze with which each challenges him. For theirs is a private world whose natural beauty is at one and the same time a projection and confirmation of their shared felicity. And, indeed, the serenely harmonious appearance of the landscape may well be a reflection of its owner's presence, for it was largely of his creation. There are numerous signs that Andrews belonged to the new breed of improving farmers. The eighteenth century was the great period for acts of parliament enclosing open country for scientific farming. The fields lying beyond the sitters to right and left have been

Fig. 41
George Stubbs
*Captain Samuel Sharpe Pocklington
with his Wife Pleasance and* [?] *his
Sister Frances*
1769

partitioned by hedgerows and fences, and within them are segregated cattle and sheep, kept in conditions providing for better methods of breeding and care of livestock than under the old open-field system. Furthermore, not only are the sheaves properly stacked in the wheatfield to the right; but the grain has been planted in drills or straight rows rather than scattered by hand, thus guaranteeing a heavier harvest in accordance with advanced principles of agricultural economy laid down in Jethro Tull's recent manual, *The Horse-hoeing Husbandry* (1731).[14]

Setting, of course, is an essential component of sporting paintings; and many of the English hunting scenes containing portraits of known individuals, originating with Jan Wyck in the seventeenth century and extending into the eighteenth in an unbroken tradition through the pictures of Peter Tillemans, John Wootton (1670s–1765), and James Seymour (1702–52), qualify as sporting conversation pieces. It remained for the great animal painter, George Stubbs (1724–1806), however, to develop the broader potentialities of this rather specialized genre in group portraits in which the human factor is imaginatively enhanced through association with elements, both animate and inanimate, from the natural world. In *Captain Samuel Sharpe Pocklington with his Wife Pleasance and* [?] *his Sister Frances* (1769, *fig. 41*), for example, the splendid horse standing at the centre provides the focal point of interest, uniting the three human beings in what has been identified as a marriage portrait. The Colonel's pose with an arm thrown across his mount's back expresses his pride in the animal which he treats as a friend and equal. Affection of another kind is conveyed through the attitude of the two women, the elder of whom in her wedding dress bends forward in her seat to offer flowers to her husband's horse. And against the Claudian landscape, suffused with light and fading into the distance, the group is encircled, as it were, in the embrace of the great tree, which, sweeping up along a line established by the inclination of the sisters' figures, spreads its boughs overhead in a protecting canopy.

In contrast to the sense of quietude and repose emanating from this picture is the controlled energy expressed in Stubbs' equestrian piece entitled *John and Sophia Musters riding out at Colwick Hall* (1777, *fig. 42*). Musters, at one time High Sheriff of Nottinghamshire, owned a famous pack of hounds with which he hunted the county for many years. The low horizon of this picture combines with the elevated foreground to project the two riders against the sky, thus emphasizing their aristocratic hauteur. The owner's splendid residence, the rebuilding of which had been completed in the previous year, here primarily serves a painterly function, in contrast to the conventional use of such architectural features as emblems of social rank. For the horses' legs, silhouetted against the severely proportioned classical façade, create a sense of purposeful movement (further accentuated by the two dogs) which contributes greatly to the dashing tone of the composition.[15]

A third artist, whose conversation pieces were much influenced by Zoffany's intimate manner and at the same time show a notable concern for situating his groups in harmonious natural settings, was Francis Wheatley (1747–1801). A charming example is *George and Mary Browne with their Five Elder Children* (c1779, *fig. 43*), in which the group's various activities conform to familiar patterns. While the mother, whose pert stance seems to invite attention, demonstrates the art of angling to her children and the eldest son removes a fish from the hook, the father makes a sketch of

Fig. 42
George Stubbs
*John and Sophia Musters riding out
at Colwick Hall*
1777

the three youngsters gathered by his side. The seven figures are skilfully composed by the stream's edge, backed by a bower of trees which opens to the left onto a receding prospect. The light flooding from this direction highlights the faces as well as the apparel of the sitters (mother and daughters in white, father and sons in darker clothes) against the shady retreat behind. Within the group the two standing girls, erect like their mother, strike similar poses, while the boy by the water echoes the more relaxed posture of his father bent over his drawing-pad. The scene was clearly designed to awaken Arcadian associations through its presentation of happy family life in an idyllic setting.

Beyond capturing a good superficial likeness, the painters of conversation pieces did not, as a general rule, try to read the characters of their subjects at any great depth

Fig. 43
Francis Wheatley
George and Mary Browne with their Five Elder Children
*c*1779

Fig. 44
Joseph Wright
Mr and Mrs Thomas Coltman
*c*1771–2

or with much subtlety of shading. Their concern, as has been said, was with the group rather than the individual. Joseph Wright of Derby (1734–97) is a striking exception to this generalization; for his conversations exhibit a fascination with the psychological interplay between closely associated persons in situations that release their feelings. The dramatic element which Wright injected into his group portraits called, among other things, for an attention to facial expression incompatible with the small size of the conversations, so that his compositions in this style approach the dimensions of formal portraiture. The fact that his patrons (almost exclusively resident in the Midlands where Wright passed virtually his entire life) were also in most cases close friends, doubtless contributed to the insight into personality traits which his pictures exhibit.

Wright's first outdoor portrait commission was *Mr and Mrs Thomas Coltman* (*c*1771–2, *fig. 44*). Coltman, who had inherited Hagnaby Priory in Lincolnshire, was a wealthy squire with sporting proclivities. He and his wife, whom he had recently married, are preparing to set out on a morning ride; she is already mounted, and he leans affectionately beside her while a groom brings up his horse. In its luminosity this picture owes something to Gainsborough, and the general composition and handling show Stubbs' influence; but the manner in which Wright has contrived to suggest the bonds of tender devotion uniting the pair is all his own. Mutual absorption in each other rules out any intrusion on their privacy, as the wife gazes adoringly down at her husband, oblivious of the sight to which he seeks to call her attention (although her extended arm with riding whip unconsciously parallels his gesture). The composition adheres to the familiar triangular pattern, in this case completed by the dog and horse whose affection for each other mirrors that of their owners. The shape of the tree is a further emblem of the union; for the trunk prolongs the sturdy thrust of the husband's torso, while the tributary branch responds to the yielding inclination of the wife's head and shoulders.

A more complex relationship is implied in the tightly knit triangle of three figures composing the conversation of *The Rev. d'Ewes Coke, his Wife Hannah and Daniel Parker Coke*, MP (*c*1780–2, *fig. 45*). The unifying motif is an aesthetic one. The clergyman, who was rector of Pinxton and South Normanton, and who had inherited the estate of Brookhill from his guardian, was himself an amateur artist, as is apparent from the engraver's burin between the fingers of his left hand draped about his wife's shoulder. That she also has artistic leanings is attested by the album which she holds upright on the table. The seated man who has taken a sheet from this album is Daniel Parker Coke, a distant relative who represented both Derby and Nottingham in parliament. The strong light from the left illuminates their faces and throws into bold relief the distinguishing characteristics of each. Pointing to the landscape of which his wife has made a sketch, d'Ewes Coke seeks to reassure her as to its fidelity. But she seems stubbornly unconvinced, as her hand in a parallel gesture draws attention back to the drawing. In the role of mediator, their guest coolly surveys the scene preparatory to comparing it with the sketch in his hand. The psychological acuteness which Wright brought to the observation of his sitters is matched by his accuracy in the rendering of incidental detail, acquired through the study of his Dutch predecessors in genre painting. One notes, for example, how Mrs Coke's green dress has taken on yellow tints from the declining sun, and the attention devoted to delineating the umbrella brought along as a sunshade, but which seems to point to the offstage spectacle on which the attention of the sitters is concentrated.

In the mid-eighteenth century, on the eve of the Industrial Revolution, there was gathered in Derbyshire and Staffordshire a company of remarkable men who embodied the spirit of the Enlightenment through their manufacturing, scientific, and humanitarian pursuits. These individuals, numbering fourteen or so, banded themselves together in a loose fellowship called the Lunar Society, which in its more modest way was the counterpart of the intellectual circle of the Encyclopédistes in

Fig. 45
Joseph Wright
The Rev. d' Ewes Coke,
his Wife Hannah and
Daniel Parker Coke, MP
*c*1780–2

France. Included among the members were Joseph Priestley, the discoverer of oxygen; Erasmus Darwin, botanist, poet, and grandfather of Charles Darwin; and Josiah Wedgwood, head of the great dynasty of potters. Wright was on friendly terms with many of the group; and from the mid-1760s to the early 1770s he perpetuated the interests growing out of their association in an astonishing series of paintings dealing with industrial and scientific subjects. Several of these fall within the category of the conversation piece, although for daring of conception and originality in treatment they have no parallel in the history of the genre. Indeed, in these works the conversation achieves the grandeur of history painting.

A Philosopher giving a Lecture on the Orrery (*c*1764–6, *fig. 46*) depicts with extreme factual accuracy an apparatus, named after the scientifically-minded Charles Boyle, fourth Earl of Orrery, for exhibiting by means of a clockwork mechanism the rotation of the planets about the sun, here represented by a concealed lamp. The individual explaining the operation of the instrument was probably Wright's friend, John Whitehurst, a well-known clock-maker and geologist of Derby; and the young man on the left taking notes is supposed to have been Peter Burdett, a local cartographer. Wright's fondness for night scenes with the light supplied by candles or other artificial illumination was derived from the Utrecht painters, Gerrit van Honthorst and Hendrick Terbruggen, and their follower, Godfried Schalcken. As employed here, the light emanating from a hidden source is only apparent from its reflection in the circle of attentive faces which seem to form a nimbus about the orrery. The effect is to add a startling element of suspense to the scene. In this demonstration to an uninformed audience of the wonders of popular science, the artist has captured in a completely convincing way the enthralment of the spectators as they watch the simulated movement of the heavenly bodies. The expressions of the young woman and man seen in profile to left and right and of the two facing children register every shade of response, from delight through awe to philosophic speculation.

Rivalling Rembrandt's *Dr Tulp's Anatomy Lesson* in its dramatic impact is Wright's *An Experiment on a Bird in the Air Pump* (*c*1767–8, *fig. 47*). The apparatus portrayed here is one observable in the background of Devis's *The Bacon Family* (*fig. 28*), which was commonly used at the time in investigations into the effect of a near vacuum on living creatures. In the globe at the top centre a dove is fluttering in pain as the oxygen in the chamber is gradually exhausted. Despite the interest of the experiment, however, the lamplight focuses attention on the expressive faces of the onlookers, which stand out from the surrounding darkness. Although none has been convincingly identified, these are clearly portraits taken from life. The young lovers at the left are too engrossed in each other to pay much attention to the demonstration. The features of the young girl facing the light are transfigured with pity, while her companion shields her eyes in distress, despite the reassurance of the older man that the bird will not be allowed to die.[16] Like the similarly placed figure in the *Orrery*, the individual seen in profile at the right broods over the implications of such scientific inquiries. Meanwhile, the boy at the window (through which the moon supplies a rival source of illumination) mysteriously catches the viewer's attention as he prepares to lower a cage to receive the revived bird. But most mysterious of all is the attitude of the experimenter whose head and arm, raised to control the globe's air-valve, form the apex of the composition. His gaze, also directed at the viewer, suggests that of a seer rapt in prophetic vision of the potential of the scientific era just opening up, an era destined conclusively to shatter the complacent and tranquil harmonies of the social world commemorated in the conversation piece.

Fig. 46
Joseph Wright
A Philosopher giving a Lecture on the Orrery
*c*1764–6

Fig. 47
Joseph Wright
An Experiment on a Bird in the Air Pump
*c*1767–8

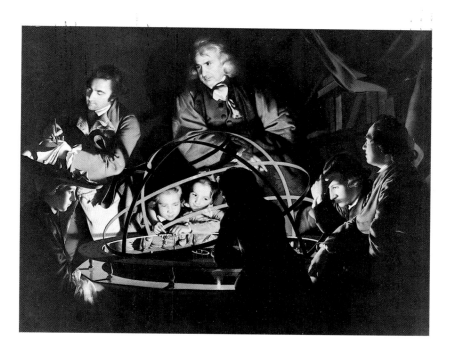

Chapter Three

THE AGE OF
SENSIBILITY

OVERSHADOWING AS HOGARTH'S PLACE WAS in the early history of British genre painting, there was one important artistic project with which he was only tangentially associated. This was the decoration of the pavilions of Vauxhall Gardens during the 1730s and 1740s under the ownership of Jonathan Tyers, who from its opening in 1732 made this resort the favourite haunt of Londoners in search of recreation. Hogarth, a friend of Tyers, may initially have suggested the plan; but he painted only one, or at most two, of the pictures on display. The artist principally responsible for carrying out the work was Francis Hayman, another close associate of Tyers and the painter of a number of conversation portraits of the Tyers family. The resulting collaboration of artist and entrepreneur established a new kind of patronage which was henceforth to be exploited in many variations.

The Vauxhall scheme called for the adornment with paintings of the fifty supper boxes surrounding the central quadrangle. The average size of these was four foot ten by eight feet; even larger pictures were commissioned for other areas. Hayman's selection of subject-matter included, in addition to conventional borrowings from historical and literary (largely Shakespearian) sources, a large number of depictions of rustic life and popular pastimes. This was virtually the first time that an artist tapped the reservoir of indigenous habits and customs on which genre painters continued to draw right through the succeeding century and a half. The scenes represented diversions – primarily of children and young people – including building card-houses, blind man's buff, leap-frog, see-saw, battledore and shuttlecock, bird-catching and bird-nesting, sliding on ice, bob-cherry, fortune-telling, dancing around the maypole, and the game of cricket. Many of these motifs had been employed by Watteau and his followers, Lancret and Pater; and Hayman would have been familiar with their practice through Gravelot, with whom he taught at the St Martin's Lane Academy, and who is indeed thought to have supplied some of the Vauxhall designs. But in a number of cases Hayman took his themes directly from the life about him. While many of the paintings are known only through preparatory drawings or engravings, about fifteen of the originals have survived. Their style exhibits an

Fig. 48
Francis Hayman
The Milkmaid's Garland, or the Humours of May Day
*c*1740

attractive blend of French rococo grace and elegance with a realistic boldness of invention that is unmistakably English. Hayman's importance as a historian of manners comes out in his Vauxhall picture, *The Milkmaid's Garland, or the Humours of May Day* (*c*1740, *fig. 48*), portraying an ancient custom which lingered on into the mid-nineteenth century. On the first of May the London milkmaids declared a holiday and donned fancy costumes and rented silver plates and mugs which they arranged into a kind of pyramid adorned with flowers and ribbons, to be carried on the head in the manner of their daily milk-pails. They then went the rounds of their customers, performing dances about this emblem to the music of fiddles and bagpipes and inviting contributions. It is an indication of the popularity of the picture that the engraving was transferred to decorate Worcester china.

There can be no understanding the rise of an art representative of popular taste in later eighteenth-century England without taking into account the phenomenal spread of the print trade. As a result, patronage of the artist, hitherto subject to control by the upper classes, expanded to the public at large. This was the audience which Hogarth had first envisaged by the sale of his pictures in engraved replicas, and whose direct support he had sought to ensure by the provisions of the Copyright Act of 1735, which he sponsored. Of the far-reaching effects of this piece of legislation Jean-André Rouquet wrote in *The Present State of the Arts in Britain* (1755): 'Before that time there were only two print shops in London; but since this act, they suddenly increased to some hundreds: and if we consider the number and abilities of the engravers who are now in that metropolis, we must allow that of all acts relative to design, that of engraving has made the greatest and quickest progress in England.'

The art of printmaking in England was at a low ebb in the opening years of the eighteenth century. This situation improved significantly with the influx of highly trained Parisian artisans following the Treaty of Utrecht in 1713, and the conclusion of a trade pact with France in 1719. Such artists as Gravelot not only set an example of high finish in their prints, but provided instruction for local engravers to supply the growing market. Meanwhile, during the decade 1740–50 many English craftsmen went to Paris to work with the great French masters, especially Jacques Philippe Le Bas (1707–83). With the establishment in 1754 of the Society for the Encouragement of Arts, Manufacture and Commerce in Great Britain, these artists came home to swell the ranks of a native school rapidly establishing its ascendancy over Continental rivals, the more so in that its numbers were strengthened by a steady stream of recruits from across the Channel. Within a few years English eminence in all graphic media was acknowledged; not only engraving and mezzotint (regarded as primarily a native mode), but also stipple and aquatint which arrived from France after the mid-century. As perfected by Francesco Bartolozzi (c1725–1815), an Italian who resided in England from 1764, colour stipple came into special esteem for the reproduction of popular subjects. It has been estimated that nearly three hundred artisans in this medium were employed in England during the last quarter of the eighteenth century.

The spread of the print trade would have been impossible without the support of a numerous company of enterprising dealers, who in many cases had themselves started out as engravers. The most ambitious and successful of these was John Boydell (1719–1804), whom Burke called England's 'commercial Maecenas'. Beginning in the mid-1740s as a purveyor of plates from the works of the Dutch and Flemish schools, he soon turned to the home front, enlisting the services of the finest engravers, such as William Woollett (1735–85), in a carefully planned patriotic campaign to establish the supremacy of the English in the fields of the graphic arts. In a letter of 1804 he commented on the success which had greeted his efforts:

> When I first began business [c1745], the whole commerce of prints in this country consisted in importing foreign prints, principally from France, to supply the cabinets of the curious in this kingdom. Impressed with the idea that the genius of our own countrymen, if properly encouraged, was equal to that of foreigners, I set about establishing a School of Engraving in England; with what success the public are well acquainted. It is, perhaps, at present, sufficient to say that the whole course of that commerce is changed, very few prints being now imported into this country, while the foreign market is principally supplied with prints from England.

In support of his assertion Boydell might have cited a statement by the Earl of Suffolk to the House of Lords that by 1778 the value of the export of English prints to France had reached an annual figure of £200,000, whereas imports had dropped to a mere £100.

Evidence of this sort should dispel the still prevalent tendency to relegate English paintings of the period to a provincial side-chamber. Engravings from the works of the more popular native artists circulated throughout Europe. The first public sale of English prints in Paris was in 1763, and others followed in 1764, 1765, 1773 and regularly thereafter. Such was the market for these works that by 1787 French buyers at print sales in London outnumbered English purchasers by three to one. Of the continuing demand for examples of the English school C. Josi, a Dutch collector and dealer who had spent five years in England as a pupil of the engraver J. R. Smith, wrote in 1821:

> The craze for English engravings during the last fifty years is extraordinary. Everyone has developed a taste for them. I am, of course, aware that they have reached an exaggerated value as mere objects of mercantile speculation, but this is only natural. They are all snapped up as soon as they are seen, bring a certain and considerable profit, and few objects have ever met with so rapid and so widely-extended a demand.

And elsewhere Josi remarks that the foreign market had resulted in a lively trade in the forgery of prints by such popular artists as Morland.

Boydell is the leading exemplar of the new type of patron who was eventually to supersede the private collector not only in the sponsorship of painting, but also in the support of the host of reproductive artists through whose engravings original works could be widely disseminated. At the time of the liquidation of his stock in 1803, following the collapse of the Continental trade brought about by the Napoleonic Wars, Boydell's catalogue listed an inventory of 4,432 prints, of which 2,293 were of English paintings. No fewer than two hundred and fifty engravers had been in his employ at one time or another. To absorb this output Boydell and his fellow dealers had fostered a widespread appetite for prints, reaching down to the humblest householder, since examples could be bought for prices ranging from sixpence or a shilling to half a guinea. The Earl of Shaftesbury had spoken prophetically when in *Second Characters of the Language of Forms* (1712) he likened the 'invention of prints . . . to printing in the commonwealth of letters'. Samuel Strutt prefaced his *A Biographical Dictionary of Engravers* (1785) with the statement that in England 'almost every man of taste is in some degree a collector of prints'. And John Pye was to write in *Patronage of British Art* (1845) that as a result of the extension of the print trade 'the British *public* became honourably distinguished as affording the first source of real patronage enjoyed by the British artist.'[1]

For those aspects of contemporary life most congenial to the public in the latter half of the eighteenth century, one must therefore look, to a very large extent, to paintings produced with an eye to their graphic reproduction. As might be expected, these pictures, like their seventeenth-century counterparts in Dutch genre painting, were small in size and mirrored the domestic concerns of the middle classes whose homes they were designed to adorn. In accordance with the inclinations of a novel-reading audience, they customarily depicted situations fraught with narrative or anecdotal interest; and before all else, they were imbued with the strongly moralistic presuppositions of the social order whose mores they flattered.

In the latter respect they retained the didactic fervour of Hogarth, but with a profound difference. For that artist's satiric impulse, which he shared with Swift, Pope and Fielding, was no longer amenable to a bourgeois mentality grounded in complacency and little disposed to have its values called in question.[2] Even while courting its favour through the sale of prints of his paintings, Hogarth had not hesitated to castigate the hypocritical pretensions of his middle-class audience. The portrait of the alderman in *Marriage A-la-Mode (fig. 10)* seems a good deal more savage than that of the earl;[3] and each of the pictures of *The Four Times of the Day (figs 2–5)*, as we have seen, ridicules some aspect of the affectations of London 'cits'. With the political and economic ascendancy of the middle class firmly established by the middle of the century, however, there grew up among its members an increasingly confident sense of their instrumental role in setting the cultural tone of national life. As a result, the kind of behaviour which excited Hogarth's mockery, while it may have persisted, ceased to be a subject for artistic treatment, and was replaced by a self-congratulatory celebration of the positive virtues making for worldly success and individual well-being.

Hogarth's posthumous reputation illustrates this important shift in the way society now expected to encounter its image in the mirror of art. With the encouragement of his widow, eager to promote the sale of her husband's prints, the Rev. John Trusler undertook to explain their subjects in accordance with contemporary ideals of conduct. Published in fourteen parts, 1766–8, the work was entitled: *Hogarth Moralized Being a Complete Edition of Hogarth's Works. ... With an Explanation, pointing out the many Beauties that may have hitherto escaped Notice; and a Comment on their Moral Tendency. Calculated to improve the Minds of Youth, and, convey Instruction, under the Mask of Entertainment.* Trusler's attempt to convert Hogarth's masterpieces into sermonizing exempla anticipated several series of pictures produced in direct imitation of the artist's moral progresses, though with their message watered down for popular consumption. The earliest of these, by John Collet (*c*1725–80) was entitled *Modern Love* (1765) in clear admission of the artist's debt to *Marriage A-la-Mode*. The series of four episodes following the courtship and elopement of a well-born couple through to eventual disillusionment with marriage retains some vestiges of Hogarth's uncompromising realism. Little of this spirit survived twenty years later in the six parts of *Laetitia, or Seduction* (1786) by George Morland (1763–1804), which trace the downfall of a country girl from seduction by a town gallant through a career as a kept woman and then a prostitute, and her final repentance and forgiveness by her parents. Clearly modelled on *A Harlot's Progress*, Morland's sequence spares his heroine the depths of degradation to which Moll Hackabout sinks and provides a happy ending through her return to the humble cottage from which she eloped.[4]

Francis Wheatley painted a set of pictures in 1791 which fulfilled Hogarth's abortive intention to match *Marriage A-la-Mode* with the depiction of a happy marriage. The titles of the four episodes are sufficient indication of the conventional stages through which the pictured narrative pursues its sentimental course: *The Maternal Blessing – Maidenhood; The Offer of Marriage – Courtship; The Wedding Morning – Marriage; The Happy Fireside – Married Life.* Although the maiden improves her social station through matrimony, the setting of each picture is rustic; and in three of the four the heroine is engaged in some domestic pursuit. A notice in the *Morning Herald* of 1792 bears witness to the artist's success in mingling moral precept with pleasure:

... by elevating the arts to the dignity of a moral in this series of pictures, he has, with singular felicity, employed his pencil in delineating the progress and manners of humble life – pursuing and attaining happiness through the channels of prudence and industry. ... The story is well told, and the scene in *The Happy Fireside* is particularly interesting. If we knew a man whose mind, soured and contracted by the presence of undeserved calamity, was verging to misanthropy, we should place this picture before him, and we think his social affections would revive.

In 1796 Reynolds' pupil, James Northcote (1746–1831), produced a feminine counterpart to *Industry and Idleness*, the most didactic of Hogarth's progresses. In the ten pictures of *Diligence and Dissipation* the protagonists are a chaste and a wanton serving-girl, who pursue courses parallel to Hogarth's two apprentices, the one being rewarded by marriage with her employer (as in *Pamela*), while the other dies in disease and poverty. Allan Cunningham states that Northcote aspired in this sequence to unite 'poetry with the realities of life' and at the same time 'to read a great moral lesson to his country'; but, despite the inclusion of details of a boldness to challenge Hogarth, posterity has sided with the Redgraves' description of the artist's achievement as 'milk-and-water illustrations of the lesser moralities'.[5]

These imitations of Hogarth's pictorial narratives are wholly devoid of the critical spirit everywhere manifest in the work of the master. They are addressed solely to the feelings, with the purpose of arousing a sympathetic response in the observer. In this respect they are symptomatic of a new insistence on the primacy of the human emotions over the rational faculties. The revolt against the cultural ideals based on reason, which had shaped neo-classical culture from the Renaissance on, was a component of the middle-class ethos and had its sources deep in the beliefs and practices of Protestant dissent. Opposition to received authority, not only in religious matters, had encouraged a direct appeal to the individual conscience, whose testimony spoke to the heart rather than the mind. By the mid-eighteenth century worldly prosperity had in large measure replaced the asperities of Puritan teaching with a deistic faith in the essential goodness of human nature. Reliance on the promptings of the intuitions as a guide to conduct was further confirmed by the sensationalist psychology of Locke and his school, and by Hume's philosophic scepticism, which denied man's capacity to attain certitude by cognitive means. 'The ultimate ends of human action', Hume asserted in *An Enquiry concerning Human Understanding*, 'can never ... be accounted for by *reason*, but recommend themselves entirely to the sentiments and affections of mankind.'

What has come to be known as the Age of Sensibility, thus prepared for, had its first popular manifestation in literature. An inkling of what was in store occurs in Fielding's *Tom Jones*. When the heroine, Sophia Western, is asked by her aunt whether she does not enjoy a good cry, she responds, 'I love a tender sensation, and would pay the price of a tear for it any time.' The temperamental effusiveness which Fielding here treats with tender mockery was to be made an absorbing concern by the novelist who succeeded him in popularity. In *Pamela* Samuel Richardson brought a finesse hitherto unimagined to the analysis of the emotional crises through which his maidservant-heroine passes as she endeavours to retain her chastity despite the solicitations of her employer. With Richardson, however, moral issues are still

Fig. 49
Francis Wheatley
Four Times of the Day: Morning
1799

paramount. In the works of his successors, Goldsmith's *The Vicar of Wakefield* (1766), Sterne's *A Sentimental Journey* (1768), and Mackenzie's *The Man of Feeling* (1771), they often seem merely a pretence for harrowing the feelings of the reader in situations primarily intended to elicit a tearful response. 'Dear Sensibility!' wrote Sterne, 'Eternal fountain of our feelings! ... all comes from thee!'[6] Sentimentality came to be regarded as a component of virtuous behaviour; and educational theory stressed the importance of cultivating the feelings.

Although it can plausibly be argued that the cult of sensibility sprang from the temperamental bent of the middle class in Georgian England, the movement was in the air and soon ignited responses throughout Continental Europe. *Pamela* was translated into Dutch, French, Danish and Italian within a few months of its publication, and everywhere was greeted as the herald of a new era of emotional hedonism. The writings of Goldsmith, Sterne and Mackenzie had their counterpart in Goethe's *The Sorrows of Young Werther*, Rousseau's *La Nouvelle Héloise*, and Gessner's *Idylls*. The earliest artistic manifestation of the movement occurred in France, where Greuze set the example for a new style of domestic genre painting, derived from the Dutch but strongly moralistic and drenched in sentiment. His episodes of village life, *La Lecture de la Bible* (1755) and *L'Accordée de Village* (1761), enjoyed a sensational success when exhibited at the Salon, and established the artist as the undisputed master of what became known as *la peinture morale*.[7] In Diderot the artist found a fervent and influential advocate for whom the ethical situations dramatized in his pictures elevated them to the dignity of history painting. In the critic's view, however, Greuze's success was clearly less dependent on intellectual content than on the emotional intensity generated by his work. Central to the expressive aesthetic of the school of sensibility was the belief that the artist must communicate his own emotional engagement with his subject in such a way as to compel an equally passionate involvement on the viewer's part. In his *Inquiry into the Beauties of Painting* (1760) Daniel Webb insisted that paintings should 'melt the soul into a tender participation of human miseries ... give a turn to the mind advantageous to society ... and quicken us to acts of humanity and benevolence.'

Engravings of Greuze's pictures were known throughout Europe, and they exercised a considerable influence on the development of sentimental genre painting in England. The French artist's example is markedly apparent in the work of Francis Wheatley. On his return in 1783 from a lengthy stay in Ireland, Wheatley virtually abandoned portrait painting and turned to a more profitable career of working for printsellers, especially Boydell. His popularity is attested by the fact that about 200 engravings were made from his paintings, a figure exceeded only by Morland. It was also during this period that the artist made illustrations for a number of the classics of *sensibilité*: among others Rousseau's *La Nouvelle Héloise*, Marmontel's *Contes Moraux*, Sterne's *A Sentimental Journey*, and Goldsmith's 'The Deserted Village'.

Wheatley's characteristic manner is evident in a series of pictures, the last he displayed at the Royal Academy, called *Four Times of the Day* (1799, *figs 49–52*), a subject which enjoyed a great vogue during the eighteenth century, as we have seen. It is when Wheatley's series is compared with that by Hogarth of 1738 (*figs 2–5*) that the full extent of the revolution in artistic taste during the period becomes apparent. Hogarth's pictures are townscapes, picturing with mordant wit the Vanity Fair of the

Fig. 50
Francis Wheatley
Four Times of the Day: Noon
1799

Fig. 51
Francis Wheatley
Four Times of the Day: Evening
1799

London streets. Only in the evening scene is there any trace of a rural setting, and it is introduced for ironic purposes. Wheatley's sequence, on the other hand, purports to present a typical day in the life of a yeoman's family. Significantly, the series of engravings carried the title *Rustic Hours*. The impression conveyed by these domestic vignettes is one of bucolic felicity. In contrast to the fuss and fret of Hogarth's London, Wheatley allows no space for the hard labour, the grinding struggle against poverty which was the small farmer's lot, the only hint of this being the weary farmer slumped over the kitchen table at the end of the day. At noon the entire family gathers for an alfresco picnic in the fields; and the other pictures dwell lovingly on the closeness and harmony of the family circle as the comely matron goes about her daily round of household chores, churning butter, folding linen, etc. The children all appear in ruddy health and are neatly dressed and obviously well cared for. The pretty cottage in its picturesque setting completes an Arcadian vision of contentment and well-being.

In the pastoral mode artists like Wheatley found a means of portraying life among the lower orders of society that would recommend itself to the middle-class public for which their paintings and prints were intended. Nothing could be further from the dispassionate realism of scenes depicting the drunken and clownish boors in Dutch genre. England's economy was still largely agrarian; and by long tradition, persistently invoked in literature, the countryside was thought of as the font of virtue and innocence in contrast to the vice and corruption of the city. The theme is central, for example, in Fielding's novels, the author declaring in the introduction to *Tom Jones*: 'We shall represent Human Nature at first to the keen appetite of our reader in that more plain and simple manner in which it is found in the country, and shall hereafter hash and ragout it with all the high French and Italian seasoning of affectation and vice which courts and cities afford.'

In presenting the town-dweller's idealized version of the rewards and pleasures of rural living, artists such as Wheatley were, furthermore, appealing to the same motive which impelled successful members of the commercial and professional classes to acquire broad acres in a society where worldly standing was so largely dependent on the ownership of land. The support of a loyal and subservient peasantry was an important adjunct of the way of life which these new landowners envisioned for

Fig. 52
Francis Wheatley
Four Times of the Day: Night
1799

themselves, as they planned the fine houses and spacious gardens commemorated in the conversation piece. And as towns in the closing decades of the eighteenth century became increasingly industrialized, so the expanding populace responded more readily to the sentimental attraction of prints that evoked the tranquil and carefree existence of the cottage dweller. Echoing the Virgilian refrain, 'O fortunatos nimium, sua si bona nôrint, Agricolas!' ('Ah blessed beyond all bliss the husbandmen, did they but know their happiness!'), the frustrated history painter, James Barry (1741–1806), was to say in a lecture during the 1780s, with regard to the charm of pastoral subjects:

> ... the simple, laborious, honest, hinds; the lowing herds, smooth lakes, and cool extended shades; the snug, warm cot, sufficient and independent; the distant hamlet; and the free, unconfined association between all parts of nature, must ever afford a grateful prospect to the mind. No doubt much of our satisfaction results from contrasting this state of things with the dark, insidious, hypocritical disguises; the hateful enormities, vanities, affectations, and senseless pageantries, so frequently found in the courts of the great, and in large cities ...

The superficiality with which popular artists pictured country people and their ways was not lost on astute critics, who also took exception to the insistent call for a sentimental response in these works. One writer, John Williams, who used the pseudonym Anthony Pasquin, remarked of Wheatley's practice: 'Whenever Mr Wheatley presents us with a rural Nymph whom he wishes to be peculiarly impressive, he decorates her head with a profusion of party-coloured ribbands, like a maniac in Coventry, which play in the breeze, offensive to thought and propriety. As this is not the character of our village Daphnes, why make them prodigiously fine at the expence of truth?' Such comments, however, make insufficient allowance for the fact that, however much artists prettified the scenes which they represented and heightened their interest with contrived situations, these scenes were nevertheless based on observation of typical activities of the rural populace and the places in which they were carried on. Thus, in noteworthy contrast to the rococo *pastorales* of such artists as Boucher, Wheatley and his English contemporaries were in fact calling attention to modes of behaviour and social relationships in rural society hitherto ignored by artists.

The proliferation of prints issued by dealers eager to supply the demands of the new public towards the end of the eighteenth century was so great that it is possible to cite only a few representative examples from the work of the better artists working for this market. A common practice was the production of pictures in pairs. Popular for their suitability as wall decorations, such pairs also expanded the artist's narrative and thematic scope. For, if skilfully chosen, the twin scenes created a reciprocal effect, each enhancing the interest of the other, and so intensifying its own inherent appeal.[8] One of the most frequent motifs inviting this treatment was that of departure and return; the going away from home and coming back of soldiers and sailors, of fishermen or hunters, of schoolchildren, of hucksters visiting market, or holiday-makers at fairs and other festivals. The potential for arousing contrasting emotional responses, ranging from the sorrow of parting to the joy of reunion, especially if the absence was of any duration and involved an element of suspense or danger, is clear enough without examples. A second type of situation lending itself to varied treatment

Fig. 53
Francis Wheatley
Scene from a Camp with an Officer buying Chickens
(The Encampment at Brighton)
1788

Fig. 54
Francis Wheatley
Scene from a Camp with an Officer buying Ribbons
(The Departure from Brighton)
1788

Fig. 55
George Morland
St James's Park
*c*1790

in paired works was the city-country dichotomy, with the opportunity to juxtapose scenes embodying conflicting values and attitudes. The proximity of the squire's manor to the tenant's cottage likewise offered the opportunity for social commentary, whether demonstrating class division or shared interest. Or, to cite a further category involving family relationships, the cruel or tender parent and the errant or dutiful child suggested episodes which could be endlessly combined in sentimental pairings.

Today's viewer naturally inclines to those portrayals of the later Georgian social scene in which the didactic, moralizing and sentimental elements are most restrained. Such a pair (1788) by Wheatley represents the military camp at Bagshot, showing respectively one officer bargaining for chickens, and a second for ribbons. When mezzotinted in 1796 these pictures were entitled *The Encampment at Brighton*

Fig. 56
George Morland
The Tea Garden
*c*1790

(*fig. 53*) and *The Departure from Brighton (fig. 54)*, perhaps because the annual assembling of militia at Brighton attracted more attention. In addition to the wealth of local colour in each, the scenes are of interest because, unlike conventional history painting, they show soldiers in peacetime, off duty and mingling with the rural populace. Another pair, engraved in 1790, and equally rich in documentary detail, is by George Morland, with the titles *St James's Park (fig. 55)* and *The Tea Garden (fig. 56)*. In the first, representing an officer with his wife and three children, the country has invaded the city; for cows were kept in Spring Gardens and driven to the park each day to provide milk at a penny a mug to citizens enjoying an outing. The dairy woman may have been a Mrs Sarah Pollock, who appears in a watercolour of a similar subject and the same period by Julius Caesar Ibbetson (1759–1817). The second picture shows a substantial merchant taking tea with his family at Bagnigge Wells, on the site of Nell Gwynn's country residence, where pleasure gardens with ponds and arbours had been built. Pictures of this kind preserve the intimate charm of conversation pieces but with anonymous sitters and the addition of a good deal of business to enliven the scene.

Pairings of a more conventional nature carry moral lessons dramatized through sentimental situations. These commonly reflect the ethical outlook of their middle-class audience, a perspective which the viewer is invited to share. Thus, a large number of pictures with their pendants preach the rewards of thrift and industry for the lower classes in contrast to the penalties of improvidence and sloth. In 1789 two plates after Morland were engraved with the titles *The Effects of Youthful Extravagance and Idleness* and *The Fruits of Early Industry and Economy*. The subjects proved so popular that the artist painted a second and wholly different pair in the following year, entitled *The Miseries of Idleness (fig. 57)* and *The Comforts of Industry (fig. 58)*. The first of these represents a destitute family in threadbare clothing and wretchedly housed. All the properties of the scene bespeak the father's feckless ways. The postures of the sleeping husband, his wife and the two older children (the boy gnawing a bone) are marked by listless dejection, while the neglected baby howls on its pallet. Although the group in the second picture is shown in an equally humble cottage room, their appearance is neat and clean, emblematic of self-respecting frugality. The stalwart farmer, who throws a guinea into his wife's lap, is clearly a good provider; for a large joint and cabbage are laid out on the table to the right. The lively gestures of the members of the family denote not only contentment with their lot, but the close bonds that unite them.

Rather more dramatic, even melodramatic, is the pairing from a few years earlier (1774) entitled *The Profligate punished by Neglect and Contempt (fig.59)* and *The Virtuous comforted by Sympathy and Attention (fig.60)* by Edward Penny (1714–91), who was the first Professor of Painting at the Royal Academy. Here the artist was less concerned with details of setting than with psychological aspects of the scenes. In every sense these pictures conform to the French term, *drames muets*. Each, furthermore, relies on its companion to generate its full impact, since illness has reduced both protagonists to a dependent state. The callous disregard provoked by the fierce, gout-ridden old reprobate in the first picture is set against the compassion with which her attendants minister to the gentle invalid in the pendant. The supplementary figures fill the role of surrogates for the viewer, whose attitude is conditioned by their behaviour, hostile in one case, sympathetic in the other. Although these works unmistakably derive from Dutch genre of the preceding century, their charged emotionalism and moral teaching are essentially products of eighteenth-century bourgeois sensibility.

According to the Protestant system of values, the conspicuous middle-class virtue which corresponded with thrift and industry among the lower orders was benevolence, manifesting itself in charitable deeds. The great Latitudinarian divines of the Restoration and early eighteenth century, such as Isaac Barrow, John Tillotson and Richard Cumberland, had argued that, since human beings are essentially good, they have an inherent inclination to perform virtuous acts. The deist Matthew Tindal was speaking for this point of view when he wrote in *Christianity as Old as the Creation*

ABOVE
Fig. 57
George Morland
The Miseries of Idleness
1790

OPPOSITE ABOVE
Fig. 58
Morland, George
The Comforts of Industry
1790

OPPOSITE LEFT
Fig. 59
Edward Penny
The Profligate punished by Neglect and Contempt
1774

OPPOSITE RIGHT
Fig. 60
Edward Penny
The Virtuous comforted by Sympathy and Attention
1774

Fig. 61
William Redmore Bigg
*The Rapacious Steward, or
the Unfortunate Tenant*
1801

Fig. 62
William Redmore Bigg
*The Benevolent Heir, or the
Tenant restored to his
Family*
1797

Fig. 63
William Ward
The Sailor's Orphans, or the Young Ladies' Subscription
mezzotint after painting by
W. R. Bigg
1799

(1730) that man is 'a social creature, who naturally loves his own species, and is full of pity, tenderness & benevolence.'[9]

Benevolence was adopted as the controlling motive in equitable social intercourse by figures as different as the third Earl of Shaftesbury and Adam Smith, and provided the middle classes with a code of conduct that allowed their members to exhibit humanitarian zeal through the channels of private munificence, while at the same time supporting the *status quo* of a hierarchic social structure. An added inducement to the relief of want and suffering among one's social inferiors was its reciprocal effect, since in alleviating need the benefactor reaped the benefits of a good conscience and rose in his own esteem.

No theme provided a wider field of subject-matter to genre painting in the later eighteenth century than that of charity. A pair of pictures by William Redmore Bigg (1755–1828), Penny's pupil, entitled *The Rapacious Steward, or the Unfortunate*

Tenant (1801, *fig. 61*) and *The Benevolent Heir, or the Tenant restored to his Family* (1797, *fig. 62*) illustrates the precarious lot of the yeomanry under the agrarian revolution that was in progress. The first shows a flinty-hearted overseer in the act of evicting a tenant farmer who has fallen in arrears with his rent. The composition suggests a *tableau vivant* in which the artist has spared no effort to harrow the viewer's feelings through the figures frozen in postures of dismay. In the pendant the same group appears under happier circumstances. The farmer has been redeemed from prison through the intervention of the compassionate squire and his wife, who stand at the right. Another picture by Bigg, here represented by the engraving (1799, *fig. 63*), indicates the educational importance attached to instilling charitable impulses during the formative years. The headmistress of a girls' seminary, shown in the distance, has brought her genteel charges to visit the home of the widow of a sailor, whose death has left his family in straitened circumstances. The scene has been conceived in such a way as to flatter without unduly upsetting the viewer's sensibilities. For the bearing of the

Fig. 64
Edward Penny
The Marquess of Granby aiding a Sick Soldier
1765

Fig. 65
Francis Wheatley
*John Howard visiting and relieving
the Miseries of a Prison*
1787

two older women is equally dignified; and, save for their clothing, there is no significant difference between the appearance or manners of the bereft children and the young ladies who shyly volunteer their offerings. The explanatory caption, printed in French as well as English, shows that the engraver, William Ward (1766–1826), was working for a Continental as well as a home audience.[10]

A fine early canvas by Penny, which was very popular as a mezzotint, bears the title *The Marquess of Granby aiding a Sick Soldier* (1765, *fig. 64*). John Manners, Marquess of Granby, was an exceptionally gallant military hero, much loved by his men because of his unfailing concern for their welfare. His readiness to relieve distress became a byword, and is commemorated in the large number of public houses still bearing his name. In this picture the restraint exhibited by officer and soldier alike establishes a bond transcending difference in rank, while the picture's overt emotional appeal is

Fig. 66
George Morland
A Visit to the Child at Nurse
c1788

Fig. 67
George Morland
A Visit to the Boarding School
c1789

relegated to the soldier's wife and children. In *John Howard visiting and relieving the Miseries of a Prison* (1787, *fig. 65*), Wheatley produced his masterpiece. Clearly patterned on compositions by Greuze, the painting shows the great prison reformer indignantly calling the gaoler's attention to the plight of the inmates. For all its deliberate assault on the feelings, the scene carries complete conviction through the sympathetic insight with which facial expressions and gestures are rendered. Howard, who was never willing to sit for a formal portrait, is especially impressive in the stern indignation of his bearing.[11]

Too often, it must be admitted, a sentimental tone incommensurate with the subjects portrayed makes the moral message these pictures were designed to convey seem perfunctory and condescending. Addressed to an audience that looked to art for a reflection of its social pretentions, the works betray in their handling the

Fig. 68
James Ward
The Rocking Horse
1793, engraving

Fig. 69
Philip Mercier
The Oyster Girl (The Fair Oysterinda)
*c*1745–50

OPPOSITE

Fig. 70
Henry Walton
Girl plucking a Turkey
*c*1776

superficiality and hollowness of the very values they are meant to vindicate. Two of Morland's most accomplished pictures in his early manner seem to comment with unwonted irony on this disparity. They depict *A Visit to the Child at Nurse (fig. 66)* and *A Visit to the Boarding School (fig. 67*, engraved in 1788 and 1789 respectively). The former records the practice among women of the middle and upper classes of consigning their babies to wet nurses until weaning, while the second relates to the custom of sending well-bred girls away from home to complete their education in finishing schools. One notices, however, that the baby clings to the foster parent, while the young daughter seems somewhat less than eager to be reunited with a parent who does not even rise to greet her. Although both scenes arouse sentimental expectations, one can hardly avoid the conclusion, conveyed subtly but with rare candour by the artist, that the mother in each is enjoying the luxury of emotion without any of the responsibility it should entail.

While carefully delineated to the observing eye, class gradations were for the most part taken for granted and passed over without comment by the artist as an integral aspect of the social fabric. Only occasionally is a note of dissonance allowed to intrude on the prescribed pattern of relationships between the upper and lower orders. A rare example of veiled commentary on privilege is *The Rocking Horse* (1793, *fig. 68*), painted and engraved by James Ward (1769–1859), Morland's brother-in-law. A pampered brother and sister divert themselves with their costly toy, oblivious of the poor woman and two children peering through the iron bars of the gates which exclude them from the park.

Subjects belonging to a small but delightful category of domestic genre paintings became known in the eighteenth century as 'fancy' pictures. As with the conversation piece, Philip Mercier deserves a major portion of the credit for developing this mode[12] in the years after he fell out of favour with his patron, Frederick, Prince of Wales, and withdrew from London to take up residence in York (1739). In 1737 Vertue, ever alert to artistic trends, described Mercier's new manner as 'peices of some figures of conversation as big as the life conceited plaisant Fancies & habits. mixt modes really well done – and much approvd off.' Mercier had formed an association with John Faber the Younger (1695–1756), dealer and engraver, who as early as 1739 published eight mezzotints from his pictures; and it seems clear that from the outset the artist exploited this vein with an eye to the print market. While his subjects in the majority of cases hark back to seventeenth-century Dutch artists, such as Dou, Metsu and Netscher, Mercier's immediate inspiration was Chardin, whose work was becoming known in England through prints.[13] Mercier, however, replaced the French artist's objectivity with an altogether more informal and intimate approach to his subjects. His fancy pictures might include as many as three or even more figures, but in their perfected form during the 1750s they were normally confined to a single portrait, usually of a woman engaged in some domestic employment. In contrast to the genre conventions prevailing later in the century, these works are devoid of moralistic intent; and the narrative element is also for the most part absent. Typical of Mercier's manner is *The Oyster Girl (The Fair Oysterinda)* (*c*1745–50, *fig. 69*). Despite her menial occupation, there is a rococo charm and elegance in the treatment of the girl's relaxed pose and dainty dress, set off against a plain background. Her pert gaze teases the viewer; yet the sentimental appeal, while present, is skilfully restrained.

Mercier's example inspired two followers, examples of whose works are regrettably rare. One was Henry Robert Morland (1730–97), father of the more famous George, whose *A Lady's Maid soaping Linen* and *A Laundry Maid ironing*, both at the Tate Gallery, are examples of the fine vein of realism the fancy picture opened up in its depiction of the labouring class at their work. A better artist was the gently born Henry Walton (1746–1813), a pupil of Zoffany, whose few known genre pictures date from 1776 to 1780. For cool lucidity of observation and exquisite tonality these little masterpieces, unrivalled in English painting, challenge Chardin's achievement. They include *Girl plucking a Turkey* (*c*1776, *fig. 70*), *A Pretty Maid buying a Love Song* (1778), *The Silver Age* (*c*1778), and *The Cherry Barrow* (1779).

Fig. 71
Francis Wheatley
The Seller of Primroses
1893, engraving

OVERLEAF LEFT

Fig. 72
Sir Joshua Reynolds
The Cottagers
1788

OVERLEAF RIGHT

Fig. 73
George Romney
The Spinstress
1787

The fancy picture achieved its greatest popular success in Wheatley's famous series, *The Cries of London*, exhibited at the Royal Academy in 1792–5. Stipple engravings of thirteen of the fourteen pictures[14] were published by the firm of Colnaghi between 1793 and 1797, coloured sets selling for 16 shillings and uncoloured for 7s. 6d., with captions in both English and French. Wheatley's *Cries* caught the taste of the day, and their appeal has never diminished. Not only is there a steady traffic in reprints of the plates, but the designs, reproduced on plates, jugs, greeting cards, fabrics and a wide variety of other articles, are constantly in circulation.

The artistic tradition of picturing the itinerant vendors who cried their wares about the city streets was an international one originating in the remote past. In eighteenth-century England, prior to Wheatley, two series of prints from drawings of the subjects had been published: that by the elder Marcellus Laroon, and Paul Sandby's *London Cries* (1759–60). Both artists clearly worked from first-hand observation, and their drawings have a Hogarthian gusto and candour, spiced in Sandby's case with raucous humour.

Colnaghi's advertisement for the prints of Wheatley's series seemed to promise a similar realism of treatment, while also voicing an element of national pride not hitherto apparent in writing about English art:

> In the civilized countries of Europe, the prevalence of polite manners softens down the rough originality of feature, and produces a similarity very unfavourable to the picturesque. It is among the lower ranks of life we are to look for the strong trait of national character. The courts of St James or St Petersburg, or Vienna or Rome, equally produce gentlemen, but the peasant of Switzerland, the *poissard* of Paris, and the *lazzarone* of Naples are genuine and original characters; and, in this point of view, few natural characters are more boldly marked than the lower order of the people in the City of London.

In actual fact, however, Wheatley's costermongers have no kinship with Hogarth's cockneys. In *Anecdotes of Painters* (1808) Edward Edwards perceptively remarked of the female figures in *Cries of London* that they were 'dressed with great smartness, but little propriety, better suited to the fantastic taste of an Italian opera stage than to the streets of London.' There is no denying, however, the sentimental charm of such a portrait as that of the seller of primroses ('Two bunches a penny primroses, two bunches a penny'), in which the girl and her two comely companions seem to share the freshness and sweetness of the flowers in their baskets (*fig. 71*). The impression instilled by the series as a whole, furthermore, points to deeper sources for their perennial appeal than may at first be apparent. However idealized, Wheatley's scenes present a composite image of eighteenth-century Londoners at work,[15] as captivating as Hogarth's account of their diversions in *The Four Times of the Day*. As a city artist, Wheatley's treatment of setting departs widely from Hogarth's. Carefully as the architectural backdrops in the *Cries* are composed, their primary function is to serve as foils to the groupings of figures, whose presence, quite apart from the services they proffer, confer grace and beauty on the bleak city streets.

The print trade led to the occasional coalescence of portraiture with the fancy piece, since, depending on its conception, the portrait could be issued as an engraving under a title in which the identity of the sitter was submerged. The fusion of the two genres is brilliantly exemplified in *The Cottagers* (1788, *fig. 72*) by Sir Joshua Reynolds (1723–92). On the one hand, this work is a pastoral conversation piece. It was commissioned by the picture and print dealer, Thomas Macklin, who employed leading contemporary artists to paint pictures for his Poets' Gallery. The spinner and the girl at the left are portraits of his wife and daughter (whose pose is modelled on Bernini's *David*). The figure in the centre carrying a sheaf of gleanings was Jane Potts, who later married the engraver John Landseer and became the mother of Sir Edwin Landseer. The scene in which they are actors, however, illustrates a literary episode dear to artists of the time, the tale of Lavinia, which occurs in the 'Autumn' section of James Thomson's immensely popular poem, *The Seasons*. The picture thus rehearses the familiar theme of the sophisticated town-dweller's yearning for the primitive joys of country life; and the subject-matter may well bring to mind such analogues as the play-acting of Marie Antoinette and her attendants at the model farm she had built at Versailles.

If, as has been asserted, the sitter in Gainsborough's unfinished oil sketch, *The Housemaid* (1782/6), was the Hon. Mrs Thomas Graham, whose magnificent portrait is at Edinburgh, then this study of a young woman engaged in the domestic chore of sweeping out a doorway is also evocative of the nostalgia for an escape to simpler modes of existence which went along with the cult of sensibility.[16] The principal celebrant of this cult under the guise of portraiture, however, was George Romney (1734–1802). During his long infatuation with Emma, Lady Hamilton, he painted her in an extraordinary variety of roles, mythological, historical and allegorical, including two portraits entitled *Nature* and *Sensibility*. His own favourite from the entire gallery was *The Spinstress* (1787, *fig. 73*), originally commissioned by Charles Greville. The notion for this work is supposed to have occurred to the artist on seeing a cobbler's wife spinning in her husband's shop. As a fancy piece, the painting is uniquely successful in its harmonious combination of portraiture with genre, of psychological insight and objective realism. Her humble occupation enhances rather than detracts from the magnetic beauty and distinction of the sitter, whose lingering glance asks the viewer's complicity in the role she is playing.

Children at play provided painters with subject-matter especially congenial to the temper of the time. Family connections were the cohesive force in Georgian society; and as is apparent from the conversation piece, the younger members occupied a prominent place in the domestic circle. Indeed, some of the most attractive group portraits by Hogarth, Zoffany and Joseph Wright were exclusively composed of children. Childhood scenes formed an entire category of genre painting in France, both in the rococo manner of such artists as Lancret and Fragonard, and, of course, in the more realistic style of Chardin. Hayman (in his Vauxhall designs) and Mercier were strongly influenced by such French artists in their frequent use of children as subjects, as was Joseph Francis Nollekens (1702–48). Born in Antwerp and a copyist of Watteau in his early years, Nollekens set up as a painter of conversations on his arrival in England in 1733, but after 1740 devoted himself to painting a series of children's diversions. These were described by Vertue after the artist's death as 'from the life & Invention several small pictures of children at different plays exercises & amusements. from the life. his own children pretty pleasant designs. which was really lately done & the best of his works.' *Two Children playing with a Top and Playing*

OPPOSITE

Fig. 74
Joseph Francis Nollekens
*Two Children playing with a
Top and Playing Cards*
1745

Fig. 75
George Morland
Blind Man's Buff
1787–8

Fig. 76
Sir Joshua Reynolds
*Lady Caroline Scott as
'Winter'*
1777

Cards (1745, *fig. 74*) illustrates two of the games most commonly portrayed in these pictures, and is pleasingly free from sentimentality, while showing a perceptive awareness of how children behave.

The readiness with which childhood lent itself to sentimental idealization made it a favourite subject in the later eighteenth century. During the mid-1780s a little-known artist, Richard Morton Paye (*c*1750–1821), issued a popular series showing the young play-acting, snowballing, playing at marbles or tops, etc. The success which Paye's work enjoyed in the form of prints inspired George Morland to enter into an agreement with the prominent engraver and print dealer, J.R.Smith, for a similar series. The first of these was entitled *Blind Man's Buff* (1787–8, *fig. 75*); and about a dozen others followed, including *Children playing at Soldiers, Children Nutting, Juvenile Navigators, Children Birds'-Nesting* and *The Kite Entangled*. As the titles indicate, the scenes take place out of doors. In Morland's treatment the youngsters' participation in their activities is remarkably wholehearted and lacking in self-consciousness. This naturalness may have resulted from the artist's reported practice of encouraging his subjects to play around him while he noted poses and attitudes suitable to his purposes. When Morland turned to other subjects in about 1790, the market for pictures of childhood was taken over by such artists as the Rev. Matthew William Peters (1742–1814), John Russell (1745–1806) and William Hamilton (1751–1801), who specialized in scenes of a rather cloying sentimentality largely absent from Morland's work in this vein.

It remained, however, for Sir Joshua Reynolds to capture the true poetry of childhood. This inveterate bachelor's fondness for children and sympathy with their ways were proverbial; and from the 1770s he found respite from his formal commissions and active public life in an astonishing array of pictures of the very young in which, by a magic all his own, portraits were transmuted into imaginative evocations of the enchanted world of childhood. Reynolds was perhaps most successful with little girls. One need only recall *The Strawberry Girl* (1773), a likeness of his beloved niece 'Offy' (Theophila Palmer, later Gwatkin); *The Age of Innocence* (1788), the portrait of her daughter, another Theophila; *Miss Bowles* (1775) with her puppy; and *Lady Caroline Scott as 'Winter'* (1777, *fig. 76*). Arch to the point of coquetry and with a dainty charm, these pictures are imbued with the sentimentality abroad at the time, yet escape its excesses by their playfulness, a quality so significantly lacking in Greuze's girl portraits. Writing of *The Strawberry Girl* to its owner, the poet Samuel Rogers, the painter, Sir Thomas Lawrence, remarked: 'That magnificent display of impudent knowledge that kicks modesty out of door, and makes you say, "Aye, let her go," has never been from my recollection or eyes since I saw it.' Yet, as images of innocence and joy, these children epitomize an aspect of the age's tendency to cherish natural purity and goodness in their primal form, which was later to find verbal expression in Blake's *Songs of Innocence* and Wordsworth's celebration of infancy. Decked out as the spirit of 'Winter' and emerging so trustfully from that snowy landscape, Lady Caroline seems a sprite from another sphere, embodying all the festive promise of the season.

More often than not a wistful and pensive tone underlies the vivacity of Reynolds' child portraits, as though the sitters were haunted, like Wordsworth's infant, by intimations of the transience of joy. This note, when present, and it is found only in the work of the true masters, adds a deeper, more philosophic dimension to the cult of sensibility. Thus, for example, pastoral motifs that seem primarily sentimental in Wheatley's handling assume an idyllic or elegiac aspect in the work of Reynolds or Gainsborough. This more poetic mood is nowhere better projected than in Joseph Wright's remarkable portrait of *Sir Brooke Boothby* (1780–1, *fig. 77*). The sitter, member of an aristocratic family and endowed with the temperament and inclinations of a scholar, is shown reclining in a woodland setting, emblematic of his retiring nature and interest in botany. The volume he holds bears the name Rousseau on its spine. Among other things, the portrait thus commemorates Boothby's friendship with and patronage of the great French philosopher, whose first dialogue, the *Rousseau Juge de Jean-Jacques*, he was instrumental in having published. More significantly, however, the portrait was designed as a partial vindication of Rousseau's primitivist teaching, which, uttered with a passionate conviction calculated to inflame emotional assent, was revitalizing the Arcadian ideal of the sanctity of living in the bosom of nature, apart from the snares and delusions of civilization. While the picture's setting clearly labels Boothby as a disciple of these views, the air of melancholy conveyed by his posture (borrowed from Renaissance tomb sculpture) further reflects a habit of mind prevalent among thoughtful Englishmen in the declining years of the eighteenth century. It finds a poetic voice in such works as Gray's 'Elegy written in a Country Churchyard', and more especially in Goldsmith's 'The Deserted Village'. Indeed, Wright's Boothby might well have in mind the lines from the latter:

> E'en now, methinks, as pondering here . . .,
> I see the rural Virtues leave the land.

Goldsmith's poem, it will be remembered, describes the afflictions of families dispossessed by the changes in land ownership that were remodelling the face of the countryside. The so-called agricultural revolution led to the absorption of small farms and village communities as well as common land into large estates under efficient management, partly in response to the need for feeding an expanding population. By the end of the century 4,000 parliamentary acts of enclosure had appropriated something like six million acres, until about half of the arable acreage in Britain was in the possession of 5,000 families and almost a quarter belonged to just four hundred families. One result was the virtual abolition of the yeoman class, members of which were reduced to tenant status or driven either to move into the towns or to emigrate. The moving message of Goldsmith's poem was enhanced by the innumerable illustrations which its successive editions inspired from contemporary artists.

The sense of impermanence accompanying social change of the kind brought about by the wholesale enclosure of land greatly heightened the appeal of the Arcadian ideal. The dream of a golden age, derived from Theocritus and Virgil, had permeated English culture from the Renaissance, assuming different forms at different times. In earlier periods the retreat to nature had generally been motivated by intellectual or ethical considerations – the need to find a refuge from the world of affairs in which to cultivate the philosophic mind and discipline the moral sense. Now, however, in the Age of Sensibility, the dominant mood became one of nostalgia for a more primitive state that would banish torpor and ennui and reawaken the faculties of joy and wonder. This temperamental shift was reflected in theories about the garden, the

Fig. 77
Joseph Wright
Sir Brooke Boothby
1780–1

OVERLEAF

Fig. 78
Thomas Gainsborough
Cottage Door with Girl and Pigs
1786

reigning metaphor for nature ordered by art. Writing in the *Spectator* in 1712, Addison could say: 'A Garden was the Habitation of our first Parents before the Fall. It is naturally apt to fill the Mind with Calmness and Tranquillity, and to lay all its turbulent Passions at Rest. It gives us a great Insight into the Contrivance and Wisdom of Providence, and suggests innumerable Subjects for Meditation.' Fifty years later in *Observations on Modern Gardening* (1770), Thomas Whateley was to write: '. . . it suffices that the scenes of nature have a power to affect our imagination and our sensibility; for such is the constitution of the human mind, that if once it is agitated, the emotion often spreads far beyond the occasion; when the passions are roused, their course is unrestrained . . .'

In Gainsborough's landscapes with figures changing attitudes can be traced, which, while they originated in personal responses, also provide an index to shadings of sensibility which have been seen to characterize the artistic temper of the age at large. The early pictures, of which *Robert Andrews and his Wife* (*fig. 40*) is the most notable example, clearly depict the Suffolk countryside in which they are set. Even in works borrowing motifs from Boucher's *pastorales*, such as *Woodcutter courting Milkmaid* (1755) and *River Scene with Figures* (mid-1750s), the young men and women are earthy English types who conduct their rustic gallantry in homely surroundings. With his departure for Bath in 1759 Gainsborough was permanently uprooted from the region he loved and to which he looked back with increasing regret from Bath, and after 1774 from London. As early as 1769 he was to write to his friend William Jackson: 'I'm sick of Portraits and wish very much to take my Viol da Gamba and walk off to some sweet Village when I can paint Landskips and enjoy the fag End of Life in quietness and ease.'

While Gainsborough always inclined to landscapes by choice, after the Suffolk years they were not based on actual observation, but were rather imaginative creations, increasingly charged with poetic feeling. Reynolds described the artist's method of composing them in his *Fourteenth Discourse* (1788): '. . . from the fields he brought into his painting-room, stumps of trees, weeds, and animals of various kinds; and designed them, not from memory, but immediately from the objects. He even framed a kind of model of landskips on his table; composed of broken stones, dried herbs, and pieces of looking glass, which he magnified and improved into rocks, trees, and water.' The principal properties of Gainsborough's landscapes are indeed few: market carts, river fords, forest glades, cottage doors – and to them he returned again and again in freshly imagined combinations.

If a remark in another letter to Jackson of 1767 is to be taken at face value, Gainsborough never regarded the figures in his landscapes as more than staffage: 'But to be serious . . . do you really think that a regular Composition in the Landskip way should ever be fill'd with History, or any figures but such as fill a place (I won't say stop a Gap) or to create a little business for the Eye to be drawn from the Trees in order to return to them with more glee . . .?'[17] Against this statement must be placed the testimony of Uvedale Price, author of *An Essay on the Picturesque*, who took frequent rides through the countryside with Gainsborough during the Bath period, and who recollected: '. . . when we came to cottage or village scenes, to groups of children, or to any objects of that kind which struck his fancy, I have often remarked in his countenance an expression of particular gentleness and complacency.'

In the groups peopling Gainsborough's great landscapes we do not look for faithful transcriptions of rustic life any more than we expect topographical fidelity. As Constable observed in a letter to Leslie: 'With particulars he had nothing to do, his object was to deliver a fine sentiment. . . .' Gainsborough's goal in the landscape art of his maturity was to create idyllic pastoral scenes in which the figures merged harmoniously with their setting. In the splendid series of canvases devoted to his favourite theme of the cottage door, he experimented with differing ways of achieving this totality of impression. In the version of 1786 (*fig. 78*, now in the Victoria and Albert Museum) he combined disparate details, as in his procedure for building up landscape effects in his studio. The girl with the broom is taken from the sketch of *The Housemaid*, while the group of the pensive girl and feeding pigs repeats almost verbatim the fancy piece of this subject, painted in 1782. With *The Cottage Door* (1780, *fig. 79*, now at the Henry E. Huntington Art Gallery) he achieved perhaps his most satisfactory resolution of the Arcadian vision. Isolated from their surroundings, the mother and her children form a masterfully composed genre study. But the triangular configuration of the group, greatly magnified, is duplicated and at the same time framed by the blasted oak (a favourite detail with Gainsborough) slanting to meet the oblique opening at the left through which the light of the declining sun falls on the figures. The composition thus takes on the monumental Rubensesque quality that characterizes the artist's other supreme landscapes, such as *The Harvest Waggon*. The setting is an immemorial one that knows nothing of enclosures or social barriers; here a natural order reigns of which the simple peasant family is just the human manifestation.

With advancing years, the elegiac spirit inherent in Gainsborough's response to nature deepened, perhaps as a result of subjective feelings of deprivation. To give it full poignancy of expression he turned to the fancy piece as a final stage in the development of his landscape art, and in so doing unfolded new layers of implication in the pastoral mode. These were the pictures which the artist himself valued most, and for which he asked the highest prices; and in the following generation his fame was to a large extent based on them. Their appeal brought into focus all of the attitudes nurtured by the cult of sensibility. The *Morning Herald* for 2 May 1786 praised 'those little simple subjects . . . that awakened in the heart the most pathetic sensations . . .' Reynolds, who greatly admired this primitivist vein in his rival and who bought his *Girl with Pigs* from the walls of the Royal Academy in 1782, found these pictures endowed with 'such a grace, and such an elegance, as are more frequently found in cottages than in courts.' But it was Constable who in his fourth lecture on landscape painting (1836) most perceptively described the impression instilled by Gainsborough's late manner:

> The landscape of Gainsborough is soothing, tender, and affecting. . . . On looking at them [his canvases], we find tears in our eyes, and know not what brings them. The lonely haunts of the solitary shepherd, – the return of the rustic with his bill and bundle of wood, – the darksome lane or dell, – the sweet little cottage girl at the spring with the pitcher, – were things he delighted to paint, and which he painted with exquisite refinement, yet not a refinement beyond nature.

Although Gainsborough was markedly influenced by the ways in which the

Fig. 79
Thomas Gainsborough
The Cottage Door
1780

Spanish painter Estebán Murillo treated beggar-boys and other urchins, his portraits of such figures were in all cases drawn from the life. Reynolds attests to the artist's habit of bringing home London waifs whose appearance attracted him to serve as models. He encountered the original of *Cottage Girl with Dog and Pitcher* (1785, *fig. 80*) in the vicinity of Richmond Hill, carrying her puppy as in the picture. This work is typical of Gainsborough's method, which was to bring forward to life-size children of the type who peopled his earlier landscapes, and, leaving the backgrounds very broadly sketched, to develop emotional intensity through concentration on the sitter's bearing and expression. The mood is invariably one of haunting sadness. Indeed, the spell which these effigies of rustic childhood cast is nearly inexpressible. They declare the unconscious grace and innocence of youth under the shadow of mutability. So engaged are these lonely figures with the settings that throw them into relief that they appear not so much knowable individuals in specific localities as emanations of the natural world, or even the tutelary spirits presiding over the scenes which they inhabit.[18]

ABOVE LEFT

Fig. 80

Thomas Gainsborough
Cottage Girl with Dog and Pitcher
1785

ABOVE RIGHT

Fig. 81

Thomas Gainsborough
The Woodman
1787, engraving by P. Simon

Fig. 83
Edward Haytley
*An Extensive View from the Terraces
of Sandleford Priory*
1744

OVERLEAF

Fig. 82

George Lambert
A Hilly Landscape with a Cornfield
1733

Gainsborough was well aware that in his later career he was breaking new ground, venturing into realms of subject-matter hitherto unexplored. In the final year of his life he produced an astonishing canvas, entitled *The Woodman* (1787, *fig. 81*), a fancy piece in which he reverted to a favourite type, but now with the intention of investing it with heroic attributes. Gainsborough regarded this work as his masterpiece, and from his deathbed sent an invitation to Reynolds to come to see it. Of the sitter we are told that he was 'a poor smith worn out by labour ... Mr. Gainsborough was struck with his careworn aspect and took him home; he enabled the needy wanderer by his generosity to live ...'

The larger than life-size painting was unhappily destroyed by fire in 1810, and is now known only by a small study, possibly by the artist's nephew Gainsborough Dupont (1754–97), and the engraving. It shows a forester who, with his dog, has taken refuge under a tree from a violent storm. The mingled fear and awe with which the man gazes up at the heavens are precisely matched in the dog's attitude; and one senses in both of them an intuitive kinship with the elemental powers which threaten them. The disturbing insights of this work look beyond the boundaries of the pastoral mode with its consoling vision of Arcadian felicity to the imaginative power of Wordsworth's 'Michael' and 'Solitary Leech-Gatherer'.

It is the Virgil of the *Eclogues* rather than of the *Georgics* that eighteenth-century paintings celebrating the gratifications of rural life most often bring to mind. Like the

subjects of the conversation piece, rustic figures are usually portrayed in moments of relaxation from their work. Such a painting as *A Hilly Landscape with a Cornfield* (1733, *fig. 82*) by George Lambert (1700–65) is almost without parallel in the period.[19] The setting is unidentified (perhaps in the Chilterns); but man has imposed his mark upon it, reclaiming a section from waste. The focal point in the prospect is the white shirt of the reaper bent to his work in the hot sunlight under the supervision of a bailiff on horseback. The scored sides of the distant hill suggest some kind of excavating operations; and it has been proposed that the figure with the sketchbook in the centre foreground may be conducting a land survey, rather than drawing for his own pleasure.

Lambert's influence is apparent in the authoritative handling of landscape in *An Extensive View from the Terraces of Sandleford Priory* (1744, *fig. 83*) by the little-known artist, Edward Haytley (active 1740–61). He contributed two roundels, *Chelsea Hospital* and *Bethlem Hospital*, to Thomas Coram's Foundling Hospital, where his *Landscape with Figures* also hangs. The present picture conforms to the conversation type with its presentation of family members on the terrace of their country estate, where they have been enjoying a game of bowls. Edward Montagu (seated) was a Member of Parliament and landowner, whose wealth was derived from coal; he was also a noted mathematician whose interests extended to astronomy (hence the presence of the telescope). His wife Elizabeth, standing to his right, was a famous hostess of the mid-eighteenth century, the intellectual tone of whose *soirées* gave rise

Fig. 84
George Stubbs
Labourers: Lord Torrington's Bricklayers at Southill, 1767
1767

to the term 'blue-stocking'. Her sister, Sarah Robinson, is at the left, while a servant brings up a chair.

The figures in the foreground, however, are dwarfed by the spreading prospect, filled in with rare topographical accuracy, showing the village of Newtown in the middle distance and the Hampshire Downs rimming the horizon. Even more unusual is the presence of harvesters at work in the adjoining meadows, providing a contrast to the atmosphere of leisure prevailing among the group on the terrace. Their activities inject a delightfully animated pastoral mood into the scene. Note, for example, the young woman trying to restrain her swain from over-indulging in the contents of the keg he has raised to his lips.

The Georgic ideal of productive toil on the land achieved its most notable expression in a few canvases by that true countryman, George Stubbs. An especially arresting example is *Labourers: Lord Torrington's Bricklayers at Southill, 1767* (*fig. 84*) commissioned by Viscount Torrington during the 1760s and existing in several versions.[20] Ozias Humphry's biographical notes on Stubbs give the following account of the inception of the work:

At Southill the Seat of Lord Viscount Torrington he painted the exhibited picture of the Bricklayers/Labourers loading Bricks into a Cart – this Commission he recd from the Noble Viscount in London who had often seen them at their Labours appearing like a Flemish subject and therefore he desired to have them represented – Mr Stubbs arrived at Southill a little before dinner where he found with Lord Torrington the duke of portland and other Noblemen and Gentlemen during dinner the old men were ordered to prepare themselves for their Labours with a little cart drawn by Lord Torrington's favourite old Hunter which was used only for these easy tasks – for this being the first Horse his Lordship ever rode was the principle motive for ordering this picture – Mr Stubbs was a long time loitering about observing the old Men without perceiving any thing that engaged them all so as to make a fit subject for a picture at length they fell into a dispute abt the manner of putting the Tail piece into the Cart wch dispute so favourable for his purpose lasted long enough for him to make a sketch of the picture Men Horse and Cart as they have been represented.

The rustics in this work are as unmistakably portraits as are the jockeys and stable-lads in Stubbs' sporting paintings. The action of fitting the tail-gate suffices as a compositional principle, the stubborn countenances of the men indicating that some sort of altercation is taking place. The comic implications of the situation are emphasized by the relaxed pose of the gaffer who looks on, as well as by the passivity of the superbly drawn horse and the dog, detached but observant of the scene.

An altogether more idyllic note is struck in Stubbs' splendid pair, *Reapers* (1784, *fig. 85*) and *Haymakers* (1785, *fig. 86*) in several versions. In both, like the artist's series of mares and foals, the figures are distributed as in a frieze before the beautiful landscapes. Their activities are allowed to speak for themselves. There is no moral bias, no trace of sentimentality, no artificial narrative heightening. Of the seven labourers in each scene, only the girl at the centre of *Haymakers* looks towards the viewer, her relaxed pose providing a counterpoise to the concentration of her fellows. The harmonious pattern provided by the diagonal and vertical thrusts of hay and

pitchforks endows the activity with a ritual significance. In *Reapers* the erect posture of the man and two women binding sheaves is played off against the three male reapers bent to their task. And there is perhaps a muted hint of dramatic tension in the watchful glances which the standing trio exchange with their master on horseback. As in somewhat similar paintings by Brueghel, time seems to have come to a standstill in the summer afternoon of Stubbs' pair, arresting change and preserving imperishably the beauty of a way of life that was passing even as the artist painted it.[21]

Stubbs' agricultural idylls have their industrial counterpart in the equally unique series of pictures of forges and blacksmiths' shops which Joseph Wright painted during the early 1770s. In a way typical of his time, Wright made no distinction between scientific discoveries and the mechanical inventions which announced the onset of the Industrial Revolution; and his subjects dealing with the latter were a natural sequel to the pictures of the orrery and air-pump of the preceding decade, exhibiting the same sense of excitement and wonder over examples of professional skill. The majestic though ruinous interiors in which these forges and smithies are set, with their curious vestiges of classical or Gothic architecture, contribute a quality of heightened grandeur to the scenes. They are artificially lit (here by molten metal), although with moonlight providing an alternative source of light; and there is a strongly emphasized contrast between the absorption of the athletic workers and the mixed emotions of the onlookers, including timid children.

In his Account Book, under 'Subject for Night Pieces', Wright projected the subject of *A Blacksmith's Shop* (1771, *fig. 87*) as follows:

> Two men forming a bar of iron into a horse shoe, from whence the light must proceed. An idle fellow may stand by the anvil in a time-killing posture, his hands in his bosom, or yawning with his hands stretched upwards, & a little twisting of the body. Horse shoes hanging upon ye walls, and other necessary things faintly seen, being remote from the light. Out of this room shall be seen another, in wch a farrier may be shoeing a horse by the light of a candle. The horse must be sadled, and a traveller standing by. ... The moon may appear, and illumine some part of the horses, if necessary.

The 'idle fellow ... in a time-killing posture' has been translated into the mysterious brooding figure seated at the right, who appears in others of Wright's scientific and industrial subjects, and who in his speculative pose may be taken as a surrogate for the artist or the viewer.

The heroic celebrations of labour by Stubbs and Wright constituted brief episodes in their artistic careers to which they did not return. And we may infer that, being so much at odds with the sentimental and moralistic nature of most late Georgian painting dealing with everyday life, they failed to appeal to the popular taste. The fact that the superlative engravings of these works excited little attention when published supports this supposition. Associated with this neglect is the virtual absence of anything resembling pure genre painting (as opposed to hybrid approximations) in the annual exhibitions of the Royal Academy down to the end of the century. Such subject-matter had still to achieve recognition as a legitimate field of serious artistic endeavour.

Chapter Four

THE TRIUMPH
OF GENRE

THE PRECEDING CHAPTER traced the rise of English subject painting in the eighteenth century in response to a new and constantly expanding public. Artistic reputation was contingent upon choosing material congenial to popular tastes, and treating it in ways that would flatter those tastes. Artist and public alike were dependent on the intervention of a new class of patron, the print-dealer, who, with the engravers he employed, fostered graphic modes expressive of the temper of the age. There resulted a body of painting that was decorative but essentially superficial in its recording of the social scene. The artist too often falsified truth of observation by making it serve a moral message designed to widen the appeal and heighten the significance of his subjects. Only infrequently, as in the case of Gainsborough, Stubbs or Wright, was an artist gifted with the clarity of vision, the imaginative power and the integrity of purpose to discover and set forth the pure ideal within the actual. The social historian on the look-out for pictures showing the familiar side of life in eighteenth-century England with unvarnished truthfulness must turn to another category of painting, not recognized as falling within the precincts of high art – the work of the topographers.

A tradition of animating architectural studies with minute figures going about the routine activities of everyday existence is traceable to Wenceslas Hollar in the mid-seventeenth century. From his early employment as draughtsman to the Ordnance Survey of the Scottish Highlands following the rebellion of 1745, Paul Sandby (1725–1809) made a practice of including vignettes from the life about him in his topographical watercolours. Later Sandby became Chief Drawing Master at the Royal Military Academy, Woolwich, and continued throughout an incessantly active career as teacher and artist to advance the cause of watercolour, both as an acceptable form of art in its own right and as a medium especially suitable to reproduction in aquatint, a process which he helped to develop. One of his principal patrons was Sir Joseph Banks, President of the Royal Society, whose collection went to swell the royal archive of more than 450 drawings. The figures who create so lively and varied a stir in Sandby's scenes, whether architectural or landscape, rarely serve the perfunctory purpose of staffage, but rather reveal the artist's talent for shrewd characterization, his careful attention to costume and occupation, and his humour. They were clearly meant to satisfy the contemporary belief that no view was truly interesting if it did not include some trace of human activity. Describing the view from Strawberry Hill to Sir Horace Mann, Horace Walpole wrote in 1753: 'Is not this a tolerable prospect? You must figure that all this is perpetually enlivened by a navigation of boats and barges, and by a road below my terrace, with coaches, post-chaises, wagons, and horsemen constantly in motion, and the fields speckled with cows, horses and sheep.'

Sandby's skill as an architectural draughtsman was rivalled by two brothers, Thomas Malton II (1748–1804) and James Malton (c1766–1803). They were primarily city artists, the former devoting himself to the topography of London, the latter to that of Dublin. In their work the formal beauty of Georgian edifices, reproduced with careful attention to perspective and tonal qualities, is brought to life by the surrounding street-life. Two other contemporary watercolourists whose work exhibits a fondness for incorporating genre activity in topographical scenes were Samuel Hieronymus Grimm (1733–94) and Michael Angelo Rooker (1743–1801).

The one artist of stature in this category who consistently painted sizeable canvases and endeavoured to endow his compositions with pictorial qualities beyond their topographical significance was Samuel Scott (c1710–72). A maritime artist in the tradition of the Van de Veldes during his early career, he was inspired by the example of Canaletto, who arrived in London in 1746, to turn to Thames-side subjects. Like Canaletto, his urban views are enriched with a wealth of local colour which, while devoid of the Venetian master's decorative sparkle, compensate with a much greater sense of reality in the introduction of incidental detail. The shipping in the background of *A Quay on the Thames at London* (c1756, *fig. 88*) includes to the left a man-of-war flying a commodore's pennant, and at the centre the stern view of a merchantman. The latter has perhaps unloaded the cargo of rum, tea, sugar and oil strewn about the quay, an inventory of which a blue-coated customs officer appears to be checking over under the scrutiny of the nonchalant figure facing him with hands in pockets. Beyond the group can be seen part of the great wheel of a treadmill crane. The dog in the foreground is thought, because of a sketch in Scott's studio sale, to have been supplied by the *animalier*, Sawrey Gilpin (1733–1807). Scott's sensitivity to atmospheric effects and the masterly disposition of light and shade, owing nothing to Canaletto, are important contributory elements in the dynamic realism of a scene that is thoroughly English in subject and feeling.

During the last decade of the eighteenth century an all-inclusive shift in artistic taste became apparent. The cult of sensibility was a short-lived phenomenon. Its uncritical acceptance of ready-made values, its complacent assumption of social stability, and its readiness to indulge in facile sentiment were swept away by the repercussions of the French Revolution, the onset of the industrial era, and the deeper emotional groundswell of romanticism, forces making for the spread of democracy and a radical revision of class relations. Expressed in terms of the rural scene, these developments produced a more clear-eyed perception of the lot of country dwellers. In literature the change of perspective can be seen in the poetry of George Crabbe, whose *The Village* (1783) and *The Parish Register* (1807) describe the harsh realities of agrarian existence with a caustic veracity at the furthest remove from the elegiac tone of Goldsmith's 'The Deserted Village'.[1] Crabbe's counterpart in painting, although

Fig. 88
Samuel Scott
A Quay on the Thames at London
c1756

without his moral indignation and didactic intent, was George Morland, who transformed the pastoral mode into conformity with the realistic prescriptions of genre painting.

Morland better than any other artist of his time exemplifies the degree to which the contemporary reputation of artists was built and sustained by the collaboration of engravers. His output of paintings, astonishing in so short a career, was about four thousand. Of these more than four hundred were reproduced in his lifetime through the media of mezzotint, stipple, etching and aquatint by some eighty-eight engravers. Recognizing the freshness of Morland's vision and the potential market for it, the eminent mezzotinter and print-seller John Raphael Smith established a Morland Gallery, based on the acquisition of thirty-six paintings by the artist from which engravings were issued in large numbers between 1787 and 1791.[2] A single dealer ordered nine dozen sets of Morland's *Deserter* series on its publication in 1791; and of the pendants *Guinea Pigs* (1789) and *Dancing Dogs* (1790) five hundred pairs were sold within a few weeks of being issued. Morland's fame spread throughout Europe, especially in France and Germany.

During the initial period of his popularity in the late 1780s, Morland, as we have seen, was content to follow the prevailing fashions, whether in the sentimental vein of the *Laetitia* sequence or in the more playful mood of his pictures of children's diversions. Like Hogarth, however, he was restless under patronage of any kind, and in about 1790 he broke free from vassalage to print-dealers, henceforth to be guided in the choice and treatment of subjects solely by his own inclinations. Morland's assertion of independence pointed the way towards a new era of autonomy for the artist, although in his own case with unfortunate results. Finding a ready market, he painted to keep both himself and the hangers-on who thronged his studio in drink, and disposed of his canvases to unscrupulous middlemen as fast as they came off the easel for whatever they would bring. As a result, Morland's work became increasingly uneven in his final years.[3]

When Morland changed his manner he was at the height of his powers; and the pictures of the early 1790s permanently altered ways of looking at rural life.[4] During this period he lived in a house in Paddington opposite the White Lion, a 'drover's house' where he could observe the coming and going of countrymen with their herds of livestock. He then moved to Winchester Row, where he maintained a virtual menagerie of models including, we are told by his biographer, George Dawe, 'an old horse, an ass, foxes, goats, hogs, and dogs of all kinds, besides monkies [*sic*], squirrels, guinea-pigs, dormice, and other animals in abundance.' Later he fled from his creditors to Leicestershire, where he became more familiar with agricultural life and the ways of the rural population.[5]

Morland was the first English painter to emulate the seventeenth-century artists of the Low Countries in finding an all-sufficient source of inspiration in peasant life; and in the formation of an appropriate style he was greatly indebted to their example. He had acquired a thorough knowledge of these schools during a long apprenticeship (1777–84) to his father, a picture restorer as well as an artist, who made his son copy and perhaps fake the Dutch little masters. During these years 'picturesque' theories of art were much in the air, fostered by William Gilpin and Uvedale Price. Among the central articles in their aesthetic doctrine was an insistence on the pictorial merits of roughness and irregularity, qualities which they specifically associated with Dutch genre. Under these influences the sentimental modishness of Morland's early style gave way to a more uncompromising directness of vision, characterized by breadth and vigour of handling. Like his Dutch progenitors and unlike English topographers of the century, Morland's canvases are peopled with types rather than individuals, the settings are rarely localized, and the actions are of everyday occurrence. The impression of veracity that they convey stems from a power of generalization that distils the timeless elements from transient phenomena. The richness of association that gives significance to Hogarth's pictures is replaced in Morland by an exclusive concentration on the pictorial constituents of his scenes.

It is generally agreed that *Inside of a Stable* (1791, *fig. 89*) announced the new style on which Morland's reputation rests. The setting is supposed to have been the White Lion, Paddington, but could represent any stable interior. It is late afternoon, the time for unharnessing, feeding and bedding down the animals. The bond built up by the day's labour still unites man and beast in their weariness. The two hands are as exemplary in the performance of their final duty to provide fodder as the two horses and pony are in the patience with which they wait to be fed. As in all of Morland's pictures, the participants are absorbed in their business and totally unaware of the presence of a viewer. Nor has the artist dressed them up for polite approval; instead he allows the ragged and dirty clothing of the men and unkempt coats of the animals to speak for the hard drudgery of their lives.

An equally good example of Morland's genius for making a workaday scene interesting without recourse to any adventitious adornment, sentimental or otherwise, is *Morning: Higglers preparing for Market* (1791, *fig. 90*), which may have been painted at Aldenham in Leicestershire, where a friend of the artist owned a farm. The time being early morning, we witness a reversal of the procedures in the preceding canvas. The hired hand leads the horse from the stable, in preparation for hitching it to the cart that will take the farm produce to market. In this moment of leisure before the day's work begins, the figures are arrested in completely natural and unself-conscious poses. While the wife pours out a bracing dram and the little daughter looks on, the farmer knots the laces at the knees of his breeches. Save for Stubbs, no other English artist has so palpably captured the hardy self-reliance, the steady endurance and the inherent dignity of workers on the land. Such is the solidity of the composition, furthermore, that the grouping of figures by the barn cannot be detached from the setting. As one early critic remarked, Morland furnished his pictures with an 'assemblage of objects always appropriate and disposed as if by accident'. Among the various properties of the scene, one notes the farmer's hat hung jauntily on the pole beside him, the manifest contentment of the two hogs on their straw bedding, and the 'picturesque' treatment of the barn's thatched and moss-covered roof.

Morland rarely portrayed his rustics engaged in the hard labour by which they earned their livelihood. As in the two pictures just discussed, he had a fondness for the early morning or evening hours which precede or follow the day's work. This in part accounts for the impression of quietude, of suspended activity so often imparted by his scenes. Another common feature of his pictures is the presence of doors of all kinds, stable doors, cottage doors, inn doors, places of meetings and encounters, of departures and returns, of hospitality and conviviality. Doorways are the spatial

OVERLEAF LEFT ABOVE

Fig. 89

George Morland

Inside of a Stable

1791

OVERLEAF LEFT BELOW

Fig. 90

George Morland

Morning: Higglers preparing for Market

1791

OVERLEAF RIGHT ABOVE

Fig. 91

George Morland

Door of a Village Inn

1793

OVERLEAF RIGHT BELOW

Fig. 92

George Morland

The Reckoning

(undated)

equivalent of those hours of the day which interrupt the flux of time, providing resting points and the leisure for shared experience.

Such a mood of harmonious social intercourse amid peaceful natural surroundings pervades *Door of a Village Inn* (1793, *fig. 91*). A traveller on horseback with the look of a prosperous farmer or squire has paused outside a humble country inn in Leicestershire,[6] and is receiving refreshment from the shy hostess. Two of her children, one holding a bowl of porridge, look on from the adjoining doorway with a curiosity in marked contrast to the detachment of an older brother burning brushwood in the rear. Again there are the slight but telling details which lend humanity to the scene – the two dogs staring suspiciously at each other, the laundry spread out to dry on the stone wall in the background. A wide prospect towards hills opens to the left, from where the evening sun floods the scene with mellow light. Commonplace enough, the episode is sufficient unto itself, inviting the viewer to linger in the present moment with no thought of before or after or any concern with extraneous meaning.

Morland's radical innovations in subject-matter have too often been allowed to overshadow the technical proficiency of his best work. Although his example produced a host of followers in the nineteenth century, no one came close to matching his artistic achievement, a fact which helps to explain his enduring popularity. *The Reckoning* (undated, *fig. 92*) is a good example of his skill in the handling of a congenial subject. There is just enough narrative content to support a representative gathering of country types. Once again it is early morning. While the portly farmer in broad-brimmed hat and capacious greatcoat settles his account with the red-waistcoated pot-boy, the ostler holds his horse in readiness for mounting. The design is in the form of a wide-angled V, the diagonal slope of the wooden partition carrying down through the great horse's back, then reascending through its head to the upper corner of the doorway. These oblique thrusts are accentuated by the shaft of sunlight falling across the stable in such a way as to create a kind of pocket of illumination which highlights and connects all the living beings, animal as well as human, while leaving the remainder of the interior in shade. The effect is to place a casual transaction at the centre of a complex pattern of relationships, suggestive of the hierarchic yet organic constitution of the rural world which Morland was portraying.

In his independence and nonconformity, his love of country people and their ways, and his broad humanity, Morland was spiritually akin to his Scottish contemporary, the poet Robert Burns. They were similar also in their artistic goals – to create a truthful and enduring image of the rural populace. But above all else, Morland's *oeuvre* impresses through its essential and ineradicable Englishness. J.R.Smith's catalogue of the engravings made from Morland's pictures (*c*1793) stated: 'His sailors are British, and have braved many a storm. . . . His fishermen, post-boys, and ostlers are . . . *English – English, Sirs, from top to toe*!'[7] Such a comment denotes the dawning awareness that a truly national school of painting was in the making. And Morland's pictures of contemporary life during the 1790s, more than any other agency, were responsible for spreading this awareness.

Any account of the trend toward greater realism in late eighteenth-century genre painting needs to take into account Morland's contemporary, Julius Caesar Ibbetson (1759–1817). During a tour of Wales with Robert Fulke Greville in 1792 Ibbetson made a number of sketches of native customs and ways of life, characterized alike by a sharp eye for eccentricities of behaviour and sprightly humour. This vein was to be developed during subsequent stays in Scotland and the Lake District. In his last years Ibbetson returned to his native Yorkshire, settling in Masham. At this time he produced a few oils of local genre scenes which are closer in manner than any other English works to the Dutch painters of common life whom he greatly admired, and whom, like Morland, he had copied in youth. Both Morland and Ibbetson were to some extent anticipated by Philippe Jacques de Loutherbourg (1740–1812). A follower of Berchem and the Italianate school of Dutch landscapists in his early career, de Loutherbourg, influenced in part by Gainsborough, adopted a more realistic manner on coming to England from the Continent in 1771. While they often include lively passages of genre, his later landscapes remained somewhat hybrid in style, too often flawed by melodramatic incident, a reflection perhaps of his vocation as a painter of theatrical scenery. Ibbetson and de Loutherbourg were among the few artists after Wright to find subjects in industrial operations, such as mining and smelting.

Morland's popularity was evidence that the public had become receptive to a more realistic approach in paintings of the contemporary social scene. The greater latitude which artists enjoyed as a result in the choice and methods of dealing with their subject-matter was ratified by a rising tide of enthusiasm for the seventeenth-century Netherlandish painters of genre who had so conspicuously influenced Morland. There had never been a time when this school had not been esteemed in England; but the traditional preference among important collectors for Italian old masters had overshadowed genre, which was principally known through engravings. The situation was very different in France, where for a number of reasons, political and economic as well as aesthetic, Dutch and Flemish paintings had throughout the eighteenth century formed the nuclei of a large number of distinguished collections. The Napoleonic Wars, following on the French Revolution, led to the dispersal of many of these, with English buyers acquiring the lion's share of the choicest examples. Among the more notable sales which laid the foundation of great collections of Dutch painting in England were those of the Duc d'Orléans (1792), the French minister Charles Alexandre de Calonne (1795), Countess Holderness, who was Dutch by birth (1802), Prince Talleyrand (1807) and Lucien Buonaparte (1815).

Foremost among English connoisseurs of Netherlandish genre painting was George IV, whose love of this school, backed by fine taste, extensive knowledge and great wealth, led to the formation of a matchless collection, based on the block of eighty-six canvases acquired from Sir Thomas Baring in 1814. Scarcely inferior to the king's holdings were those of the future prime minister, Sir Robert Peel, which were ultimately purchased by the National Gallery in 1871, a transaction involving seventy-seven paintings. Other superlative collections of Netherlandish art assembled in the opening years of the century were those of Alexander Baring (Lord Ashburton), Thomas Hope, the Marquess of Westminster, the Duke of Bridgewater and the Duke of Wellington. Mention should also be made of the Earl of Yarmouth, later third Marquess of Hertford, and Sir Peter Francis Bourgeois, whose masterpieces of this school now hang in the Wallace Collection and Dulwich Picture Gallery respectively.

The taste for Dutch genre was furthered by the British Institution, which in 1813 began to hold annual exhibitions of paintings loaned from private collections. Its exhibition of 1815, devoted entirely to Dutch and Flemish works, was the first public showing of the older schools to be held in Britain. The six exhibitions of Continental paintings held at the British Institution between 1813 and 1823 included 509 works by artists from the Low Countries, nearly double the number from all other foreign countries (Italy, France and Spain). Nor was this vogue short-lived. Recording his visit to the annual show at the British Institution in 1835, Waagen wrote: 'In number, as well as in value, the pictures of the Flemish and Dutch schools of the seventeenth and eighteenth centuries have on the whole a decided preponderance; for of the 176 Pictures, 108 belong to them.' The claim of Dutch genre to serious critical recognition was confirmed by the publication in nine volumes (1829–42) of the monumental *Catalogue Raisonné of the Works of the Most Eminent Dutch, Flemish, and French Painters*, compiled by John Smith, a print and picture dealer.

Awakened interest in Netherlandish painting helped promote appreciation of native English art, which exhibited so many of the same characteristics. The British Institution assumed a leading role in upholding the reputations of British artists of the preceding age. Its first loan exhibition was devoted to Reynolds, and that in the following year to Hogarth, Wilson, Gainsborough and Zoffany, drawing attention to the importance of Hogarth's oil paintings after half a century during which they had been neglected in favour of the engravings. The preface to the catalogue, in remarking on this fact, spoke of Hogarth's originality in adopting 'a new line of art, purely English . . .'[8]

The rise of a school of British art was fostered by a new generation of collectors who made a practice of patronizing their countrymen. In the vanguard of these was John Boydell, who commissioned works not only for his Shakespeare Gallery but also as a personal memorial at the Guildhall.[9] During the opening years of the nineteenth century Sir John Fleming Leicester, first Baron de Tabley, who founded the British Institution, formed the first gallery of paintings devoted exclusively to contemporary English artists. Of de Tabley's collection, which was kept in his house in Hill Street and open to the public without charge, William Carey, whom the owner employed to prepare a *Descriptive Catalogue* of his holdings, wrote in 1819: '. . . in that season of false taste, when a British picture, in the higher classes, was not to be found upon the walls of the first residences in England, he led the way to the brilliant prospects of the present era.' The preponderance of landscapes and fancy pictures reflected the rather nostalgic tastes of the owner. Carey's hope that this collection would 'prove a triumph to the English school and a powerful blow against Prejudice' was vindicated at the sale in 1827 following de Tabley's death, when his pictures realized substantially more than had been paid for them. Outstanding among other aristocratic patrons of contemporary English art were Turner's friend, the Earl of Egremont of Petworth House, and Sir George Beaumont of Coleorton Hall, himself an amateur artist and friend of Wilkie and Constable.

At the beginning of the nineteenth century there was an important development in the history of patronage, as members of the mercantile class joined the ranks of serious collectors of contemporary painting. Three are especially worthy of mention. One was John Sheepshanks, a prosperous Leeds cloth manufacturer who retired to Blackheath. After selling his original collection of Dutch and Flemish etchings to the British Museum, he used the proceeds to start forming a gallery of the English school. This eventually numbered 233 oils and 298 drawings, which were bequeathed to the nation in 1857, and are now in the Victoria and Albert Museum. The second was Robert Vernon, a large part of whose fortune had been amassed through supplying horses to the British army during the Napoleonic Wars. Vernon's collection of 152 contemporary English paintings, matching Sheepshanks' in quality, was presented to the National Gallery in 1847, and subsequently transferred to the Victoria and Albert Museum. The owner had exercised great independence of judgement in its formation, buying as his fancy dictated from the walls of the Royal Academy or British Institution, at auctions, from the artist's studio, or on direct commission. The third of this early trio of middle-class patrons was William Wells, former sea-captain and shipping magnate, whose extensive holdings in British art were located at Redleaf, near Tunbridge Wells, where he kept virtual open house for his favourite painters, including Sir Edwin Landseer.[10]

The change from aristocratic to primarily middle-class patronage, although not fully confirmed until Victorian times, was fraught with major implications for the subsequent progress of British painting. At the same time, it must be granted that the motives inducing such collectors as Sheepshanks, Vernon and Wells to concentrate on the works of their countrymen were not wholly disinterested. Aware of their lack of knowledge, of the scarcity and costliness of old masters, and of the concomitant prevalence of fake works passing under time-honoured attributions, they were more inclined to acquire pictures of whose genuineness they could be confident. Furthermore, as their rivalry in seeking out good examples by rising artists attests, they were not unaware of their potential value as investments, or of the social status conferred by owning them.[11] Yet, it is clear that these collectors took a good deal of patriotic pride in the thought that their wealth was being devoted to encouraging the development of home-grown talent. Vernon and Sheepshanks, indeed, both hoped that their collections would become the foundation of a national gallery of British art.

Although in early nineteenth-century England there was thus a more and more clearly defined sense that a distinctive national school of painting was in the making, many of its characteristics remained those which under similar conditions had shaped Dutch genre of the seventeenth century, and the seeds of which were already present, as we have seen, in British art of the eighteenth century. There was a continuing demand for pictures small enough to find a place on the walls of private houses, portraying familiar types engaged in customary activities, and with enough anecdotal or narrative content to sustain interest in the situations depicted. The one element from the previous age that had largely disappeared (although only for the time being) was the intrusion of sentimental morality; and it is in this respect, perhaps, that the influence of the current vogue for Dutch genre pictures with their dispassionate realism can be most readily perceived. The guiding considerations which Richard Redgrave attributed to Sheepshanks in the formation of his collection may well stand as a résumé of the prevailing tastes of the time:

> The present collection . . . consists of pictures of cabinet proportions, illustrative of every-day life and manners amongst us, appealing to every man's observation of nature and to our best feelings and affections, without rising to what is known as historic art; and as such, they are works that *all* can understand and all more or less

appreciate. And this is especially to be insisted on, since a wrong impression is all too widely entertained that art does *not* appeal to the multitude but only to those specially educated to appreciate it.

The time was therefore right for the arrival of a powerfully original artist who would focus these tendencies into modes of expression at once genuinely new and widely popular in appeal. He appeared in the person of Sir David Wilkie (1785–1841). Wilkie's Scottish nationality is of extreme importance, since it meant that he was heir to traditions alien to the tired conventions preserved by academic inertia in England. Unlike England, Scotland was a land in which rich and poor shared a common culture, nurtured on the popular traditions of an inherently democratic society.[12] Its literary origins went far back to the vernacular poetry of the ballads, which mingled humour and tragedy with a bold realism characterized by its 'sharp and fresh presentment of incident and scene', as Allan Cunningham observed in the Preface to his collection of *The Songs of Scotland, Ancient and Modern* (1825). Wilkie, it should be remembered, was a contemporary of Burns and Scott, in whose writings these earthy traditions enjoyed their great romantic revival. A second, specifically artistic influence particularly congenial to the Scottish temper of mind flowed from the Low Countries, with which Scotland had maintained closer relations, cultural as well as political and economic, than England. In the early years of the eighteenth century Sir John Clerk of Penicuik had begun to buy Dutch paintings, and he was followed by such members of the Scottish aristocracy as the third Earl of Bute, the seventh Earl of Wemyss and Sir James Erskine, who were forming their important collections of the Netherlandish schools well before anything of the sort was undertaken south of the border. Engravings of the work of such artists as Ostade and Teniers circulated freely in Edinburgh during Wilkie's student days; and he would certainly have been familiar with the three massive volumes of plates from original paintings by the Edinburgh seal-engraver, David Deuchar, published in 1803 under the title *A Collection of Etchings after the Most Eminent Masters of the Dutch and Flemish Schools*.

The father of Scottish genre painting was David Allan (1744–96). Back in Edinburgh after thirteen years of study in Italy and unconfident of his ability to support himself by portrait painting, he wrote to Sir William Hamilton in 1780: 'If I have health and time I intend to do groups of the manners in Scotland, which would be new and entertaining and good for engraving.' Allan is best remembered for his twelve illustrations (1787) of Allan Ramsay's early eighteenth-century pastoral drama, *The Gentle Shepherd*. In contrast to the artificial evocation of pastoralism in England, Ramsay had sought to give a truthful picture of Scottish rural life in all its rude and uncouth humour and pathos; and the illustrator spared no effort to be faithful to his text. In a letter of dedication of 1786 to his countryman, the painter Gavin Hamilton, he declared:

> This piece, it is well known, he [Ramsay] composed in the neighbourhood of Pentland Hills, a few miles from Edinburgh, where the shepherds to this day sing his songs and the old people remember him reciting his own verses. I have studied the same characters on the same spot, and I find that he has drawn faithfully and with taste from Nature. This, likewise, has been my model of imitation, and while I attempted in these sketches to express the ideas of the Poet, I also endeavoured to

Fig. 93
David Allan
The Penny Wedding
1795, watercolour

preserve the costume as nearly as possible by an exact delineation of such scenes and persons as he actually had in his eye.

On his return, Allan transferred the skills which he had developed in his Italian carnival scenes to humorously realistic drawings of Scottish customs, including a series of Edinburgh street types. Representative of his work in this vein is the watercolour of *The Penny Wedding* (1795, *fig. 93*), a subject of which virtually every Scottish genre artist produced his own version down to the middle of the nineteenth century. The name derives from a practice at country weddings by which each guest made a donation to help towards the cost of the celebration, the residue being given to the couple to help set up home.[13] Allan's picture reveals his keen eye for detail, the ability to draw a variety of types of character, and the boisterous humour which from the outset distinguished Scottish treatments of contemporary life. Allan was Master of the Trustees' Academy in Edinburgh from 1776 until his death a decade later; and he and his successor, John Graham, imparted to a whole generation of talented students, including Wilkie, the realism of approach and accompanying skills which gave its characteristic features to Scottish genre painting.

A favourite subject of this school was the village fair, which was an important occasion in the calendar, bringing together the local populace for business and pleasure, and thus offering a panoramic spectacle of regional life. Allan had made a drawing of Glasgow's *Muzzling Fair* at the age of twenty in 1764 before his departure for Italy; and at the same age in 1804 Wilkie selected for his first major oil painting the fair at Pitlessie near the parish of Cults in Fife, where his father was pastor of the Presbyterian church (*fig. 94*). The scene is an accurate rendering of the town square; and many of the figures in a throng numbering no fewer than 140 were portraits of Cults parishioners, covertly sketched by the artist on blank pages of his Bible during Sunday morning service. John Gibson Lockhart, Scott's son-in-law, hailed the originality of Wilkie's accomplishment, writing: 'It is a canvas 44 × 25 inches; into this space the artist has compressed such a panorama as never before was, never again will be, produced of the rural life of a province ... it is to Wilkie much what Border minstrelsy was to Scott'; and Allan Cunningham, Wilkie's biographer, called it 'the portrait of a village'. In his handling of setting Wilkie showed his debt to Ibbetson, whose pictures had been exhibited in Edinburgh and whose treatise, *Painting in Oil* (1803), he had copied out by hand. The rowdy behaviour of some of the groups was taken over from Brouwer and Ostade, whose influence in this respect the Scottish artist was soon to outgrow.

Pitlessie Fair was purchased for twenty pounds by Charles Kinnear, a Fife landowner, who allowed Wilkie to take it with him to London in 1805. Wilkie was tireless in seeking to perfect his technique, and the early years in London were ones of rapid development. Morland's realism struck a responsive chord, recorded in a letter to a fellow student: 'He seems to have copied nature in every thing, and in a manner peculiar to himself. When you look at his pictures you see in them the very same figures that we see here every day in the streets, which, from the variety and looseness in their dress, form an appearance that is truly picturesque, and much superior to our peasantry in Scotland.' But it was in the Netherlandish genre pictures beginning to flood London that Wilkie took special delight; and he lost no opportunity to study them, whether in examples borrowed from patrons, in auction rooms, or in the collections to which he was granted admission, such as those of Thomas Hope, John Angerstein, Sir George Beaumont, the Marquess of Stafford, or Sir Peter Francis Bourgeois. The influence of these masters, and especially Teniers, is apparent in his increased compositional skill in the handling of groups, in closer attention to accuracy in the rendering of detail, and in the brighter palette of such a canvas as *The Village Festival* (1811), which Cunningham called 'a joyous image of social England'. It is indicative of the rapidity with which Wilkie was establishing his reputation that he received eight hundred guineas from the prominent London collector, John Angerstein, for this canvas completed only six years after *Pitlessie Fair*.

From the outset of his career Wilkie unabashedly courted popularity, finding no difficulty in accommodating his artistic conscience to public demand. In his *Remarks on Painting*, assembled in 1836, he perceptively pointed out: 'The taste for art in our isle is of a domestic rather than a historical character. A fine picture is one of our

Fig. 94
Sir David Wilkie
Pitlessie Fair
1804

household gods, and kept for private worship: it is an every-day companion; and, unseen in holy places associated with holy things, becomes too familiar for awe ...' From this it followed that: 'To know ... the taste of the public – to learn what will best please the employer – is to an artist the most valuable of all knowledge ...' In summary, he concluded that art 'is like water spilt in a desert, unless the mind moulds and forms its speculations to the circumstances of its situation and the ruling desires of the times.'

Wilkie recognized that the awakening interest in a native school of British art was dependent on such patrons as Beaumont and Sheepshanks, whose support the artist was well advised to seek. 'Let us', he wrote, 'cultivate and improve that patronage which is extended to art; that employment almost unknown in other nations which we owe to the taste and refinement of prominent gentlemen.' Wilkie's pictures throughout his career were largely produced on commission; and the warmth of esteem and friendship he enjoyed from his sponsors reflected a significant rise in the social standing of the artist. This fact is illustrated by the instructions accompanying the commission for a picture (*Blind Man's Buff*, 1812) from the Prince Regent: 'let Wilkie make choice of the subject – take his time in painting it – and fix his own price.' With his astute business sense the artist was also mindful of the market for prints of his works; and he was fortunate in commanding the services of two of the most accomplished engravers of the time, Abraham Raimbach (1776–1843) and John Burnet (1784–1868), whose plates spread his reputation throughout Europe.[14]

For all their colourful animation, Wilkie's early pictures show that he had still to attain clarity and precision in handling panoramic scenes. While carefully studied, the separate clusters of figures in *Pitlessie Fair* and *The Village Festival*, making love, bartering, roistering, are lost in an overall welter of activity that bewilders the eye. *The Blind Fiddler* (1806, *fig. 95*), produced when Wilkie was only twenty-one, marks a significant stage forward in his mastery of pictorial narrative. Although he is said to have painted this work with a picture by Teniers, borrowed from Beaumont, beside him, the strongly defined narrative emphasis derives from Hogarth rather than from the Dutch, in whose pictures it is rarely a prominent feature. In contrast to the chaotic jumble of *Pitlessie Fair*, the itinerant musician provides the focal point for a complex pattern of response, as the viewer's gaze moves from group to group, much as in the act of reading.[15] The old wife's stony passivity in the presence of an all too familiar act contrasts with the rapt attention of the two children and elderly man at the centre who, alone of the audience, are truly under the spell of the music. The father snaps his fingers in time with the tune to interest the baby in the performance, but instead draws its attention to his own antics. The mother, oblivious to all else, is lost in loving contemplation of their child. And the two boys concealed at the right, one of whom is sawing away on a bellows with fire-tongs, gaze out at the viewer, as if inviting us to relish their impudent mimicry in preference to the serious concert. *The Blind Fiddler* admirably illustrates the artist's theories about composition, contained in his notes. The student is instructed to 'see that the minutest object obtained its due share of thought; that all the auxiliaries of the picture contributed to its sentiment; and that he put in no article of furniture merely to fill blanks; that all were required as matters of harmony, or confirmation to the story.'

Wilkie's next stage was to reduce yet further the number of figures in his composition in the interests of fuller psychological characterization. As all critics have observed, he was a past master in projecting graphic equivalents of states of mind.[16] In his proposals concerning physiognomy, published in the 1770s, the Swiss philosopher and mystic, Johann Kaspar Lavater, had immensely elaborated Le Brun's teaching that the conformation and expressions of human features are an index of character and behaviour. And Wilkie would have been familiar with such speculations through a friend, the distinguished Scottish anatomist, Sir Charles Bell (1774–1842), who set out to establish a physiological basis for the pseudo-science of physiognomy. Soon after his arrival in London the painter heard the series of lectures by Bell published in 1806 under the title *Essays on the Anatomy of Expression in Painting*.[17] Bell, himself an accomplished draughtsman, maintained:

Fig. 95
Sir David Wilkie
The Blind Fiddler
1806

Anatomy stands related to the arts of design, as the grammar of that language in which they address us. The expressions, attitudes, and movements of the human figure, are the characters of this language; which is adapted to convey the effect of historical narration, as well as to show the working of human passion, and give the most striking and lively indications of intellectual power and energy. The art of the painter, considered with a view to these interesting representations, assumes a high and dignified character.

The study of physiognomy became one aspect of the insistence on the uniqueness of each individual – and the resulting interest in distinguishing psychological traits – which characterized the romantic spirit in contrast to the eighteenth-century's generalizing habit of mind.

Wilkie's deftness in portraying the dramatic interaction of differing temperaments is shown in a remarkable small oil (24 × 20 inches), *The Letter of Introduction* (1813,

fig. 96), painted for a London merchant, Samuel Dobree. The subject originated in an incident which took place on the artist's first arrival in London. He had brought with him a letter of introduction from Sir George Sandilands, Vice-President of the Society of Arts, to a fellow Scot, Caleb Whitefoord. A wine merchant and political journalist with a reputation for acerbic wit, Whitefoord was also a recognized connoisseur, the friend of leading artists including Reynolds, and himself the possessor of a notable collection. Struck by his caller's gauche appearance, Whitefoord asked his age. Wilkie, who was not lacking in Scots pride, thought the question impertinent and stammered out, 'Really now!' to which his host retorted: 'Ha! introduce a man to me who knows not how old he is!'

To lend authority to an encounter which made a lasting impression on him, Wilkie based the composition of his picture on a work of 1658–9 of nearly the same dimensions by the Dutch master Terborch, variously entitled *Officer writing a Letter* or *The Despatch (fig. 97)*. Whatever their other comparative merits, the British picture, developed from the series of preliminary drawings which the artist usually made, certainly surpasses its Dutch counterpart as an evocation of a dramatic situation. Wilkie here appears as Hogarth's heir in suggesting traits of character by the play of facial expression and bodily gesture, with this difference: whereas Hogarth (and even more Wilkie's Dutch models) dealt with types, Wilkie's figures, however typical they may seem, almost invariably started as portraits of actual individuals.[18]

The meeting in *The Letter of Introduction* between a carefully dressed youth, whose attitude of brash self-reliance does not disguise the fact that he is shy and ill at ease, and an elderly eccentric in nightcap and carpet slippers (Wilkie, we are told, was careful to preserve Whitefoord's informal eighteenth-century style of dress), suspicious, as is his dog, about this invasion of treasured privacy, fairly crackles with explosive innuendo. The viewer's eye oscillates back and forth between the pair, awaiting whatever outburst is in store. The picture is evidence of Wilkie's skill in investing with dramatic tension and pungent humour a trivial episode which in the hands of a lesser artist would have offered merely passing anecdotal interest.

Having refined his approach to depicting aspects of contemporary life through technical mastery over the presentation of narrative and methods of characterization, Wilkie was equipped to take on a subject of major thematic significance. The opportunity came in 1816, when the Duke of Wellington commissioned from him a work relating to the Battle of Waterloo. Battle scenes, of course, were a staple of history painting; and by long and academically sanctioned tradition they were habitually presented in archaic guise, with the figures conventionally, even if anachronistically, garbed as classical heroes. In 1770 the American-born artist, Benjamin West (1738–1820), made a sensational departure from this practice in his painting of *The Death of General Wolfe*, in which the figures are clad in the appropriate military dress of the time.[19] Despite this token nod towards contemporaneity, West's piece, which exists in several versions, is a very stagey and inflated affair. To lend pathos to the expiring general, for example, the artist modelled his posture on Van Dyck's *Deposition of Christ*. Thirteen years later in *The Death of Major Peirson* (1782–4, *fig. 98*) another American resident in England, John Singleton Copley (1737–1815), gave far more lifelike treatment to a similar scene, derived from an encounter between British and French forces on the island of Jersey in 1781.[20]

Fig. 97
Gerard Terborch
Officer writing a Letter (The Despatch)
1658–9

OPPOSITE

Fig. 96
Sir David Wilkie
The Letter of Introduction
1813

Despite some melodramatic heightening of the action, there are also passages which ally the work with domestic genre, notably the distraught group of civilians fleeing to the right, for which the artist used his wife, their children and the family nurse as models.

In contrast to conventional depictions of Waterloo as a military engagement, Wellington's original proposal, to which Wilkie fully acquiesced, was for a picture in which genre should be the main element. Writing to Beaumont on 12 December 1816, Wilkie said of the projected work: '[Wellington] wants it to be a number of soldiers of various descriptions seated upon the benches of the door of a public house, with porter and tobacco, talking over their old stories.' In another letter to the painter Haydon he wrote: 'I said this would make a most beautiful picture, and that it only wanted some story, or a principal incident, to connect the figures together. He said [clearly with the example of such painters as Teniers in mind] perhaps playing skittles would do, or any other game, when I proposed that one might be reading a newspaper aloud to the rest, and that in making a sketch of it many other incidents would occur.' From this suggestion grew the all-important conception that would bring the picture within the province of history painting: the introduction as a focal point of interest of the bulletin announcing the British victory on the field of Waterloo, which had occurred in the previous year.

As was his wont, over a period of several years Wilkie made a large number of preparatory sketches, not only of the architectural setting in Jew's Row, the picturesque street leading from Pimlico to Chelsea Hospital, but also of various groupings of disabled or retired veterans of the country's far-flung wars.[21] More than eighty of these drawings and at least four oil sketches survive, and they form a fascinating record of the gradual evolution of *Chelsea Pensioners reading the Gazette of the Battle of Waterloo (fig. 99)*, which Wilkie finally completed in 1822. The preliminary studies show among other things the artist's scrupulous concern at every stage in the picture's progress for accuracy of detail. For example, in an early drawing the despatch-rider wore the uniform of the Life Guards; but when it was pointed out that this regiment saw action at Waterloo, the figure of a lancer was substituted.

Although there are no fewer than sixty figures in a picture which measures only $36\frac{1}{2} \times 60\frac{1}{2}$ inches, they do not appear posed as in Wilkie's earlier crowd scenes, but rather fall into natural groupings, forming a great crescent, a compositional principle borrowed from its successful use in *The Penny Wedding* (1819, *fig. 100*), which the artist had painted for the Prince Regent as a pendant to *Blind Man's Buff*. Nor does the artist in any way strain after effects to enhance the inherent drama of the *Chelsea Pensioners*. The attitude of the old warriors, whose easy conviviality has been interrupted by the news of Britain's great victory, bears witness to the historic nature of the occasion. At the same time, the carefully observed uniforms, emblematic of gallant actions of former days, challenge the informed viewer (of whom there were, of course, many at the time) to reconstruct the scene's context in appropriately heroic terms.

One might linger indefinitely over the reading of Wilkie's masterpiece; but identification of some of the participants will serve to suggest its imaginative scope. The despatch has been delivered by an orderly of the 7th Lancers, the Marquess of Anglesey's regiment; and it is being read aloud to the jubilant gathering by an old

soldier who was on the 'heights of Abram' with General Wolfe.[22] The listeners include: a sergeant of the 42nd Regiment, a Glengarry Highlander named MacGregor, who fought at Barossa in Spain under General Graham; a member of the Hanoverian Legion, a corps which distinguished itself at Waterloo; a Life Guardsman belonging to the regiment that helped break the charges of the French cuirassiers; a Negro from St Domingo, a member of the 1st Regiment of Foot Guards, who was in France during the Revolution and present at the death of Louis XVI; a veteran of the Indian Wars who fought at Assaye; an Irishman of the 12th Dragoons at the end of the table, relaying the news to a deaf old-timer, who had served with General Elliot at the siege of Gibraltar, and who has dropped his pipe in astonishment; and another soldier of the Foot Guards leaning out of the window of the Duke of York public house.

The spectacle is further diversified by the woman who anxiously bends forward to hear the roll of the dead of her husband's regiment, which suffered heavy losses, and by the black dog at the feet of the sergeant of the Oxford Blues, which was at the Battle of Vittoria and followed its master's regiment throughout the Peninsular Campaign, acquiring the name of 'Old Duke'. Nor should one overlook the originality of the domestic touches which the artist has introduced into the scene through the figures at the right – the jovial family group with the sergeant holding up his baby, and, in contrast, the exquisite Watteau-like seated woman, who does up her hair with the unruffled serenity of a seasoned camp-follower.

For the *Chelsea Pensioners* Wilkie received from Wellington twelve hundred guineas, the highest price that had ever been paid for a British painting. There had never been anything like the public acclaim that greeted the picture when it went on view at Somerset House. So great was the daily crush surrounding it that for the first time in the history of the Royal Academy it was necessary to erect a guard-rail to prevent damage to the canvas from the eagerness of viewers, many of whom recognized the portraits of their fellow soldiers. Wilkie, by general agreement, had produced a 'great national work'; but, more important, he had given the quietus to history painting in the grand manner. In the *Chelsea Pensioners* he showed that the assimilation of history painting into the popular mode of genre, first apparent in Hogarth's *March to Finchley* (where, however, the intent was primarily satiric, *fig. 13*), was commensurate with the loftiest goals of subject painting.[23]

Overnight, Wilkie's success inspired throughout Great Britain a flowering of genre painting in his manner. Not surprisingly, many of his followers were in Scotland where the Trustees' Academy, under John Graham's leadership, fostered the tradition of recording native habits and customs. Perhaps the most original of Wilkie's Scottish contemporaries was Alexander Carse (*c*1780–1832), a pupil of David Allan and a stay-maker by trade, whose pictures of tent-preaching, holy fairs and ale-house brawls exhibit a licentiousness suggestive of the artist's debt to Brouwer and Ostade, and not found elsewhere in British painting. Carse's *The Penny Wedding* (1819, *fig. 101*), although far inferior in artistry to Wilkie's version of the same subject painted a year earlier, is a good deal richer in incident and entertaining detail. The career of a fellow student of Wilkie at the Trustees' Academy, William Home Lizars (1788–1859), was unfortunately cut short when in 1812, at the age of twenty-four, he was obliged to take over his father's business. His last works, *A Scotch Wedding* and *Reading the Will*, exhibited at the Royal Academy in 1812, show his exceptional

Fig. 101
Alexander Carse
The Penny Wedding
1819

OVERLEAF

Fig. 102
Sir George Harvey
The Curlers
1835

promise as a painter of group activity. In 1837 John Burnet, Wilkie's leading engraver, exhibited his canvas of *Greenwich Pensioners commemorating the Anniversary of the Battle of Trafalgar*, designed as a companion piece to *Chelsea Pensioners*, but sadly lacking in the cohesiveness and broad humanity of the latter. Two other Scottish artists active during the early decades of the nineteenth century, who made a speciality of country fairs and similar local festivals, were Walter Geikie (1795–1837), who enjoyed the patronage of the Earls of Hopetoun, and Alexander Fraser (1786–1865), for many years Wilkie's assistant. Several views of All Hallows Fairs (1828–9) by the former are at Hopetoun House, while the Art Gallery at Dundee has *A Scotch Fair* (c1834) by the latter. Although slightly younger, Sir George Harvey (1806–76) belongs with this group. The splendidly spirited depiction of a curling-match (1835, *fig. 102*), like its pendant, *The Bowlers*, illustrates his humorously sympathetic perception of typical scenes from the life of the times.

Much work still needs to be done on the rise of provincial art centres in England during the early decades of the nineteenth century; and a fascinating study could be written of Wilkie's followers who sought to record the special features of life in specific regions. As in Scotland, the annual fairs which brought together cross-sections of the

local populace were a favourite subject. The Bath artist, Thomas Barker, who worked in many styles, depicted the motley gathering at *Lansdown Fair, near Bath* (1812), which also exists in a totally different version. Joseph Parry (1744–1826), an artist of more local reputation who was clearly influenced by Teniers, from as early as 1808 painted pictures in which he captured the turbulence of *Eccles Wakes*, an annual fair in a suburb of Manchester (*fig. 103*). Another Manchester artist was the short-lived Henry Liverseege (1803–32), whose livelihood was in large part dependent on the sale of engravings of his pictures, many of which were dedicated to local patrons. Newcastle is associated with the name of Henry Perlee Parker (1795–1873), who, in addition to some remarkable pictures of the coal-mining populace, recorded such bustling scenes of community life as *The Fish Market*. A central figure in the lively artistic life of Liverpool was Alexander Mosses (1793–1837), who specialized in portraits of typical regional types. *The Savoyard* (*c*1832, *fig. 104*) shows an itinerant boy musician with his dog and monkey entertaining a group of rustic children. Among other artists associated with specific localities were William Shayer (1788–1879), a native of Southampton who imitated Morland in his scenes of gipsy life and gatherings outside country inns, especially in the region of the New Forest in Hampshire, and Joseph Rhodes (1782–1854), a Leeds painter best known for his naive but animated portrayal of street activity around the *The Old Moot Hall, Brigate, Leeds*.

Stimulated by an unusually dedicated sketching society, made up of both amateur and professional artists, and by the patronage of local industrialists, Bristol – the peak of whose prosperity as a seaport for overseas trade had largely passed before the onset of the Industrial Revolution – was unique among provincial cities for the abundance of its artistic life in the opening years of the nineteenth century. A school of genre painting was led by Edward Bird (1772–1819), who had moved from Wolverhampton to Bristol by 1797. Bird was for a time regarded as a serious rival to Wilkie. The Prince of Wales had acquired his painting, *Country Choristers*, when it was exhibited at the Royal Academy in 1810, and on the basis of this purchase commissioned Wilkie to paint a companion to it, *Blind Man's Buff*.[24] In contrast to Wilkie, Bird's scenes from contemporary life lack conviction because of their sentimentalizing tone inherited from the previous age, as is apparent from a series of six pictures depicting the downfall and regeneration of a poacher (1813). His masterpieces were *The Raffle for the Watch* (undated), and *The Reading of the Will Concluded* (1811, *fig. 105*), both favourite subjects in genre painting of the age.

The latter substantiates the praise of a fellow artist, Edward Villiers Rippingille (1798–1859), who spoke of Bird's 'great power of seizing character, in furnishing illustrative incident, and the employment of episodes suitable to his object.' One notes, for example, the contrast between the humble gratitude of the naval officer and his family at the right, who have received a bequest, and the churlish attitudes of the trio of raffish sporting types by the table to the left, who have been disappointed.

Rippingille was Bird's principal successor. His first great success, *The Post Office* (1819), took for its subject a topic which was fresh and original at the time, and which was to enjoy continuing popularity into the Victorian period. Following Hogarth's example, although without the satiric bite to temper the obtrusive moral, Rippingille painted a sequence of six pictures, *The Progress of Intemperance* (c1840), tracing the ruin through drink of a guileless young farmer who falls into the clutches of a 'gang of depredators' on a visit to town. The artist is seen at his best in *The Recruiting Party* (1822), of which the crowded setting is a fair, and *The Stage Coach Breakfast* (1824, *fig. 106*). The latter work is unique among genre paintings for the richness of its literary associations, which have been spelled out by Sir Arthur and Lady Elton for whose family the canvas was originally painted:

> It portrays many of the contributors to *The London Magazine* and a number of members of Sir Charles Abraham Elton's family. Charles Lamb is handing Rippingille the bill. Coleridge is holding out a boiled egg for Wordsworth to sniff while Dorothy Wordsworth in a black bonnet sits at the table with folded hands. Robert Southey ogles Julia Elizabeth, Charles Abraham's daughter, pouring out tea while her father looks on grinning. ... To the right another Elton daughter, Caroline Lucy, laughs as an ostler tries to extract a tip from a mean old lady. On the extreme left, Caroline Lucy's twin sister, Lucy Caroline, prods a porter with an umbrella. Another Elton daughter, Laura Mary, is leaning against an old lady at the bottom of the stairs. Her mother, Sarah, clasps her youngest sons, Arthur Hallam and Edmund William.

A local artist of whom little is known was Samuel Colman (active 1816–40), who in addition to apocalyptic visions in the manner of John Martin painted *St James's Fair*,

Fig. 107
Samuel Colman
St James's Fair, Bristol
1824

OPPOSITE ABOVE

Fig. 105
Edward Bird
The Reading of the Will Concluded
1811

OPPOSITE BELOW

Fig. 106
Edward Villiers Rippingille
The Stage Coach Breakfast
1824

Bristol (1824, *fig. 107*), a festival dating from the thirteenth century. Colman's treatment is remarkable for the satiric boldness with which he depicts the thieving, lechery and general immorality for which this annual market had become notorious and which led to its being abolished in 1838. Hogarth's influence is apparent in the bawd soliciting the country lass at the right, while the would-be seducer lurks in the doorway, an episode lifted directly from the first plate of *A Harlot's Progress*. A version of St James's Fair which was very much more demure was painted by Rolinda Sharples (1793–1838), the most talented of a Bristol family of artists. She was content to record the passing show of the city's life without commentary, and her pictures invariably include a large number of local portraits. Their titles indicate her surprisingly wide range of interest: *A Market* (1820), her first success at the Royal Academy; *The Village Gossips* (1828); *The Stoppage of the Bank* (1825–31), a subject recommending itself 'as well suited to a great variety of expression'; and *Clifton Race Course* (1836). Eager to promote her reputation, Sharples missed no opportunity to show examples of her work at the provincial exhibitions which were becoming a regular feature of the artistic scene.

It is supremely ironical that Benjamin Robert Haydon (1786–1846), the foremost champion of history painting, should have significantly contributed to genre's rise to the dominant place it came to enjoy under Wilkie's leadership. Haydon's personal liking for Wilkie was tempered with bitter disapproval of the influence which he exerted. On 6 February 1824 he wrote in his *Diary*: 'Wilkie by his talent has done great injury to the taste of the Nation. Nothing bold or masculine or grand or powerful touches an English Connoisseur – it must be small and highly wrought, and vulgar & humorous & broad & palpable. I question whether Reynolds would now make the impression he did, so completely is the taste ebbing to a Dutch one.' And six years later, on 29 January 1830, he was still harping on the same theme: 'The Village Politicians [1806] changed the whole system of Art in the domestic style, and to that Picture is domestic life in the present high rank in England, owing entirely to that style.' Driven by financial necessity, Haydon produced only a handful of genre pictures, but they are of such interest that one can only wish that he had abandoned his principles and followed the trend of the times in Wilkie's wake.

Haydon's incarceration for debt in the King's Bench Prison in July 1827 was immediately responsible for a remarkable pair of pictures, entitled *The Mock Election* (1827, *fig. 108*) and *Chairing the Member* (1828). The former was inspired by a spectacle which he described as follows:

Before me were three men marching in solemn procession, the one in the centre a tall, young, reckless, bushy-haired, light-hearted Irishman, with a rusty cocked-hat under his arm, a bunch of flowers in his bosom, his curtain rings round his neck for a gold chain, a mopstick for a white wand, tipped with an empty strawberry-pottle, bows of ribbons on his shoulders, and a great hole in his elbow, of which he seemed perfectly unconscious; on his right was another person in burlesque solemnity with a sash and real white wand; two others, fantastically dressed, came immediately behind, and the whole followed by characters of all descriptions, some with flags, some with staffs, and all in perfect merriment and mock gravity, adapted to some masquerade. I asked what it meant, and was told that it was a procession of burgesses, headed by the Lord High Sheriff and Lord Mayor of the King's Bench Prison, going in state to open the poll, in order to elect two members to protect their rights in the House of Commons!

Of the immediate impression that this strange sight made on him Haydon wrote: 'I saw in an instant the capacity there existed in this scene of being made morally instructive and interesting to the public, by the help of an episode in assistance. I told Mr _____, the banker, who stood by me, I would paint it, and asked him if he believed there ever were such characters, such expressions, and such heads, on human shoulders, assembled in a group before?' After his release, Haydon returned repeatedly to the King's Bench to sketch from the life the cast of characters for his picture, which was to be, as he wrote in his *Diary*, 'a sort of Beggar's Opera'. Virtually all of the figures have been identified as portraits of actual inmates. The original of the person playing the Lord High Sheriff, for example, was an Irishman, named Jonas Alexander Murphy, who was later released after his friends paid his debts. When the painting was exhibited, Haydon published an explanation of all the details. This is too lengthy to quote in full; but the following description of the impressive figure seated in profile at the right, a Major Campbell, shows that the subject called forth the full imaginative effort that the artist was accustomed to expend on his historical themes:

In the right hand corner, sipping claret, sits a man of family and a soldier, who distinguished himself in Spain; he was imprisoned in early life for running away with a ward in Chancery; embarrassment followed, and nine years of confinement have rendered him reckless and melancholy; he has one of the most tremendous heads I ever saw in nature, something between Byron and Buonaparte; it was affecting to see his pale determined face and athletic form amongst the laughing afflicted, without a smile! without an emotion! Indifferent to the humour about him, contemptuously above joining in the burlesque, he seemed, like a fallen angel, meditating on the absurdities of humanity!...

In the picture I have made him sit at ease, with a companion, while champagne bottles, a dice-box, dice, cards, a racket bat and ball on the ground announce his present habits.

Encouraged by George IV's purchase of *The Mock Election*, Haydon produced in the following year its sequel, *Chairing the Member*, also based on an actual prison experience:

The scene now painted and represented to the public is The Mock Chairing, which was acted on a water-butt one evening, but was to have been again performed in more magnificent costume the next day; just, however, as all the actors in this eccentric masquerade, High Sheriff, Lord Mayor, Head Constable, Assessor, Poll Clerks and Members were ready dressed and preparing to start, the Marshal interfered and stopped the procession! Such are human hopes!

The moment chosen by the artist was that of the ill-advised arrival of the guardsmen to break up the performance. Many of the characters in *The Mock Election* reappear, and Haydon added a portrait of himself watching from the prison window. The artist's debt to the final painting of Hogarth's *Election* series (*fig. 17*) is clearly apparent in the exuberantly burlesque handling of the scene.

In the following year Haydon produced his masterpiece in the genre mode. Its alternative titles, *Punch, or May Day* (1829, *fig. 109*), suggest the scope of the artist's conception. The subject – a popular form of street entertainment, the puppet show, on a traditionally festive holiday – provided a matchless opportunity to survey the motley pageantry of the city streets. The canvas is a microcosm of *Life in London*, and this, indeed, was its original title. Entranced by the performance, a farmer with his dog stands in front of the booth, unaware that an urchin, hidden by a confederate's cloak, is about to pick his pocket, while a flashily dressed man, another accomplice, distracts his attention. The thieves in turn are unconscious of the scrutiny of a Bow Street officer, truncheon in hand. Among the figures in the audience are a sailor, a Life Guard veteran of Waterloo, a nursemaid holding up her charge, a street-sweeper whose posture mimics Punch, and an Italian vendor of images carrying on his head a tray of casts of Theseus and Apollo. At the left an apple-girl dozes by her stall below the showman. Opposite her a group of sweeps frolic in the spirit of May Day revels, flourishing their ensign, a Jack-in-the-Green. Above them passes a coach carrying a newly married couple from the church (St Mary-le-Bow); its bravery of display stands in contrast to the blackness of the funeral procession emerging from a side street.

Haydon's repeated assertion in his *Diary* entries that he hoped to make *Punch* into a

humorous moral satire indicates the extent of his conscious debt to Hogarth. And in this, as in the two prison pictures, he was seeking to exploit Hogarth's master theme – the interplay of actuality and make-believe, of real-life drama and its simulation in play-acting. Haydon, however, lacked Hogarth's ability to establish a thematic as well as a compositional unity in his crowd scenes. Instead, the somewhat haphazard composition based on an artificial juxtaposition of details, such as the wedding and the funeral, or the soldier and the sailor, suggests that the artist was painting to fulfil a self-imposed prescription rather than out of any true depth of conviction. And just as Haydon shows no trace of Hogarth's generous indignation, so he also lacks the capacity for kindly sympathy which informs Wilkie's paintings. Despite their animation and individuality the figures are as much puppets as Punch and Judy; and like their performance, Haydon's picture is best viewed as an entertainment, filled with lively and accurate reportage.

Fig. 108
Benjamin Robert Haydon
The Mock Election
1827

Fig. 109
Benjamin Robert Haydon
Punch, or May Day
1829

Wilkie's pictures conform to two general types. The first is panoramic in scope, presenting numerous figures engaged in some activity which gives them a group identity. It was in this mode, inspired by Hogarth and now revived after being neglected throughout the eighteenth century, that Wilkie's practice was most immediately influential, as is apparent from the prevalence of fairs, markets, raffles, and other such gatherings in early nineteenth-century British art. This, furthermore, was the strand of genre painting which most nearly approximated history painting in scope and significance. The second category over which Wilkie demonstrated equal mastery was private rather than public in reference, concerned with individual behaviour expressed through the responses of a limited number of characters to highly dramatic situations. Wilkie's rival and in some respects his superior in this field was

William Mulready (1786–1863), whose Irish origins, like Wilkie's Scottishness, may in part account for the freshness and originality of his approach to the contemporary scene. Like Wilkie as well, Mulready enjoyed the privilege of painting primarily for private patrons who treated him as an equal and encouraged the natural development of his talents. In early years his students bought many of his works; and he was to become a favourite artist of such collectors as Sheepshanks, a voracious client, Sir Thomas Baring, and Sir John Swinburne and his family.

The anecdotal style of treating domestic incidents on which Mulready's reputation rests may well have been developed in response to the prompting of Wilkie, who wrote to him in October 1813: 'Think of a subject of interest & with not too many figures in it.' *The Convalescent from Waterloo* (1822, *fig. 110*), completed in the same year as the *Chelsea Pensioners (fig. 99)*, shows how germane Wilkie's advice was to Mulready's natural bent in choice of subject. As he was to remark to a friend, Sir Henry Cole, many years later in 1849, mindful perhaps of the contrast between his way of responding to a great historic event and Wilkie's: 'Civilian life had as many stirring incidents in it as one at Sea or in the army & more touching too.'

In his sketchbook Mulready tersely set down his artistic goals as follows: 'Story Character Expression Beauty'. The narrative interest in his pictures relates less to the type of incident, which is usually banal enough, than to his skill in choosing precisely the most effective moment for its presentation. In painting after painting the action, which has gathered to a head, is arrested on the threshold of dénouement, its issue in precarious balance and unresolved. There is thus an element of ambiguity in Mulready's work that teases the viewer into trying his own conclusions; and one must assume that this ambiguity was deliberate, since the artist, contrary to conventional practice, never volunteered explanations of his meaning. Redgrave relates an anecdote about George IV's fondness for Mulready's work which illustrates how readily it invited an interpretative response: 'Mr Sheepshanks told Lord Palmerston that Mulready's "Wolf and Lamb" was a great favourite with George IV, and that when it came back to Mulready to be looked over, the whole bottom of the frame was a mass of wax, which had dropped from the candle when the King, from time to time, stood before it explaining the story.'

Mulready was especially given to portraying unruly boys, probably because he had four high-spirited sons of his own whom he raised single-handed after his early separation from their mother. These lads are said to have provided the portraits for *The Fight Interrupted* (1815–16, *fig. 111*), the earliest example of the style of genre painting in which he had no rival. The light falling from the left leads the eye to read the narrative sequentially from left to right, as in Wilkie's *The Blind Fiddler (fig. 95)*. The schoolmaster has stopped a fist-fight between two of his pupils, and is trying to apportion blame from the stories of a pair of onlookers, each of whom gestures at one of the combatants. The smaller of the pugilists, whom he holds by the ear, would appear to have had the upper hand, judging from the swollen lip which his adversary by the pump is fingering. One guesses from the toadies gathered about the latter that he is the school bully who retains his following even in defeat. Nevertheless, the viewer is left uncertain how to distribute his sympathies, since it is the victim in his master's clutch who seems destined for punishment.

The Wolf and the Lamb (1820, *fig. 112*) reveals Mulready's growing skill in

Fig. 110
William Mulready
The Convalescent from Waterloo
1822

Fig. 111
William Mulready
The Fight Interrupted
1815–16

delineating 'character' as a component of 'story'. For the two boys embody in human form the generic traits of the animals which give their names to the picture. And as 'story' is instigated by 'character', so 'character' is dependent on 'expression'. In contrasting his two protagonists, Mulready has exploited every expressive resource at his command – facial expression, gesture (note especially the attention devoted to hands), bodily posture, even clothing. For the French critic Théophile Gautier this was the most notable aspect of Mulready's style, and one that he associated with the special genius of British painting. Of *The Wolf and the Lamb*, which Mulready exhibited along with eight other pictures at the Exposition Universelle des Beaux-Arts in Paris (1855), Gautier had this to say: 'Ce petit drame est rendu avec ce sentiment exquis de l'expression et de la pantomime qui, depuis Hogarth, semble être l'apanage des peintres anglais. . . . ils apportent à leurs ouvrages une finesse d'analyse, un soin de composition et une recherche de physionomie tout particuliers.'[25]

Mulready's attention to facial expressions was undoubtedly stimulated by his brother-in-law, the artist John Varley, who in 1828 published *A Treatise on Zodiacal Physiognomy*, in which he advanced the eccentric notion that physical appearance is governed by the signs of the zodiac.[26] Another artist, William Powell Frith, relates that Mulready's fascination with the appearance of criminals led him to attend the trials of notorious offenders.[27] Of greater importance was Mulready's lifelong attendance at the life classes of the Royal Academy, not only as the much-loved drawing master but also for the sake of keeping up his own skills as a draughtsman. Like Wilkie, he habitually made pen and ink drawings, chalk studies, watercolours and oil sketches before arriving at the final versions of his pictures. They show how meticulously the artist worked out the expressive features of his finished works.

There are several sheets of preparatory drawings to *Giving a Bite* (1834, *fig. 113*), for example, the immensely more sophisticated reworking of an earlier picture of 1819. These sketches show that the artist was especially concerned to capture the attitude of the boy at the left, who has been cowed into sharing his apple, but whose clutching hands and covetous expression betray how reluctantly he has given in. Mulready was conscious of the kinship of men and animals in even more subtle ways than Landseer; and in this painting, as in many others, the animals play a central role. The rigidity of the boy with the apple carries vertically down through the identical posture of the performing monkey frozen in terror of the dog, whose menacing manner in turn echoes the predatory forward thrust of its greedy master's body.

Mulready's portrayal of belligerent boys stands at the farthest possible remove from the gently sentimental presentations of youth in later eighteenth-century painting. Such pictures as *The Fight Interrupted, The Wolf and the Lamb, The Dog of Two Minds* (1829–30, derived, as has been suggested, from Gainsborough's *Two Shepherd Boys with Dogs Fighting*, 1783) and *Giving a Bite* have a common basis in aggression and the threat of physical violence. This strain in Mulready's work is in part at least attributable to his temperament. He was himself an accomplished pugilist and, according to F.G.Stephens, provided most of the engraved illustrations for Pierce Egan's *Boxiana: or Sketches of Antient and Modern Pugilism* (1812). Frith recalled that Mulready 'always took great interest in street fights when opponents were equally matched. I saw him one day with an intense expression of interest on his face, looking from the street into a small alley which ran at right angles with it; and

ABOVE LEFT

Fig. 112

William Mulready
The Wolf and the Lamb
1820

ABOVE RIGHT

Fig. 113

William Mulready
Giving a Bite
1834

when I reached him, I saw the cause of his interest in the form of two boys who were pummelling one another, displaying what he called true British pluck.'

The reference to 'true British pluck' provides an additional key to Mulready's predilection for situations calling for the display of physical courage and hardihood. Thomas Hughes, a leader of the movement popularly known as 'muscular Christianity', voiced this mood in his novel, *Tom Brown's Schooldays* (1857), the hero of which proclaims: 'After all, what would life be without fighting? ... From the cradle to the grave, fighting, rightly understood, is the business, the real, highest, honestest business of every son of man.' A writer in the *New Monthly Magazine* made out an ingeniously original case for the appeal of *The Fight Interrupted* on grounds deriving from John Bull's love of a good scrap:

The interest which this picture excites would doubtless astonish, and perhaps disgust a foreigner, who, unused to such scenes, might censure the taste of the artist in the selection of his subject, but for our part we prefer the representation of a fight of this sort, which is purely national, to all the pictures of Waterloo which we have seen: – in fact, we have now no small authority for our preference, for, at a late public dinner, a gallant general, who has fought and bled for his country, declared that he owed all his success and reputation to the first black eye he received at Westminster, and 'no less strange than true', this remark was followed by a similar avowal from a British judge.

In *The Convalescent from Waterloo* (fig. *110*) the two sons locked in struggle playfully carry on the warlike impulse which has crippled their father and deprived their mother, in mourning dress, of a near relation.[28]

It is not unlikely that the contentious atmosphere which so frequently pervades Mulready's paintings had a still deeper origin. He may have been responding, whether consciously or not, to the new temper of mind which was coming to dominate social relations in the age of industrial competition, and which was in due course to find sanction in the Darwinian stress on conflict as the natural condition of survival. Exposed to the deterministic pressures of *laissez-faire* economics as well as biological theory, the eighteenth-century dream of paradisal joy and well-being as the heritage of the young and innocent dissolved. Contemporary patrons, such as Sheepshanks and Vernon, possibly relished Mulready's portraits of pugnacious boys so keenly because they provided surrogates for their own acquisitive impulses – the more so since the artist's ambivalent detachment in presenting his subjects could be construed as flattering the self-assertive spirit at large in the world.[29]

In mid-career Mulready began to alternate his more dramatic subjects with pictures best described as domestic idylls of young love. Indeed, Palgrave noted their congruity with Tennyson's *English Idyls* of the same period, which he described as 'not more finished, glowing, and poetical' than Mulready's canvases. *The Sonnet*

ABOVE LEFT

Fig. *114*
William Mulready
The Sonnet
1839

ABOVE RIGHT

Fig. *115*
William Mulready
The Bathers Surprised
c1852–3

(1839, *fig. 114*) is the masterpiece of a series which includes such charming works as: *Open Your Mouth and Shut Your Eyes* (1835–8), *First Love* (1838–9), *Crossing the Ford* (1842), and the paintings which Mulready developed from his extraordinarily popular illustrations for *The Vicar of Wakefield* (1843), such as the pastoral *Haymaking: Burchell and Sophia* (1846–7). Virtually devoid of incident, in their frank appeal for emotional response these pictures barely skirt the sentimentality which was to be the bane of the next generation of such paintings. Yet they exhibit qualities that redeem the apparent triviality of their content. Among the factors heightening the viewer's response are the artist's 'borrowings' from the Old Masters, a practice in which he was the disciple of Hogarth and Reynolds. Thus the postures of both figures in *The Sonnet*, that of the boy shyly peering over his shoulder and of the reading girl, hand drawn across her mouth, are lifted from Michelangelo's *Jeremiah* in the Sistine Ceiling. The harmonious grace of Mulready's compositions in these paintings is supported by their tonal values, which were an achievement of his mature technique. He had seen examples of Titian and Tintoretto exhibited at the British Institution, and henceforth endeavoured, as he said, 'to graft the principles of the Venetian school of colour on subjects of the Dutch school.' By applying bright colours to a wet white ground, he achieved a luminescence of tone which was to influence the Pre-Raphaelites in the middle of the century.[30]

One other aspect of Mulready's art responded to an element in the temper of his times, although it was perhaps the result of inherent inclination rather than of deliberate intent. The great romantic writers, such as Wordsworth and Coleridge, had dwelt on the elements of mystery and strangeness lurking just below the surface of everyday experience. Mulready's scenes of domestic life frequently carry disturbing hints of a preternatural dimension, hovering ominously in the background and at variance with their apparent content. An example is *The Bathers Surprised* (c1852–3, *fig. 115*). On first glance this picture seems simply an accomplished study of female nudes, rivalling Mulready's friend, William Etty (1787–1849).[31] But then one notes the figure with raised arm in the left background, signalling some urgent warning which has been picked up by the standing woman at the right and to which the bathers in the middle distance are responding in a frantic scramble, although the girl in the foreground is as yet undisturbed. The source of the menace and its nature are left entirely to the viewer's imagination.

Mulready regarded as his masterpiece a picture painted for Sir Thomas Baring (who also owned *The Bathers Surprised*), which carries the cumbersome title from the Book of Proverbs: *Train up a Child in the Way He should go; and when He is old He will not depart from It* (1841, *fig. 116*). The artist was here addressing himself to the theme, so popular in the preceding century, of the importance of implanting charitable impulses in the young. Two older girls are encouraging their brother to give his alms to three beggars huddled by the wayside. But Mulready has gone out of his way to invest this familiar situation with truly frightening attributes. The dark and threatening cliffs in the background create a setting of Gothic gloom, and the beggars crouching to the right are dark-skinned Lascars with glaring eyes. No wonder that the boy is braced for flight even as he thrusts out a penny.

A similar atmosphere of lurking evil invests *The Toyseller* (c1857–63, *fig. 117*), which the artist left unfinished at his death. This was the final and most disturbing

Fig. 116
William Mulready
*Train up a Child in the Way He
should go ; and when He is old He will
not depart from It*
1841

version of a subject which he had worked on as early as 1835. Again, the episode of an itinerant vendor offering his wares is familiar in genre painting; but it here takes on overtones of menace from the hypnotic gaze of the huge blackamoor. The object in his hand may be a rattle but looks more like a magic talisman than a toy, and is being held up in such a way as to terrify rather than placate the child, whose averted eyes express panic dread in the face of some threat that invades the security of his mother's embrace. Not even Dickens, whose *Oliver Twist* and *The Old Curiosity Shop* had appeared not long before, offered more devastating portraits of children at the mercy of an alien and inscrutable world.

The wave of pictures of scenes of childhood that rose in the late Georgian period was to assume tidal proportions in the nineteenth century. Indeed, it may be questioned whether any other subject-matter was as popular throughout the entire period. Victorian domestic mores were circumscribed by the family circle, and at the heart lay the cult of the child, the ultimate guarantee of the sanctity of the home and the prepotency of the hearthside virtues. At the same time, the darkening social prospect that accompanied the onset of the industrial age for so many of the population introduced new ways of thinking about the blissful state of childhood. What the city dweller, trapped in the deadening routine of the struggle for subsistence, looked for in pictures evoking the happiness of childhood were not visions of paradisal innocence and purity, but rather believable representations of carefree joy and freedom from the restraints and anxieties of adulthood. And if artists continued in large measure to derive their subjects from rustic life, this was not so much because country ways seemed to embody the pastoral ideal as because they were unsullied by the blighting gloom of cities. In his description of the Vernon bequest, written in 1850, Samuel Carter Hall commented on the considerations governing contemporary taste:

> Apart from the natural beauties which are scattered so profusely over the face of our country, there is much in the occupations and amusements of our peasantry, and more especially of their children, to call the artist into their society; and the popularity of such subjects with us is an additional inducement for him to answer the appeal. Who can think of these things and deny the superiority of his [the rural child's] lot – even with all its poverty – to those 'cribbed and confined' in pent-up cities or overgrown towns, where the Industrial Arts flourish? What painter would ever think of selecting for a picture a group of factory children, or the tenants of some crowded court or alley, except for the purpose of exciting commiseration, or to show how much squalor and wretchedness thousands of our fellow-creatures are doomed to endure? Who would gaze on such a picture with other feelings than those of distress, or without uttering a wish that each and all of them were permitted to taste the breath of heaven 'pure and undefiled'?

Although Mulready's originality and uncompromising approach to his subjects discouraged direct imitators, his practice set patterns for the treatment of scenes of childhood which were carried on in the best examples of the genre. In contrast to the vignette-like quality of much work in the later eighteenth century, Mulready, following Wilkie's lead as we have seen, introduced a much more prominent narrative element into typical situations. Likewise, the use of types was replaced by highly

Fig. 117
William Mulready
The Toyseller
c1857–63

individualized characterizations revealing sympathetic insights into the habits of mind that determine behaviour. Finally, although these tendencies were to be reversed with the onset of Victorianism, Mulready presented his scenes (again like Wilkie) without any trace of a moralizing or didactic purpose, while playing down their sentimental appeal through a strong infusion of humour.

Thomas Webster (1800–86) so conclusively appropriated the world of boyhood as his artistic domain that he won the soubriquet of 'Do-the-Boys' Webster. When he moved to the Kentish village of Cranbrook in 1857, he became the leader of the most important group of rustic genre painters in Victorian England, the so-called Cranbrook School. Long before this, however, he had established his manner through such popular works as the paired *The Smile* and *The Frown* (1841) and *A Village Choir* (1847), in which he displayed his talent for expressing idiosyncrasies of character. No setting relating to children occurs more frequently in genre pictures than school-rooms, education being, of course, a dominant concern of the age. Like many of his contemporaries, including Mulready (see his painting *The Last In*, 1835), Webster found a favourite subject in the truant, perhaps because such rebels against authority struck a responsive chord in viewers condemned to lives of insipid conformity. In *The*

Fig. 118
Thomas Webster
The Boy with Many Friends
1841

Fig. 119
Thomas Webster
Sickness and Health
1843

Boy with Many Friends (1841, *fig. 118*) Webster presented a more original classroom scene. One of the pupils has just received a hamper of goodies and is being besieged by his fellows to divide up the spoils. Despite the somewhat overcrowded composition, the artist has skilfully distinguished between the various kinds of approach to which the victim is being subjected. One lad offers a handful of marbles for barter, another a dog-eared book, while a third is reduced to the role of plain beggar. Reared pugnaciously behind is the school bully who, we may assume, will exact a high price for his protection, much like Steerforth on David Copperfield's arrival at Blimber's Academy.

Unusually sentimental for Webster, but demonstrating his sympathetic understanding of the joys and sorrows of youth, is *Sickness and Health* (1843, *fig. 119*). The artist's narrative skill is apparent in the composition, which effectively supports the picture's title through the arrangement of the two contrasting groups of figures in parallel diagonals. The one to the left consists of the dancing children and hurdy-gurdy player, and the other of the ailing girl with her elders and seated brother. The light, falling from the left, as in *The Boy with Many Friends* and so frequently in Webster's work, picks out the light-coloured dresses of the three sisters. The compassionate response which the picture is designed to arouse in the viewer rings true, since the musician is playing for the older girl as well as for her two sisters, just as their dancing is quite as much to cheer the invalid as for their own obvious enjoyment.

Another artist devoted to child subjects was William Collins (1788–1847), whose work, although nearly contemporary with his friend David Wilkie's and Mulready's, shows less affinity with theirs than with that of the preceding age. Indeed, in manner and content he may be said to provide a bridge between the sentimentality of the late eighteenth century and its re-emergence in Victorian painting. For his first important canvas he chose a subject well calculated to stir up a heartfelt response, *The Sale of the Pet Lamb* (1813), the engraving of which sold between fourteen and fifteen thousand impressions. Throughout his career Collins was to seek to adapt his pictures to prevailing trends in taste. As Wilkie Collins, his son and biographer, wrote: 'His efforts, from first to last, were addressed to every grade of his fellow beings who were likely to behold them; and were tried in his own mind by no other final standard than that of general approbation.' Like Wilkie and Mulready, the artist worked almost exclusively for private patrons, commonly selling his pictures from the studio before they were exhibited, and making several versions of those that proved popular. He also capitalized on the market for engravings, and took advantage of the new field for tender domestic scenes opened up by the vogue for Keepsake Annuals.[32] He had studied with Morland for a time in his youth, and always thought of himself as working in and promoting a native tradition; and this aspect of his performance was remarked on by the sculptor Thomas Woolner as largely responsible for the wide appeal of his pictures: 'Collins is thoroughly English, and in his country lanes, cottage doors, sweeps of landscape, and seaside views he presents the ideal of all a tired citizen would wish to behold when enjoying his annual holiday. And it is this ability to satisfy the wholesome and natural craving of so many of his countrymen that has made his works deservedly popular.'

A representative canvas by Collins is *Happy as a King* (1836, of which several versions exist, *fig. 120*). Set in Frognal Grove, Hampstead, the subject, according to Wilkie Collins, was suggested to his father 'by the story of a country boy whose ideal of happiness was swinging upon a gate and eating fat bacon.' The artist does not attempt to rival the narrative or expressive skills of Wilkie or Mulready; the situation has only anecdotal interest, and the figures, despite their ragged garb, are prettified types. But the group's happy-go-lucky abandon to a simple rural pastime, especially the lad with upraised arms on top of the gate, is admirably calculated to awaken in the viewer nostalgia for the unclouded joys of childhood. And this response is enhanced by the attention lavished on the beauty of the natural background in which the children are so much at home.[33]

In about 1816 Collins turned to painting shore scenes; and many of his best pictures are set by the seaside. An admirable late example is *Seaford, Sussex* (1844, *fig. 121*). Here the artist again achieved a happy counterpoise between setting and the human element enlivening it. The youngsters are busy building a toy boat, an action which recurs in innumerable genre scenes of child life. Such is their absorption in this occupation that they are wholly oblivious of their surroundings. Yet the grandeur of the prospect, with the broad sands below and the sweep of the bay rounding to the distant cliffs under a radiant sky, imparts an immemorial quality to a trivial pastime, and endows the children with a commensurate dignity.

The rise of the great British school of landscape painting was concurrent with the

Fig. 120
William Collins
Happy as a King
1836

Fig. 121
William Collins
Seaford, Sussex
1844

spread of genre in the early nineteenth century; and many rural scenes with figures are on the borderline between the two categories, provoking responses that will vary, depending on whether the artist has placed emphasis primarily on the human or non-human elements in his picture. Popular preference clearly inclined to works in which the landscape was conceived as an arena for some kind of activity; and during the first half of the period there was a market for *paysages de genre* of the type painted by William Collins. Some of the best examples were produced by artists better known for work in other modes. A list of representative pictures, all from the early years of the century, would include: *Boys sailing a Little Boat* (c1821, *fig. 122*) by the Bristol artist Francis Danby (1793–1861), who specialized in more fanciful subjects; Mulready's early oil of a place near his home in London, *The Mall, Kensington Gravel Pits* (1811–12); *Londoners gipsying* (1820, *fig. 123*) by Charles Robert Leslie (1794–1859), who was to turn almost exclusively to literary genre; and *The Hop Garland* (1834) by William Frederick Witherington (1785–1865), an artist whose facile talent was

Fig. 122
Francis Danby
Boys sailing a Little Boat
c1821

particularly suited to exploiting popular themes. Despite the charmingly detailed and sensitive treatment of landscape in all these works, it is the playful presence of the actors in the scenes which draws and holds the viewer's attention.

The relationship to genre of the two great masters of landscape, John Constable (1776–1837) and Joseph Mallord William Turner (1775–1851) is more difficult to specify. Constable was so inextricably wedded to the populous Suffolk scenes in which he had grown up that a visit to the Lake District in 1806 left him unmoved. His artist friend and biographer, C.R.Leslie, wrote: 'I have heard him say the solitude of mountains oppressed his spirits. His nature was peculiarly social and could not feel satisfied with scenery, however grand in itself, that did not abound in human

Fig. 123
Charles Robert Leslie
Londoners gipsying
1820

Fig. 125
John Constable
The Leaping Horse
1825

associations. He required villages, churches, farmhouses, and cottages; and I believe it was as much from natural temperament as from early impressions that his first love, in landscape, was also his latest love.' Constable's notebooks bear witness to the truth of this observation with their sketches not only of figures employed in the seasonal round of agricultural labour, but also of the implements used in these chores. Nor was the artist unaware of the extent to which the inclusion of human interest in his pictures increased their attraction for potential buyers. Of *The Cornfield* (1826, *fig. 124*), which the artist habitually referred to as *The Drinking Boy*, he wrote to his friend Archdeacon Fisher: 'I do hope to sell this present picture – as it certainly has got a little more eye-salve than I usually condescend to give to them.'[34]

At the same time, Constable detested the popular manner of Collins, of one of whose canvases he remarked, 'a coast scene with fish as usual, and a landscape like a large cow-turd'; and he was equally repelled by the pastoral manner stemming from French practice in the eighteenth century.[35] According to Leslie, John Thomas ('Antiquity') Smith, who was to become Keeper of Prints and Drawings at the British Museum, had cautioned Constable when a young man: 'Do not set about inventing figures for a landscape taken from nature; for you cannot remain an hour in any spot, however solitary, without the appearance of some living thing that will in all probability accord better with the scene and time of day than will any invention of your own.' How much the artist took this advice to heart is apparent in such pictures as *Boat-building near Flatford* (1815) and *View on the Stour near Dedham* (1822). The activities of the shipwrights in the former and of the bargemen in the latter are accurately observed, but only in the most general way, as aspects of the surrounding landscape with which they merge harmoniously.

OPPOSITE

Fig. 124
John Constable
The Cornfield
1826

The Leaping Horse (1825, *fig. 125*), the last of Constable's great series of canal scenes, was inspired by the practice of training the horses that towed the canal barges to leap over the barriers erected along the towpath to prevent cattle from straying. Yet, the artist made no effort to individualize the great horse or its rider; his interest in this local custom was confined to its strength as a compositional motif about which to construct a natural scene alive with corresponding movement. The description of the picture to Archdeacon Fisher omits any mention of this focal point, and makes the figures in the scene of less significance than the natural objects along the margin of the canal: 'It is a canal and full of the bustle incident to such a scene where four or five boats are passing with dogs, horses, boys & men & women & children, and best of all old timber-props, water plants, willow stumps, sedges, old nets, &c. &c. &c.'

Turner, with his extraordinary experimental flexibility, was in touch with genre traditions at every stage in the development of his mature style. *Sun rising through Vapour, Fishermen cleaning and selling Fish* (1807) derives from the Dutch school, although already, as the first part of the title indicates, the artist was concerned with the atmospheric effects which he was the first to exploit. *A Country Blacksmith*

Fig. 126
Joseph Mallord William Turner
A Country Blacksmith disputing upon the Price of Iron, and the Price charged to the Butcher for shoeing his Poney
1807

Fig. 127
Joseph Mallord William Turner
Ploughing up Turnips, near Slough
('Windsor')
1809

disputing upon the Price of Iron, and the Price charged to the Butcher for shoeing his Poney
(1807, *fig. 126*) is equally unmistakably a genre scene in the manner of Morland, with
perhaps an added debt to Wilkie in the elaboration of narrative content. In *Ploughing*
up Turnips, near Slough (1809, *fig. 127*) the artist deliberately played down the
picturesque appeal of Windsor Castle in the background in order to emphasize the
theme of agricultural labour, although again one feels that he was chiefly attracted to
the scene by the technical challenge posed by the shrouding haze. For *Crossing the*
Brook (1815) Turner chose a favourite subject among artists of the time, including
Mulready; but in his handling the humble activity in the foreground gives access to a
vista of Claudian magnificence. In all these pictures the inclusion of material normally
found in genre painting is incidental to other considerations of a more painterly kind;
and by the time of the great *Rain, Steam, and Speed – The Great Western Railway*

(1844) the reality of a familiar aspect of the industrial landscape has been translated into the higher reality of the glorious chromatic fantasies of the artist's final manner.[36]

Among the British picture-viewing public in the nineteenth century animals rivalled children in popularity.[37] The native love of horses and dogs is manifest, as we have seen, in painting of the eighteenth century; but as in so many other ways, the new age brought with it radically changed attitudes towards this traditional proclivity. The sense of kinship with the natural world that characterized the romantic spirit carried over to animals, inspiring, among other things, more humane behaviour towards them.[38] In painting, *animaliers* such as Sawrey Gilpin and especially James Ward (1769–1859) replaced the objectivity of Stubbs with an attempt to humanize animals by dwelling on the expressive qualities of their behaviour, in accordance with Charles Bell's theories of physiognomy. This tendency reached its apogee in the work of Sir Edwin Landseer (1802–73), whose anthropomorphized portraits of animals erase all barriers between the human and non-human. Hogarth's painting had proposed a similar identity of relationship, but in a fundamentally opposed perspective. For Hogarth, like Swift, was struck by the brutish propensities of man, whereas Landseer's pictures – in the spirit of a more sentimental age – insist on the human attributes of animals.[39]

Landseer's success from the outset of his career, as spectacular as that of Wilkie, bears witness to how shrewdly he gauged the artistic tastes of the age. His list of patrons extended from the Queen, with whom he was always a special favourite, to prominent families of the nobility and such leading collectors as Wells, Sheepshanks,

Fig. 128
Sir Edwin Landseer
Windsor Castle in Modern Times
1841–5

RIGHT

Fig. 129
Sir Edwin Landseer
Shoeing
1844

BELOW

Fig. 130
Sir Edwin Landseer
The Old Shepherd's Chief Mourner
*c*1837

and Vernon; and everywhere his charm and affability made him a privileged friend. Before all else, however, he capitalized on the market for engravings, spreading ever more widely through an increasingly literate public. It has been estimated that 434 different plates were made from his pictures by 126 engravers, a number of whom, such as Samuel Cousins (1801–87) and Charles George Lewis (1808–80), made their fame and fortunes from these reproductions. Henry Graves, the leading print publisher of the time, is said to have paid Landseer £60,000 in copyright fees, including £3,600 for the fine conversation piece of Wellington and his daughter, *A Dialogue at Waterloo* (1851), and almost twice that figure for *Stag at Bay* (1846).

Landseer's claim to recognition as a historian of manners rests not on his sentimental portrayal of animals parading as human types, but on those paintings which, while remaining faithful to the inherent nature of the creatures depicted, stress their central role in the life of the age. The highly finished conversation piece entitled *Windsor Castle in Modern Times* (1841–5, *fig. 128*) forms an instructive contrast to eighteenth-century works in a similar mode. While the Green Room at Windsor seems a strange place for dead game demonstrating the Prince Consort's prowess as a hunter, and it is stranger still to see the trophies of the hunt turned into playthings by the Princess Royal, the artist has clearly lavished as much care on the portraits of the three Skye terriers, Dandie, Islay, and Cairnack, and the Consort's favourite greyhound, Eos, as on the royal couple and their child. These dogs share in the domestic atmosphere of the scene and also contribute to the sense it conveys of providing a glimpse behind the official façade and into the bosom of the sovereign's family life. The pleasure which Victoria derived from the picture was recorded in a diary entry for 2 October 1845: 'Landseer's Game Picture (begun in 1840!!) . . . is at last hung up in our sitting room here, & is [a] very beautiful picture, & altogether very cheerful & pleasing.'

Shoeing (1844, *fig. 129*) recognizes without falsification the close relationship that may exist between a man and his animal dependants. Jacob Bell, who managed Landseer's finances, posed for the farrier; and the mare, Old Betty, her stablemate the donkey, and the bloodhound, Laura, all belonged to him. The gaze of each animal directs attention to another, leading back to the smith in a circular composition that locks the four figures in bonds of affectionate intimacy of which the keynote is patient trustfulness. The continuing popularity of Landseer's best-known painting, *The Old Shepherd's Chief Mourner* (c1837, *fig. 130*) rests on the kind of sentimental reading that led Ruskin to term the picture 'a work of high art'. This moving evocation of a dog's capacity for devotion invites, however, a deeper response. The bleak light of the declining day and the details which it accentuates – the coffin nailed shut, the shepherd's crook and tam-o'-shanter discarded on the floor, the Bible with the spectacles lying where they were last put down – emphasize the finality of death. Yet it is refuted by the steadfastness of the dog whose inability to understand the loss only intensifies its deepest instincts, loyalty to its master's memory and to the way of life they shared.

Chapter Five

VICTORIAN PERSPECTIVES
(I)

THE SUCCESS which Wilkie and his contemporaries enjoyed during the early decades of the nineteenth century firmly established genre as the dominant mode in British painting; and its spread kept pace with the vast expansion of the picture-buying public in the Victorian age. Christopher Wood's *Dictionary of Victorian Painters* lists the names of more than 11,000 artists; and in recent years the London sale-rooms, especially Sotheby's Belgravia, have shown how large a percentage of these worked in categories of genre. If evidence were wanting that paintings of contemporary life had achieved a place in the forefront of Victorian art, it would have been supplied by the prominence accorded to them in the great exhibitions held around the middle of the century. Two hundred and thirty-two oils by ninety-seven British artists were shown at the Exposition Universelle des Beaux-Arts in Paris in 1855. Although only examples of living painters were included, the French press, as reported in the *Art Journal*, spoke of Hogarth as 'the real father of the English school', and of Wilkie as its 'very embodiment'. Mulready (represented by nine examples) and Webster (four) were two artists selected for special praise as exemplifying 'the singularity and thorough originality of the English school'.[1] The exhibition of the Art Treasures of the United Kingdom at Manchester in 1857 was the first large public exhibition of works of art loaned from private English collections, including that of the royal family. Conceived to compensate for the absence of paintings from the Great Exhibition of 1851, it was principally sponsored by magnates from the industrial centres of the Midlands. While the exhibition amply displayed the superb holdings of the Old Masters in the British Isles, there were also nearly seven hundred examples of the modern British school, including twenty-two works by Landseer, eighteen by Wilkie, eleven by Collins, and nine each by Mulready and Webster. Five years later the International Exhibition at South Kensington again bore witness to the popularity of the native school of genre painting. Among the 790 British pictures were fourteen by Wilkie, twelve by Collins, nine by Landseer, eight by Mulready, and four by Webster.[2] In the catalogue accompanying the British section, Francis Turner Palgrave accounted for the conspicuous vogue for genre as follows: 'Yet it is indisputable that the growth of the Incident style in painting runs parallel with the great outburst of novel writing from about 1790 onwards, with the social change that gave the patronage of art rather to the mercantile than to the educated classes, with that fusion of ranks and interests which (in another sphere) found expression in Burns, Scott, Crabbe, and Wordsworth.'

The lists of those who loaned pictures to these exhibitions point to the radical shift in the patronage of contemporary British art that had taken place. Such pioneers as Sheepshanks, Vernon and Wells in the early part of the nineteenth century formed only the vanguard of the host of middle-class collectors whose tastes controlled the Victorian art market. In a letter to his sister of May 1851, the artist Charles Robert Leslie wrote: 'The increase of the private patronage of Art in this country is surprising. Almost every day I hear of some man of fortune, whose name is unknown to me, who is forming a collection of the works of living painters; and they are all either men in business, or who have made fortunes in business and retired.' The emergence of this new class of patrons, brought into existence by the Industrial Revolution, signalled a transfer in economic wealth and influence from London to the rapidly growing cities of the Midlands and north. Here were the factories and mills on which these 'captains of industry' (as Carlyle called them) founded their fortunes. With financial prosperity came the desire to build and adorn showy residences; and motivated by the pride of possession but also by a genuine eagerness to acquire the culture befitting their newly won social standing, these self-made men competed to form collections of pictures – no longer the Old Masters which were in short supply, but rather the works of living or recently dead British artists, who portrayed the kind of familiar scenes at which their owners liked to look. The roll of this new class of art collectors, which could be indefinitely extended, includes the following representative figures: Joseph Gillott (Birmingham), mass-producer of pen-nibs, who once said, 'the best is good enough for me'; Thomas Plint (Leeds), stockbroker; Thomas Fairbairn (Manchester), engineer; Sam Mendel of Manley Hall (Manchester), cotton merchant; John Naylor (Liverpool), banker; Thomas Miller (Preston), head of the firm of Horrocks; Francis McCracken (Belfast), shipping agent; James Leathart (Newcastle), partner in a lead-works; and Thomas Taylor (Wigan), cotton manufacturer.

Several of these men showed considerable independence of mind and self-reliance in making their collections, commissioning works directly from painters and forming close associations with the art world in the process. Plint, Fairbairn and Leathart, for example, bought pictures by the Pre-Raphaelites when it took courage to do so.[3] The ardour for acquiring pictures, however, could hardly have been so widespread if it had not been fostered by another class of influential patrons, the art dealers who served as middlemen between artists and buyers. The leadership for this greatly expanded traffic in picture dealing was provided by the firm of Thomas Agnew and Sons, still active today. This house was established in Manchester in 1817, primarily as print-sellers and purveyors of scientific instruments, and under the guidance of Thomas Agnew and his sons, William and Thomas junior, had opened offices in London and Liverpool by 1850, numbering among its clientele the majority of Midlands industrialists who were forming art collections. Of Thomas Agnew's role in promoting the cause of contemporary British painting, the *Art Journal* wrote on his retirement in 1861:

The principal support of British Art proceeds from wealthy Lancashire. Some twenty years ago, the merchants and manufacturers there were collectors of 'old masters' – they paid large sums for 'names' with bad pictures. Of late, however, fabricators of Titians and Raphaels make no sales in that district: undoubtedly, the change was mainly effected by the judgment and energy of Mr Agnew – whose perseverance has been rewarded by the knowledge that works of British artists are now the luxuries (they have become almost the necessaries) of the rich men of that rich county; and he may justly claim the gratitude of many who have prospered by the transfer of Art-patronage from the dead to the living.

By shortly after the middle of the century the Agnews' success was rivalled by two enterprising entrepreneurs of foreign extraction, Ernest Gambart, a Belgian, and Louis Victor Flatow, a Polish Jew, who combined the sponsorship of contemporary British and sometimes Continental artists with a highly lucrative trade in engravings from paintings of which they had acquired the copyright.[4]

Indeed, the growth of the print trade was probably the single most important factor in spreading the taste for pictures of familiar subject-matter. The circulation of engravings was helped enormously by Thomas Lupton's perfection of the steel plate process in 1822; for whereas the copper plate yielded editions of only about three hundred, steel-plate engravings could be produced in issues of as many as fifteen thousand impressions, a fact responsible for the wide circulation and popularity of Keepsake Annuals, which first exploited this technique. The introduction of the method of electrotyping in 1845 removed all limits from the size of editions of engravings.[5] The year 1836 saw the emergence of a new source of art patronage in the first Art-Union, founded in London on the model of similar bodies in Germany, and under the presidency of Prince Albert. Between 1840 and 1842 its membership increased from two to nearly twelve thousand; and by 1840 there were thriving branches in Liverpool, Birmingham, Manchester, Leeds, Norwich, Bath and Bristol. In addition to providing subscribers with copies of engravings, they organized annual lotteries offering as prizes paintings and prints, which in many cases had been commissioned directly from artists and engravers.[6] The establishment in 1847 of the Printsellers' Association to register and monitor the publication of prints encouraged an increasingly lively spirit of speculation in the trade, since the Association's lists provided members with information about both the price of prints, especially proofs, and the size of editions.[7]

Paintings themselves testify to the enthusiasm for popular art that pervaded all classes of Victorian society. *Public Opinion* (1863, *fig. 131*) by George Bernard O'Neill (1828–1917), who was a member of the circle of artists who gathered around Webster at Cranbrook in Kent, portrays a scene at the annual exhibition of the Royal Academy, then held in a wing of the National Gallery. The work communicates the excitement of the viewers, from the smiling elderly couple in the centre to the woman who is instructing her son in the right-hand corner. The fact that the picture enjoys the unusual distinction of being protected by a rail suggests that this by popular acclamation was the picture of the year. The aptly titled *One Touch of Nature makes the whole World Kin* (1867, *fig. 132*) by a more obscure artist, Thomas P. Hall (active 1837–67), shows the equally enthralled response of a gathering of spectators to a

Fig. 133
Thomas Faed
The Mitherless Bairn
1855

Fig. 133
Thomas Faed
The Mitherless Bairn
1855

OPPOSITE ABOVE

Fig. 131
George Bernard O'Neill
Public Opinion
1863

OPPOSITE BELOW

Fig. 132
Thomas P. Hall
One Touch of Nature makes the whole World Kin
1867

painting in the window of an art-dealer. All classes are represented, including the crossing-sweeper in the centre foreground, the pipe-smoking drayman behind, and the silk-hatted connoisseur to the left, whose attention is apparently otherwise engaged. The conductor of the omnibus in the background seems to be trying to call his passengers, who have been distracted by the painting.

Despite the proliferation in the Victorian age of artists who sought to portray the life of the times, comparatively few produced work of sufficient originality to call for more than passing notice. Given the temper of the predominantly middle-class public for whom these pictures were made, it is not surprising to find that the pictorial field was almost entirely confined to domestic scenes of kinds already popularized by earlier genre artists, but with sufficient change in details to bring them up-to-date. Wilkie and Mulready had laid the heroic pretensions of a West, Barry, or Haydon to rest, with the exception of the ill-fated competition to provide frescoes on historical themes to decorate the new Houses of Parliament. As Thackeray observed: 'The younger painters are content to exercise their art on subjects far less exalted: a gentle sentiment, an agreeable, quiet incident, a tea-table tragedy, or a bread-and-butter idyll, suffices for the most part their gentle powers.' One voluminous category of subject-matter was devoted to occasions celebrating the continuity and cohesiveness of family life: courting, marriages, christenings, birthdays, anniversaries; another portrayed the annual spectrum of holidays: Sunday church-going, Christmas, New Year, May Day, the Harvest Home, Guy Fawkes' Night. Equally in favour were all kinds of popular pastimes such as games, fairs, or the spectacles provided by puppeteers and strolling players. Throughout all such scenes the predominant impression is one of the carefree enjoyment of moments of relaxation and leisure, so that, for example, agricultural labourers were invariably shown during their midday

Fig. 134
John Phillip
Collecting the Offering in a Scottish Kirk
1855

rest. That paintings were meant to deal only with the lighter moments of daily life is illustrated by an anecdote concerning the Bristol manufacturer and patron, D. W. Acraman. He had commissioned the landscape artist William James Muller (1812–45) to paint a picture, entitled *Forging the Anchor* (1836), to be sent as a present to Mahomet Ali, for one of whose ships his firm had made an anchor. Liking the work, Acraman commissioned a duplicate for himself, but on its delivery declared to the artist that he could never hang it with the rest of his gallery because it would remind him too much of the 'shop'.

Among the most successful artists of the time was a group of Scottish genre painters, most of whom had been trained in the folk tradition imparted by John Graham at the Trustees' Academy in Edinburgh. Of these the most gifted was Thomas Faed (1826–1900), whose painting *The Mitherless Bairn (fig. 133)*, exhibited in 1855, established his characteristic blend of realism with pathos in the portrayal of peasant life in cottage settings. In a more humorous vein Faed was rivalled by Erskine Nicol (1825–1904). Other Scottish artists working in a similar manner were John Faed (1820–1902), brother of Thomas, and the brothers John Burr (1831–93) and Alexander Hohenlohe Burr (1835–99). All of these artists settled in London around the middle of the century, but continued assiduously to cultivate the native strain on which their popularity rested. An altogether more considerable figure was John Phillip (1817–67), whose early reputation as a painter of Scottish scenes, such as *Collecting the Offering in a Scottish Kirk* (1855, *fig. 134*), was effaced by his later concentration on Spanish subjects.

The talented coterie of painters that gathered around Thomas Webster after he went to live in Cranbrook in 1857 continued, through their somewhat idealized pictures of homespun rusticity, to provide subjects dear to the hearts of the British public. The isolation of the place had preserved the traditional ways of life of which these pictures are a strikingly accurate record. Webster's associates shared his fondness for young people, and in depicting typical activities of their daily lives the artists of this school provided patterns for the treatment of child subjects that were imitated by other artists throughout the century. By and large, the world represented is one devoted to play. While schoolroom scenes are common, they are usually presented under a comic aspect, as in *The Captured Truant* (1850, *fig. 135*) by Thomas Brooks (1818–91); and gainful employment, whether shrimping, hop-picking, or gleaning, is made to seem a lark. Among the most engaging works in this category are those showing children converting into games the serious business of the grown-up world. In *Children at Play* (1847, *fig. 136*) Charles Robert Leslie suggests the romantic spell which the heyday of coaching exercised over the youthful imagination. Similarly, Frederick Daniel Hardy (1826–1911), a leading member of the Cranbrook colony, painted in rapid succession (1860–3) pictures of children drilling in emulation of the volunteer militia of the time, operating a make-believe photographer's studio, and playing at doctors and pharmacists (*fig. 137*). One of the most perceptive recorders of the world of childhood was Charles Hunt (1803–77), who was particularly attracted to scenes of children play-acting, as in *Trial Scene: 'The Merchant of Venice'* (1867, *fig. 138*). Among the numerous other artists influenced by Mulready and Webster and deserving attention for their handling of child subjects are Henry Le Jeune (1819–1904), William Hemsley (b. 1819 – active 1848–93), William Henry Knight

Fig. 135
Thomas Brooks
The Captured Truant
1850

Fig. 136
Charles Robert Leslie
Children at Play
1847

(1823–63), John Morgan (1823–86), George Smith (1829–1901), William Bromley III (active 1835–88), Charles Green (1840–98), Alfred Provis (active 1843–86) and Mathias Robinson (active 1856–84).

At its best, as in the examples illustrated, Victorian domestic genre offers the viewer narrative pictures which are interesting in content, and which involve believable and well-defined characters within carefully observed settings. Soon after 1850, however, a progressive decline in quality set in; and the market began to be flooded with mawkishly sentimental and facetiously humorous representations of simpering lovers, namby-pamby nursery scenes and rustic buffoonery, addressed to the tastes of an undiscriminating public for whom art at best provided momentary distraction from the tedium of daily existence. As recorded in his *English Notebooks*, Nathaniel Hawthorne, then United States Consul at Liverpool, brought away from his visit to the Manchester exhibition of 1857 the impression that British painting was devoted to: 'Pretty village-scenes of common life – pleasant domestic passages, with a touch of easy humor in them – little pathoses and fancynesses ...' Yet, the aspects of contemporary art that made it seem so trivial to the American visitor constituted its appeal to the public at large. In its remarks on the Royal Academy exhibition of 1863, the *Art Journal*, which had from its first publication championed the cause of British art, stated: 'England, happy in her homes, and joyous in her hearty cheer, and peaceful in her snug firesides, is equally fortunate in a school of Art sacred to the hallowed relations of domestic life.' An anonymous reviewer in *Blackwood's Magazine* for July 1860 was even more complacent in his acceptance of current artistic trends:

OPPOSITE ABOVE

Fig. 137
Frederick Daniel Hardy
Playing at Doctors
1863

OPPOSITE BELOW

Fig. 138
Charles Hunt
Trial Scene: 'The Merchant of Venice'
1867

Painters dream not of anything so unpictorial as extended suffrage and vote by ballot. They go into the lanes and rural homes of what once was, and still is happy old England; and as long as an interesting mother dotes over her lovely infant – as long as the husband is prosperous in his work and happy in his pipe and ale – as long as the bonny sunburnt children bring home the russet fern upon their shoulders, or go forth in joyous bands to glean the harvest field – as long as sunshine streams in at the cottage window, and content smiles from every face – what cares the painter or the peasant for the politician's suffrage? – what can the statesmonger add when kind nature has given her all?[8]

A notable exception to the general chorus of approbation was a long and thoughtful article in the *Quarterly Review* by the excavator of Nineveh, Sir Austen Henry Layard, who traced to the pressure of market demands the decline in artistic standards of which he saw evidence among the living artists whose works were on display at Manchester:

> If a painter has gained a reputation by painting a picture with certain effects, every collector of pictures thinks it necessary to have a similar specimen of the artist. . . . Mr Cope [Charles West Cope, 1811–90, best known for historical genre] paints some trivial domestic subject which amuses the visitors to the Exhibition, and is favourably noticed by the critics. He abandons a class of painting in which he gave good promise, and prostitutes undoubted talents in painting 'Baby's Turn', and a succession of babies bobbing at cherries and sucking sugar. Surely, even if the higher aims of art be discarded there is something better to be done in its most humble sphere than to paint pictures to amuse nursery maids and their charges. The Manchester Exhibition shows few English painters who have not fallen, or do not threaten to fall, into this snare of continual repetition and constant exaggeration and mannerism so fatal to the development of genius and the accomplishment of great works.

Layard found that even the work of such reigning favourites as Landseer, Mulready and Webster had over recent years deteriorated in acceding to popular demand.

Revealing as it often is as an index to domestic manners and morals in the Victorian age, genre painting could hardly have retained the esteem which Wilkie had won for it if its scope had been confined to so limited a sphere. William Michael Rossetti recognized the truth of this in an article on the Royal Academy exhibition of 1861, originally appearing in *Fraser's Magazine*, in which he proposed that the modern age provided subject-matter far more challenging to the artistic imagination:

> Of subjects recommendable to our school as a body . . . the best, we think, are clearly those of our own day. But there is a distinction here. Mere domestic art, as mostly understood and practised, is a very meagre affair . . . boys playing games, girls listening to organ-grinders, cottagers smoking quiet pipes, or preparing homely dinners. Or we have a touch of the most poverty-stricken religious feeling – a grace before meat, or a girl at a tombstone. . . . Such art as this is strictly analogous to the juvenile tale or the religious tract; and it would be just as sensible to exhort our men of letters to disport themselves in those mildest fields of literature as to

inspirit our painters to corresponding relaxations in art. Modern art, to be worthy of the name, must deal with very different matter; with passion, multiform character, real business and action, incident, historic fact.

And Rossetti concluded: 'If we go back to the beginning of our English school, we shall find a model of the vital modern art ready to our hands. Our great Hogarth led the van of all modern-life art worthy of the name.'

In examining important new areas opened up by genre painters in their exploration of the Victorian social scene, the broad distinction between public spectacles inviting panoramic treatment, and more intimate glimpses of episodes from private life still holds good, if not too rigorously applied.

The mantle of Hogarth and Wilkie was to fall on the shoulders of William Powell Frith (1819–1909). His early reputation had been made through the approved appropriation of subjects from literary sources, a particularly popular example being his portrait in several versions of Dolly Varden from Dickens' *Barnaby Rudge*. In his entertaining autobiography he states, however, that he had from early on been drawn to scenes of modern life, and was only deterred from undertaking them by the ugliness of contemporary dress. In the year 1851 he at last came on 'a theme capable of affording ... the opportunity of showing an appreciation of the infinite variety of everyday life.' Of this turning-point in his career he wrote: 'My summer holiday of 1851 was spent at Ramsgate. Weary of costume painting, I had determined to try my hand on modern life, with all its drawbracks of unpicturesque dress. The variety of character on Ramsgate Sands attracted me – all sorts and conditions of men and women were there. Pretty groups of ladies were to be found, reading, idling, working, and unconsciously forming themselves into very paintable compositions' (*fig. 139*). With the encouragement of such colleagues as James Ward, Augustus Egg, Webster and John Leech, Frith worked steadily on his picture throughout the next three and a half years, developing it, after the manner of Wilkie, from innumerable preparatory sketches. The composition illustrates his belief that in large subject pictures, 'There must be a main incident of dramatic force, and secondary ones of interest.' The pretty child to left of centre who at the urging of her mother so gingerly dips her toes in the water forms an apex from which the surrounding throng of holiday-makers fans out and up on either side. Such was Frith's attention to accuracy of detail that the work might serve as a manual for popular fashions of dress in the mid-nineteenth century.[9] And the behaviour of the figures is unmistakably transcribed from life, with a gusto that communicates itself to the viewer. Of the authenticity of the entertainment with performing animals in the mid-centre, for example, the artist wrote:

A couple of men were joint proprietors of a 'happy family', consisting of cats and mice, dogs and rabbits, and other creatures whose natural instincts had been extinguished so far as to allow for an appearance of armed neutrality, if not of friendship, to exist amongst them. When the cat had played with the mice, and had allowed the canaries to peck it without resenting the liberty, a hare was made to play upon a tambourine, and during the finale, the proprietor's friend and assistant on the drum made the usual collection. The drummer wore a wonderful green coat; he was very ugly, but an excellent type of his class. As I made up my mind to introduce the whole of the show, taking the moment of the hare's performance as the chief

OVERLEAF

Fig. 139
William Powell Frith
Ramsgate Sands
1854

point; it was necessary to enter into negotiations with the proprietors. I found, as I expected, that they hailed from London; and I also found that they would sit, and the animals should sit, if they were sufficiently well paid for doing so. The chief proprietor's name was Gwillim. . . . He came to see me in London, and a day was fixed for the beginning of *my* performance.

Ramsgate Sands was shown at the annual exhibition of the Royal Academy in 1854, under the more general title, *Life at the Seaside*. It was purchased by the prominent dealer Lloyd for one thousand guineas; but Queen Victoria on visiting the exhibition fell in love with the picture and Lloyd agreed to part with it to her at the original purchase price, with the understanding that he might borrow it for three years to have an engraving made (he presumably did not lose by the transaction, since he is said to have sold the plate to the London Art-Union for £3,000). For the first of his panoramic spectacles of the Victorian social world, Frith had chosen a scene that could hardly fail to have a wide appeal. With the development of transport by rail, seaside resorts had superseded the inland spas of the eighteenth century, such as Bath, as the favourite holiday resorts of Victorian families. Arthur Boyd Houghton (1836–75), best known for his woodcut illustrations, painted a number of seaside scenes, including one of *Ramsgate Sands* (c1861, *fig. 140*). Among the most winning of these pictures of holiday activity at the shore, with its display of animal-drawn carts, is *Weston Sands in 1864* (1864, *fig. 141*), a joint product of William H. Hopkins (active 1853–92) and Edmund Havell, Jr (1819–94). Other paintings of pleasure-seekers thronging marine resorts include *Brighton Front* (c1859) by Abraham Solomon (1824–62); *On the Beach: A Family on Margate Sands* (1867) by Charles Wynne Nicholls (1831–1903); and *Scarborough Spa by Night* (1879) by F. Sydney Muschamp (active 1870–1903).

For the subject of his next great spectacular piece Frith chose the most popular of all outings in the British calendar, Derby Day (*fig. 142*). Ben Marshall (1767–1835), the sporting artist, described it in 1830:

Thursday morning arrived, a day of extraordinary excitement and interest to all sportsmen and to millions of others in every part of England from the manufacturer of twelve stories high, to the Yorkshire ploughman; from the Cockney behind his counter, down to the cellarman at Hatchett's; and after all there was very little difference between this and former years, except that the art of cramming horses down people's throats had been practised more successfully than ever was known.

It was on going to the races at Hampton Court in 1854, where he saw the attempted suicide of a man ruined by betting, that the idea first came to Frith that 'if some of the salient points of the great gathering could be grouped together, an effective picture might be the result.' An initial visit to Epsom Downs in May 1856, the year that a horse named Ellington won the Derby, brought into focus his plans for dealing with a great race meeting. 'My first Derby', he was to write in his autobiography, 'had no interest for me as a race, but as giving me the opportunity of studying life and character, it is ever to be gratefully remembered. Gambling-tents and thimble-rigging, prick in the garter and the three-card trick, had not then been stopped by the police.' A longish period of gestation ensued, during which he refined his

Fig. 140
Arthur Boyd Houghton
Ramsgate Sands
c1861

Fig. 141
Edmund Havell, Jr and William H. Hopkins
Weston Sands in 1864
1864

composition. His method of working may be inferred from the words of Daniel Maclise (1806–70), who, on visiting Frith's studio, found him 'dropping in here and there little gem-like bits into the beautiful mosaic' which he had 'so skilfully put together'. As in all his major works, he depended on living models for the majority of his figures. For example, he found the originals of the acrobat and his son in the Drury Lane Pantomime. The horse-dealer Tattersall provided a jockey named Bundy to pose on a wooden horse; and Frith was also helped by the well-known *animalier*, John Frederick Herring, Senior (1795–1865). The pharmaceutical tycoon Jacob Bell, who had commissioned *Derby Day* and who appears to have been a prominent man about town, produced most of the female models. 'What is it to be this time?' he would say. 'Fair or dark, long nose or short nose, Roman or aquiline, tall figure or small? Give your orders.' Finally, the artist was among the first to call on the nascent art of photography, enlisting an individual named Robert Howlett 'to photograph for him', as he said, 'from the roof of a cab as many queer groups of people as he could.'

After 'fifteen months of incessant labour' the canvas was ready to go on view at the Royal Academy in the spring of 1858.[10] It was immediately and enthusiastically greeted as the picture of the year; and for the first time since the exhibition of Wilkie's *Chelsea Pensioners* in 1822 it was necessary to put up a railing to fend off the public. This distinction was accorded to Frith five more times during his career as an Academician. Although Bell had paid £1,500 for the painting, he died in 1859 before he could enjoy its possession. His fine collection of contemporary art was willed to the nation; but six years were to pass before *Derby Day* came to rest in the National Gallery; for Gambart had acquired the copyright with rights of exhibition for an additional £1,500. Not content with having an engraving made, he capitalized on its enormous popularity by touring it about England, and then sent it, despite public protest, on a world tour to Paris, Vienna, the United States, and as far away as the gold fields at Ballarat and Geelong in Australia.

Despite the disappointment of some viewers that Frith had not followed in the great tradition of British sporting painting, he insisted that such had not been his intent. 'My determination to keep the horses as much in the background as possible', he wrote, 'did not arise from the fact of my not being able to paint them properly, so much as from my desire that the human being should be paramount.' And he explained: 'The acrobats with every variety of performance, the nigger minstrels, gipsy fortune-telling, to say nothing of carriages filled with pretty women, together with the sporting element, seemed to offer abundant material for the line of art to which I felt obliged – in the absence of higher gifts – to devote myself . . .'

The *Athenaeum* perhaps best summarized public response in calling *Derby Day* (originally entitled *The Humours of a Race-Course*) 'a panoramic epitome of English character in the year 1856'. A more searching criticism suggested that the picture's merit resided solely in its admittedly very great documentary significance. Ruskin was the most outspoken advocate of this point of view in his scornful comment: 'It is . . . quite proper and desirable that this English carnival should be painted; and of the entirely popular manner of painting, which, however, we must remember is necessarily, because popular, stooping and restricted, I have never seen an abler example. . . . It is a kind of cross between John Leech and Wilkie, with a dash of daguerreotype here and there, and some pretty seasoning with Dickens's sentiment.'

Fig. 142
William Powell Frith
Derby Day
1856–8

Fig. 143
William Powell Frith
The Railway Station
1862

Such criticism, however, fails to take account of the consummate skill with which Frith developed the dramatic potential of his spectacle through a series of interlocking episodes, each arresting in itself (Walter Sickert wrote: 'Surprises lurk in the *Derby Day* like Easter eggs'). Crowded as the canvas is with racing fans milling about in their separate pursuits, the motley throng nevertheless resolves itself in the foreground into three groupings, to form a kind of triptych, reminiscent of the composition of Hogarth's *March to Finchley (fig. 13)*.

The cluster at the left centres on the thimble-rigger, with the tools of his fraudulent trade set out on the table before him and his raffish accomplices. It is clear from the dejected bearing of the top-hatted lad, hands thrust in empty pockets, that he has just been fleeced of all his money.[11] The country yokel on the other side is being drawn into the game despite the restraining hands of his wife (while his faithful dog faces up to the sharper's truculent terrier), comically re-enacting the time-honoured motif of Hercules between virtue and vice. In the background another man is being gulled by a sleight-of-hand artist with his deck of cards. Balancing this group on the right are the figures gathered round the sulky crinolined beauty who reclines beneath her parasol. A gipsy woman offers to tell her fortune; and this piece of business presumably relates to her connection with the dandy lolling in front. He may be buying his mistress a nosegay from the little flower-girl, but his supercilious manner hardly inspires confidence in the steadiness of his devotion. Unobserved beneath the carriage, an urchin snatches at a wine bottle.

The central and dominant group is composed of the acrobats and their audience. In this passage the relationship between spectators and entertainers is subtly and tellingly reversed. On the two wings of the composition the former are being victimized by the professional tricksters; but here it is the well-to-do spectators who are the agents of corruption. The goodhearted innocence of the troupers is exemplified by the girl with tambourine tenderly peering at the infant whose mother is receiving alms from a charitable youngster. In contrast, her fellow performer on stilts is being enticed into accepting a glass of champagne from the drunken toff on the charabanc. Meanwhile, the father and leader of the company, with outstretched arms, seeks in vain to divert his son's attention from the lavish picnic spread on the ground.

Frith's great canvas is happily devoid of the kind of moral commentary which invalidates so much Victorian subject painting. The picture's theme, so far as there is one, relates to the way that such festivals as the Derby release the irrational impulses inherent in human nature, promoting a universal capacity for self-deception. Quite as much as the racehorses on whose performances fortunes will be won and lost, the mountebanks and charlatans who caught the artist's eye from the outset are all merchants of dreams, good or bad. Their stock-in-trade is make-believe; and just as Frith invites participation in his scene through the realism of every detail, which promotes a 'willing suspension of disbelief', so at the same time he insinuates that the viewer is drawn into the scene by his participation in the very illusions and delusions of which it is the breeding-ground.

The railway, which in the previous generation had united the entire nation within its network of tracks, symbolized more than any other social phenomenon the arrival of the industrial era, but Frith nevertheless had doubts at first whether Paddington, the setting of his next major picture, *The Railway Station* (1862, *fig. 143*), was sufficiently 'picturesque'. The reception of the work, which the journalist Tom Taylor called 'one of the points at which the life of our century is brought into focus', laid any such uncertainty at rest; 21,150 viewers paid the fee to see it during the first seven weeks after it was placed on display by its owner, the dealer Flatow. Onto a canvas larger than *Ramsgate Sands* or *Derby Day* the artist crammed every imaginable episode that could attend the departure of a great Continental express. Such was the mastery which Frith had by now attained over the deployment of crowds that the eye moves naturally from one grouping to the next: the family despatching two sons to school, the foreigner haggling over his fare with a cabby, the adieus of the wedding party, the fleeing criminal arrested at the last moment by officers of the law (for whose portraits two famous detectives of the time, Haydon and Brett, posed).[12] As in Hogarth's paintings, the total impression is built up by a cumulative process, which in this case produces a heightened sense of the excitement and urgency of the occasion, disrupting settled patterns of life and precipitating change. The impassive splendour of the wrought-iron-ribbed structure spanning the crowds seems at once to give unity to the human spectacle and to intensify by contrast its dramatic components.[13]

Not surprisingly, pictures involving travel by rail constitute a distinct category of Victorian genre painting. One of the most informative as well as entertaining is *To Brighton and Back for 3/6* (1859, *fig. 144*) by Charles Rossiter (1827–90). The passengers here have taken advantage of the cheap excursion rates originally instituted to promote travel to the Great Exhibition of 1851. The metropolitan omnibus system provided equally attractive pictorial possibilities. William Maw Egley (1826–1916) was one of the first to capitalize on this subject-matter in his *Omnibus Life in London* (1859, *fig. 145*), described by the *Illustrated London News* as 'a droll interior, the stern and trying incidents of which will be recognised by thousands of weary wayfarers through the streets of London.' As the two pictures (which were exhibited in the same year) demonstrate, the inconvenience resulting from the crowding of many people within a closely confined area allowed not only for the juxtaposition of types representative of all social classes, but also for humorous psychological interplay among those who found themselves jostling each other.

The gambling instinct illustrated in *Derby Day* continued to fascinate Frith. In 1871 he exhibited a remarkable picture of the fashionable world gathered round the tables in a gambling casino, entitled *The Salon d'Or, Homburg*; and in 1878 this was followed in a more moralistic vein by *The Road to Ruin*, a sequence of five pictures showing how a well-born young man's passion for gaming destroys his family and eventually leads to his own suicide. Although the series was clearly derived from Hogarth's *A Rake's Progress*, Frith modestly disclaimed rivalry with his great predecessor: 'Without any pretension to do my work on Hogarthian lines, I thought I could show some of the evils of gambling; my idea being a kind of gambler's progress, avoiding the satirical vein of Hogarth, for which I knew myself to be unfitted.' Two years later followed a second series of five, called *The Race for Wealth*, tracing the calamitous career of a promoter of bubble companies. The 1870s were a period of wildcat speculation, represented by such figures as Baron Albert Grant in life, and Auguste Melmotte in Trollope's *The Way We Live Now* (1875) in fiction; and Frith had thus chosen a topical theme in his wish 'to illustrate ... the common passion for speculation, and the destruction that so often attends the indulgence of it, to the lives

and fortunes of the financier's dupes.' The fact that fifteen thousand photogravure prints of this series were issued attests to the artist's continuing responsiveness to the temper of the times. His adherence to the documentary reportage which had guided his practice from the beginning appeared again in his last ambitious composition, and the sixth to require a guard-rail when it was exhibited at the Royal Academy in 1883. Entitled *A Private View at the Royal Academy in 1881*, it satirized the 'aesthetic craze' as exemplified by Oscar Wilde, whose portrait appears among other celebrities.[14]

Nothing in Frith's career gives cause for greater regret than his failure to paint the series of three London street-scenes, entitled *Morning, Noon,* and *Night,* commissioned by Gambart in 1862. Although the dealer had contracted to pay the staggering sum of £10,000 for the trio, Frith gave up the project to undertake, at the Queen's request, the demanding and ultimately unrewarding task of painting the throng attending *The Marriage of the Prince of Wales* (1864). From the artist's description of his plans for the series, which was to be set in Covent Garden, Regent Street, and the Haymarket, and from the preliminary sketches he made, one can imagine works which in richness of incident and evocative atmosphere would have challenged Hogarth's *The Four Times of the Day*.

Fig. 144
Charles Rossiter
To Brighton and Back for 3/6
1859

Fig. 145
William Maw Egley
Omnibus Life in London
1859

One of the first artists to endeavour to paint the face of Victorian London with Hogarthian breadth was George Elgar Hicks (1824–1914). Early in his career (1859) he exhibited a crowded canvas inspired by the investment habits of an affluent and conservative middle class, entitled *Dividend Day at the Bank of England*. Its success was such that in the years immediately following, before turning to work in a more conventional manner, he painted several more panoramic scenes, including *The General Post Office, One Minute to 6* (1859–60, fig. 146) and *Billingsgate* (1861), depicting London's tumultuous fish-market. Hicks' pictures do not exhibit Frith's talent for the dramatic grouping of figures; but he did achieve a sense of the frantic hurry and bustle of life in the metropolis. This quality becomes especially apparent if the rush at closing time in London's central post office, St Martin's-le-Grand, is compared with representations of the leisurely pace of the mail delivery in country towns, a familiar scene in Victorian genre painting. Significantly, the artist derived his conception from a description in Dickens' weekly, *Household Words*:

A fountain of newspapers played in at the window. Water-spouts of newspapers broke from enormous sacks and engulphed the men inside. . . . Now and then there

Fig. 146
George Elgar Hicks
*The General Post Office:
One Minute to 6*
1859–60

Fig. 147
Arthur Boyd Houghton
Holborn in 1861
1861

was a girl; now and then a woman; now and then a weak old man; but as the minute hand of the clock crept near to six, such a torrent of boys, and such a torrent of newspapers came tumbling in together pell-mell, head on heels, one above another, that the giddy head looking on chiefly wondered why ... the boys didn't post themselves nightly along with the newspapers, and get delivered all over the world. Suddenly it struck six. Shut, sesame![15]

Although small, the few street scenes painted by Arthur Boyd Houghton early in his career exhibit an originality unmatched by any other painter of the time. These include a *Punch and Judy* (*c*1860) which brilliantly evokes the varying responses of the motley group of onlookers, and *Holborn in 1861 (fig. 147)*, in which the artist's alert and roving eye, surveying a crowded street corner in a district of small shops, takes note of every gradation in social station as conveyed by occupation, dress and behaviour, and in so doing subtly communicates an awareness of class inequality and the accompanying social injustice. Isolated examples by lesser known artists which capture the look and spirit of mid-nineteenth-century London include: the sunlit gathering of tranquil pleasure-seekers on the edge of the Serpentine, entitled *A Summer Day in Hyde Park* (1858, *fig. 148*), by John Ritchie (active 1858–75);[16] and the German-born Phoebus Levin's (active 1855–74) engrossingly detailed pair from 1864, showing popular gathering-places in full swing, *The Dancing Platform at Cremorne Gardens* (1864, *fig. 149*) and *Covent Garden Market from James Street*.

The splendid ceremonial occasions of Victorian times, such as the opening of the Great Exhibition, were often painted by artists; but the interest of these is for the most

Fig. 150
William Holman Hunt
London Bridge by Night on the Occasion of the Marriage of the Prince and Princess of Wales
1863–6

OPPOSITE ABOVE

Fig. 148
John Ritchie
A Summer Day in Hyde Park
1858

OPPOSITE BELOW

Fig. 149
Phoebus Levin
The Dancing Platform at Cremorne Gardens
1864

part only documentary, since they were likely to have been commissioned to provide a historic record of actual people and places. Sometimes, however, spectacles of this nature inspired the artist to an imaginative re-creation of the scene. Such was Holman Hunt's response to the jubilant crowd on London Bridge, celebrating the marriage of the Prince of Wales to Princess Alexandra on the night of 10 March 1863 (*fig. 150*). The originality of Hunt's *tour de force* (1863–6) becomes clear if it is compared with Frith's official portrait of the wedding ceremony in Westminster Abbey, with its massed portraits of the participants and guests.[17]

Of his attraction to the subject and the progress of his work Hunt wrote:

Being fascinated by the picturesque scene, I made sketches of it in my note-book, and the next day, feeling how inadequate lines alone were to give the effect, I recorded them with colour on a canvas. When I had completed this, the Hogarthian humour that I had seen tempted me to introduce the crowd; but to do this at all adequately grew to be an undertaking. I was led on and felt that the months ... would not be ill spent in perpetuating this scene of contemporary history.

The composition is so congested with incidents that the artist, following Haydon's example, felt it necessary to provide an explanatory pamphlet when it was placed on view in 1864 at an exhibition of his work in a Hanover Street gallery. Indeed, without this assistance the viewer would have difficulty in sorting out individual episodes from the 'river of life' which surges across the 'river of water'. The most prominent (perhaps suggested by a similar passage in Haydon's *Punch, fig. 109*) involves the pickpocket at the lower left clambering along the scaffolding. Having snatched a watch from the individual above, he is handing it on to a better dressed confederate, who in turn is about to be apprehended by one of the two police officers in top hats. A sailor with a concertina observes the action.

Princess Alexandra was a member of the Danish royal family; and Hunt remarked that the festivities took place 'on a spot full of memories of Danish exploits of ancient times', as he had found them recorded in the *Anglo-Saxon Chronicle*. And, indeed, in his presentation the scene far transcends the 'humorous incidents and characteristic points of English manners' described in the pamphlet. The parallel rows of tall standards with their streaming banners disappearing into the distance make the bridge seem like a majestic avenue of march. The smoky glare of the flaming braziers and the light of the gas street lamps together cast a lurid red glow over the milling throng, hotly reflected in the Thames below, while in the upper left the moon breaks through heavy clouds to lay a path of silver across the distant water. The total effect is one of barbaric splendour, converting the helter-skelter rabble into a triumphal procession driven by fierce exultation.

Outstanding among panoramic Thames views in the nineteenth century were several paintings by Walter Greaves (1846–1930), boatman for Whistler and his close associate for many years. His extraordinary 'primitive' early picture, *Hammersmith Bridge on Boat-Race Day* (c1862), was followed in 1871 by *Chelsea Regatta (fig. 151)*. The occasion was the last rowing of the annual boat race from the Royal Hospital to Cremorne, when two-oared sculls competed for a prize contributed by the citizens of Chelsea, before the old Chelsea waterfront was destroyed to make way for Sir Joseph William Bazalgette's embankment. The work, painted before Greaves fell under the domination of Whistler's manner, is imbued with love of the river he knew so intimately. Although he made little effort to distinguish individuals, the handling of the crowd conveys the excitement of the race. The high vantage point from Battersea Bridge, with a long view downstream over the uprights of the steamboat pier, dramatizes the event. The Adam and Eve tavern is prominent among the carefully drawn buildings along the shoreline, its three crowded balconies displaying the pennons of boat clubs, while the river's edge presents a dense mass of spectators, gesticulating as they cheer on the oarsmen.

Near the end of the century Edward John Gregory (1850–1909) produced one of the most animated of all scenes of Londoners in a holiday mood, *Boulter's Lock – Sunday Afternoon* (1897, *fig. 152*). In this period when boating excursions along the Thames were all the rage, it has been said that the traffic through Boulter's Lock on a fine Sunday might exceed 800 pleasure craft, and as many as seventy steam launches. The artist has shown the stretch of water at the time of its greatest congestion with boats of every variety, from canoe to punt to six-oared gig. The figure reclining in the stern of the boat at the right and observing the various displays of watermanship churning all about him was a self-portrait.[18] In the words of the critic in the *Art Journal*: 'It is the kind of picture which foreign critics recognise as national; it is in fact

Fig. 151
Walter Greaves
Chelsea Regatta
1871

the three-volume novel in art, the guide-book and encyclopaedia of the manners and customs of English people.'

Most Victorian genre scenes show people in moments of relaxation. In sharp contrast is the *chef d'oeuvre* of Ford Madox Brown (1821–93), *Work (fig. 153)*, on which he was sporadically engaged between 1852 and 1865. Brown's picture was among the first serious attempts by a British artist to represent the working class in an urban environment, as against the innumerable portrayals of agricultural activity. For his subject he chose the excavations for the laying of a sewage system off Heath Street in Hampstead, an area which is virtually unchanged to this day. Brown made preliminary sketches on the spot throughout the summer of 1852, observing the digging operations from an improvised shelter when the weather was inclement; and the figures were actual portraits of navvies, often Irish immigrants, who cleared the ground for railways and metropolitan improvements in Victorian England. In the lengthy catalogue description of *Work* which he wrote to accompany its first showing in 1865, the artist stressed the originality of his conception. In revolt against the current vogue for insipidly prettified portrayals of Italian peasant life by such artists as Thomas Uwins (1782–1857) and Penry Williams (1798–1885), his purpose was to disclose the inherent dignity of the British labourer, who was a product of the Industrial Revolution and whose lot had up to this time been ignored by artists. In his own words:

At that time extensive excavations, connected with the supply of water, were going on in the neighbourhood, and, seeing and studying daily as I did the British excavator, or *navvy* ... in the full swing of his activity (with his manly and picturesque costume, and with the rich glow of colour which exercise under a hot sun will impart), it appeared to me that he was at least as worthy of the powers of an

Fig. 153
Ford Madox Brown
Work
1852–65

OPPOSITE

Fig. 152
Edward John Gregory
Boulter's Lock – Sunday Afternoon
1897

English painter as the fisherman of the Adriatic, the peasant of the Campagna, or the Neapolitan *lazzarone*. Gradually this idea developed itself into that of *Work* as it now exists, with the British excavator for the central group, as the outward and visible type of *Work*.[19]

Brown received encouragement to proceed with his canvas in November 1856, when Thomas Plint of Leeds, the great collector of contemporary art, agreed to buy the finished work.[20] In concluding terms for its purchase, however, Plint made certain suggestions about the treatment of the subject which led Brown greatly to expand its social message. 'Cannot you', Plint wrote, 'introduce *both Carlyle*, & *Kingsley*, and change one of the *fashionable* young ladies into a *quiet, earnest, holy* looking one, with a book or two & *tracts*? I want *this* put in, for I am much interested in *this* work *myself*, & know others who are.'

Through the surviving drawings it is possible to trace the growth of Brown's original plan as it took on an increasing burden of social import, to become in the end a profoundly searching comment on Victorian class structure. Against their architectural backdrop all the ancillary figures are so disposed as to set off the central group of navvies. The eye travels downward, surveying the strata of society from top to bottom. The man and his daughter on horseback at the apex represent the ruling class, as do the two fashionably dressed gentlewomen descending to the left. The younger one in front is primarily concerned that her dress should not be dirtied. Her older companion is distributing temperance tracts, entitled 'The Hodman's Haven, or drink for thirsty souls', one of which flutters unregarded among the workers. In accepting Plint's proposal for this figure, Brown converted it to his own satiric ends.[21] The inefficacy of the propaganda is mockingly emphasized by the presence of the potman dispensing drink to the navvies. His trade calls to mind Hogarth's *Beer Street*, with its hearty celebration of beer as the wholesome drink of the working classes.[22] In the foreground, representing the nether fringes of society, the artist has placed a group of street urchins, in which the older girl shows a mother's solicitude for her orphaned brothers and sister. These contrasts are very boldly and disturbingly reinforced by the figures who enclose the composition on either side. The uncouth, barefooted man at the left is a seller of wild flowers, bringing his wares to the city for sale. In the explanatory text Brown described him as 'a ragged wretch who has never been *taught to work*'; and there is implied menace in the accusing glance he directs at the viewer through the broken brim of his hat.[23] The spectators at the right are portraits of two of the great Victorian prophets of reform, called by Brown the 'brain-workers'. The figure in front was Frederick Denison Maurice, leader of the Christian Socialist movement, substituted by the artist for Charles Kingsley, whom Plint recommended. To improve the opportunities of members of the working class through education he established the Working Men's College, at which Brown took over the life-class from Dante Gabriel Rossetti in 1858. Behind him is Thomas Carlyle, of whose social philosophy Brown was a disciple, a message subtly yet forcibly inculcated in the ordering of the pictorial details in *Work*.

Harking back to the Middle Ages, Carlyle preached that society, properly constituted, is a hierarchic organism in which class is bound to class through an interlocking network of shared responsibilities, which he called 'organic filaments'. To this ideal dispensation he opposed, in a devastating chapter of *Past and Present* entitled 'The Gospel of Mammonism', the situation prevailing in Victorian England. 'We call it a Society', he wrote, 'and go about professing openly the totalest separation, isolation. Our life is not a mutual helpfulness; but rather, cloaked under due laws-of-war, named "fair competition" and so forth, is a mutual hostility. We have profoundly forgotten everywhere that *Cash-payment* is not the sole relation of human beings.' In diagrammatic form the hierarchic ordering of society was often represented as a pyramid, with the governing minority at the peak, reaching down to provide an example of leadership for the middle classes and combining with them in paternalistic regard for the welfare of the lower orders. And it is the ideal embodied in this configuration that the composition of *Work* parodies. For the representatives of wealth and privilege at the top, their progress symbolically blocked, are cast in deep shadow, which divorces them from the brilliantly highlighted navvies, who are in turn separated by a parapet from the ragged children below and the unemployed migrant farm workers resting on the slope at the right. The strong lateral thrusts of the navvies' brawny arms, repeated in the girl's arm reaching to grasp her brother's hair, reinforce the impression of social stratification conveyed by the railings. These implicit hints of

Fig. 154
James Sharples
The Forge
1854–9, engraving

class antagonism carry over into the animal world through the behaviour of the dogs, a late addition, at the base of the triangular design. For the greyhound, effetely jacketed despite the heat, and obviously the household pet of the two ladies, is about to be set upon by the mongrel-terrier peering around the skirt of his young mistress.

As a panacea for the evils besetting society, Carlyle never tired of extolling, in his words, the 'perennial nobleness and even sacredness in Work'; and it is this activist gospel that Brown's painting, as a kind of *allégorie réelle*, proclaims. Among the numerous figures in the scene only the navvies are presented as beings of heroic stature, exemplary in devotion to their productive labours, which they carry on in proud self-reliance and utter disregard of the idlers looking on.

Brown's presentation of the urban worker in heroic guise had been anticipated by James Sharples (1825–93), who in 1845–7 painted *The Forge (fig. 154)*, a work which invites comparison with Wright of Derby's treatment of similar material. Sharples, a member of the Amalgamated Society of Engineers and an engine smith throughout his life, was self-taught. The picture is best known through the steel engraving to which Sharples devoted his free time over a period of five years and which enjoyed immense success on its publication in 1859. A critic in the *Athenaeum* wrote: 'It has been wisely published at the earnest desire of the artist's brother-workmen, who look upon it as gratifying evidence of social progress – of the spread of Art among our labouring population.'[24] In contrast to the natural appearance of Sharples' hands in their industrial setting, the figures of the mill girls, disposed with the elegance and grace of a classical frieze in *The Dinner Hour: Wigan* (1874, *fig. 155*) by Eyre Crowe (1824–1910), are ill-assorted with the harsh angularity of the buildings of the cotton

Fig. 155
Eyre Crowe
The Dinner Hour: Wigan
1874

factory in the background. This picture is the urban counterpart of idealized country scenes of farm labourers enjoying their midday rest. Even so, critics took exception to the subject-matter, the writer in the *Athenaeum* declaring that it was 'a pity Mr Crowe wasted his time on such unattractive materials'.

A painting influenced by Brown's *Work*, although without its moralistic impulse, was the last of the eight large canvases illustrating the history of Northumberland which William Bell Scott (1811–91), a close associate of the Pre-Raphaelites, painted to decorate the enclosed central courtyard of Wallington Hall, the home of the Trevelyan family. Entitled *Iron and Coal* (1861, *fig. 156*), it depicts the industrial activity of Tyneside. The ostensible setting is an engineering workshop where three muscular 'strikers' are hammering out molten iron. The mechanical drawing in the right foreground shows one of the steam-engines built by Robert Stephenson and Co., Engineers, Newcastle-upon-Tyne, an example of which is crossing Stephenson's High Level Bridge in the distance. The newspaper folded over the drawing carries the date 11 March 1861, along with references to Garibaldi's victory at Caserta and to activities in the Newcastle art world. The little girl seated on an Armstrong gun to the left has both her father's lunch and a schoolbook of arithmetic in her lap. Other objects in the shop include an anchor, a marine air-pump and a heavy chain with pulley. In the background stands a pit-boy with a whip and a Davy safety lamp. The dock scene on which he looks down shows fishermen, a milk girl and a photographer. A coal barge passes on the river. The picture's caption proudly proclaims: 'In the Nineteenth Century the Northumbrians show the World what can be done with Iron and Coal'.

Scott's picture might have been painted in response to the plea in a piece entitled 'Modern Giants' (1850) in the Pre-Raphaelite publication, *The Germ*, written by the critic Frederick George Stephens under the pseudonym Laura Savage:

> And there is something else we miss; there is the poetry of the things about us; our railways, factories, mines, roaring cities, steam vessels, and the endles novelties and wonders produced every day; which if they were found only in the Thousand and One Nights, or in any poem classical or romantic, would be gloried over without end; for as the majority of us know not a bit more about them, but merely their names, we keep up the same mystery, the main thing required for the surprise of the imagination.

Spectacles of the kind painted by Frith and his imitators show how completely by the mid-nineteenth century British genre had usurped the province once reserved for history painting. Yet such ambitious subject-matter is not common in the pictures of the period, and is not as a general rule typical of the artists who produced them. The dominant vein remained an essentially domestic one, directed much more at the concerns of private life than to public occasions. This was true even of the numerous canvases reflecting a sense of Britain's growing prestige as a world power. Battle scenes or related works celebrating the nation's military and naval prowess are relatively rare, the theme of patriotism being conveyed in much less heroic terms.[25] Typical in this respect is *Hearts of Oak* (1875, *fig. 157*) by James Clarke Hook (1819–1907), whose shore scenes, usually with children, carried on the mode made popular earlier in the century by William Collins. Without the punning title, evocative

Fig. 156
William Bell Scott
Iron and Coal
1861

Fig. 157
James Clarke Hook
Hearts of Oak
1875

of oak vessels manned by men with hearts of oak, this depiction of a small boy who has abandoned his toy wagon to watch with rapt attention while a sailor carves a ship model would hardly convey the artist's appeal to pride of nationality. So that there might be no doubt of this purpose, the work was shown with the following lines from Shakespeare's *King John*:

> ... that England, hedged in with the main,
> That water-walled bulwark, still secure
> And confident from foreign purposes.

Victorian artists' favoured method of representing their country's far-flung wars, whether in the Crimea, India, or South Africa, was through the impact of these events on non-combatants, such as the numerous pictures showing the arrival at home of letters from sons or husbands fighting on remote fronts. Especially compelling in their emotional appeal were scenes of leave-taking. The finest of these, *Eastward Ho! August 1857* (1858, *fig. 158*) by Henry Nelson O'Neil (1817–80), represents the embarkation of troops at the time of the Indian Mutiny. Within its striking diagonal design the artist has movingly represented the varying manifestations of grief of the families left behind.[26]

Even when the scene occurred in the battle zone, the Victorian artist tended to concentrate attention on the pathetic plight of the victims. *In Memoriam* (1858, untraced, engraved by William Henry Simmons, 1862, *fig. 159*) by the Scots disciple of the Pre-Raphaelites, Sir Joseph Noel Paton (1821–1901), was 'Designed to Commemorate the Christian Heroism of the British Ladies in India during the Mutiny of 1857, and their Ultimate Deliverance by British Prowess'. In the original version the prisoners were shown at the mercy of invading sepoys with fixed bayonets; but the horrors of the massacre of Cawnpore were so fresh in the public's memory that

ABOVE

Fig. 159
Sir Joseph Noel Paton
In Memoriam
1862, engraving by William Henry
Simmons

ABOVE

Fig. 160
Sir John Everett Millais
Peace Concluded
1856

RIGHT

Fig. 158
Henry Nelson O'Neil
Eastward Ho!
August 1857
1858

the artist decided to spare their feelings by replacing the mutineers with Scottish Highlanders coming to the relief of Lucknow.

The vogue for patriotic subjects, initially inspired by the Crimean War, found still more effusive expression in the many pictures showing wounded heroes restored to the blessings of domestic life. According to Holman Hunt, the original intention of Sir John Everett Millais (1829–96) in *Peace Concluded* (1856, *fig. 160*) had been to show up the abuse of influence which allowed British officers in the Crimea to enjoy home leave when no such opportunities were available to soldiers in the ranks. While he was at work on the picture, however, peace was declared; and as Hunt continued: 'The call for satire on carpet heroes was out of date; the painter adroitly adapted his work to the changing circumstances, and put *The Times* in the hands of the officer, who has read the news which they were all patriotically rejoicing over; he with a sling supporting his wounded arm to represent that he had nobly done his part towards securing peace.' Millais' wife, Effie, posed for the loving spouse; and the officer was a portrait of the artist's friend, Colonel Malcolm, while the dog was the household pet, Roswell. The daughters are unidentified; one holds out a dove, signifying peace, while the other grasps a medal awarded to her father for valour. In good Pre-Raphaelite fashion the toys in the officer's lap are emblematic of the antagonists in the Crimean War: the menacing lion for England, the suppliant bear for Russia, the belligerent game-cock for France, and the turkey for Turkey!

The popularity of pictures designed to awaken a patriotic response indicates how large a public there was for scenes dealing with the significant issues of the day.[27] Many of the best examples of Victorian genre as a result reflect the critical temper of an age characterized by moral zeal and the reforming impulse. This humanitarian spirit, which was given expression in the novels of social protest written during the 1840s and 1850s by Dickens, Disraeli, Kingsley and Elizabeth Gaskell, found its principal artistic voice in the Pre-Raphaelite Brotherhood. It is too often forgotten that the Pre-Raphaelites were in revolt as much against the triviality of most contemporary subject-painting as against the stale and outmoded formalism of academic training. 'The name of our Body', wrote Holman Hunt, 'was meant to keep in our minds our determination ever to do battle against the frivolous art of the day, which had for its ambition "Monkeyana" ideas, "Books of Beauty", Chorister Boys, whose forms were those of melted wax with drapery of no tangible texture.'

The articles of the Pre-Raphaelite aesthetic creed were twofold. First, the painter was to aim at a completely literal transcription of the scene which he had chosen to paint, rendering it faithfully in every detail. In the words of Ruskin, who appointed himself monitor of the movement, he 'should go to Nature in all singleness of heart . . . having no other thought but how best to penetrate her meaning; rejecting nothing, selecting nothing, and scorning nothing; believing all things to be right and good, and rejoicing always in the truth.' As Robin Ironside has written: 'It was as if the Brotherhood looked at the world without eyelids.' An example is Millais' picture of *Ophelia* (1852) in which the flowers and vegetation surrounding the drowning girl were painted with such microscopic exactitude that the work was used to instruct a class in botany. In an effort to achieve the effect of natural light, the members worked out-of-doors and on the spot whenever possible, painting on a wet white ground with bright pigments which imparted to their canvases that jewel-like brilliance that is a hallmark of their style. When combined with close observation, the successful application of this technique produced a startling sense of the actuality of natural phenomena.

The Pre-Raphaelites, however, deemed truth to nature in its surface manifestations insufficient unless accompanied by the revelation of the spiritual meanings immanent within appearances. In a passage about a fellow artist which brings to mind what the poet Gerard Manley Hopkins meant by 'inscape', Hunt wrote:

> Cecil Lawson [1851–82], in his 'Minister's Garden', seemed well capable of representing not only the literal truth but the healthy poetic spirit of our principles. It was apparent, however, that many who deluded themselves that they were adopting our ideals went out to the fields, and sitting down transcribed chance scenes touch by touch, without recognising that art is not prosaic reproduction. Every hour a view, indoors or outdoors, near or far, changes its phase, and the artist must capture that which best reflects the heavens. The dull man does not discern the image of the celestial in earthly things, and his work accordingly may be deservedly admired for its care and delicacy, but the spectator passes by and forgets it.

Elsewhere he concludes: 'It has been seen how in a quite child-like way we at the beginning set ourselves to illustrate themes which we conscientiously persuaded ourselves to be connected with the pathetic, the honest, the laudable, the sublime interests of humanity.'

One of the artist's principal ways of providing insight into the realms of meaning beneath the surface of reality was to endow details in his pictures with symbolic or emblematic significance. Thus, the Pre-Raphaelites revived one of Hogarth's principal pictorial devices, though with a soberness of purpose essentially Victorian.

As men of their age, the Pre-Raphaelites coupled a strongly defined social conscience with their artistic precepts. Unlike their contemporaries in France, such as Courbet and Millet, in their concern for human welfare they lacked the broad-based political and economic sanction springing from revolutionary upheavals on the Continent during the first half of the nineteenth century, which had no counterpart in Britain. Rather, the members of the Brotherhood and their affiliates, reflecting the prevailingly domestic temper of their society, directed their attention to the dramas of private life. To the portrayal of situations of personal crisis and the disturbed states of mind arising from them, these artists brought all the psychological realism and mastery over expressive means that had come to be recognized as distinguishing characteristics of the British artistic genius.[28] They added to these faculties, however, a quality wholly new in British art. Born of the deep emotional commitment and acuteness of perception whose fusion embodied the Pre-Raphaelite ideal, this quality is best described as *intensity*; and it gave to Victorian genre painting a compelling immediacy of appeal and urgency hitherto absent from the mode.

The advocacy of subject-matter drawn from contemporary life was a central article of the Pre-Raphaelite creed. In the second of two articles on 'The Subject in Art', published in 1850 in the short-lived periodical of the group, *The Germ: Thoughts towards Nature in Poetry, Literature, and Art* (renamed *Art and Poetry* after the second issue), John L. Tupper, a minor disciple, proposed: 'If, as every poet, every

painter, every sculptor will acknowledge, his best and most original ideas are derived from his own times: if his great lessonings to piety, truth, charity, love, honour, honesty, gallantry, generosity, courage, are derived from the same source; why transfer them to distant periods, and make them *not things of today*?' In developing this argument, he was led to the conclusion 'that Art, to become a more powerful engine of civilization, assuming a practically humanizing tendency (the admitted function of all Art), should be made more directly conversant with the things, incidents, and influences which surround and constitute the living world of those whom Art proposes to improve . . .' With memorable exceptions, however, the vision of the central figures of the Pre-Raphaelite movement was nourished by the imaginary realms of literature, religion, and history rather than by the life about them. As a result, it is to their teaching and example, as much as to their pictures, that one must look for evidence of how profoundly they influenced the practice of serious genre painting among their contemporaries.

The Victorian artist who sought to handle crucial issues of the day in a responsible manner more often than not found himself cast in the role of social commentator. A topic which inspired innumerable paintings of the period was emigration. The years 1840–50, known as the 'hungry forties', were a period of severe distress attendant on the growing pains of the Industrial Revolution; and British citizens were moved in growing numbers to seek a better way of life in Canada or Australia. (The annual emigration figures increased from 90,000 to 280,000 during the decade.) In dealing with this state of affairs, artists frequently chose to show its impact on the family circle in scenes representing either the receipt or answering of letters from distant relations; and in such examples the sadness of separation is often mitigated by pride in the closeness of Britain's ties with her overseas colonies.[29] A more pathetic note is struck in Abraham Solomon's *Second Class: The Parting* (1854, *fig. 161*), which unites the theme of emigration with the equally popular one of travel by rail. The wide-eyed lad is about to take leave of his sorrowful mother and sister; and as the placards on the wall of the compartment advertising job opportunities in Australia indicate, his destination is that remote continent, so that the absence is likely to be a long one. The subtitle, 'Thus part we rich in sorrow, parting poor', suggests that an element of class awareness is also present, which is substantiated by a pendant, *First Class: The Meeting and at first meeting loved* (1854, *fig. 162*), in which the figures, a father, his daughter, and the latter's admirer, travelling in comfort and engaged in pleasant dalliance, clearly belong to the upper middle class. The contrasting views from the train window, a dreary industrial landscape in the former and an outlook of pastoral beauty in the latter, emphasize the contrast in social station of the two groups.[30]

The most poignant of all handlings of the emigrant theme is Ford Madox Brown's *The Last of England* (1852–5, *fig. 163*),[31] inspired by the departure of his friend, the Pre-Raphaelite sculptor Thomas Woolner, for the Australian gold-fields, and praised by the *Athenaeum* for its 'Hogarth fertility of thought'. The artist was in a depressed state of mind that brought thoughts of emigrating; and he used himself and his wife, Emma, as models. In the catalogue description of 1865 Brown wrote of the picture's inception:

This Picture is in the strictest sense historical. It treats of the great emigration movement, which attained its culminating point in 1852. [It is said that in this year alone 369,000 Britons departed from their homeland.] The educated are bound to their country by quite other ties than the illiterate man, whose chief consideration is food and physical comfort. I have, therefore, in order to present the parting scene in its fullest tragic development, singled out a couple from the middle classes, high enough, through education and refinement, to appreciate all they are now giving up, and yet depressed enough in means, to have to put up with the discomforts and humiliations incident to a vessel 'all one class'.

The ship, outward bound, is passing the cliffs of Dover in a blustery sea. Of the conditions under which he worked by choice, the artist wrote in his diary:

To insure the peculiar look of *light all round* which objects have on a dull day at sea, it was painted for the most part in the open air on dull days, and when the flesh was being painted, on cold days. . . . The minuteness of detail which would be visible under such conditions of broad day-light I have thought necessary to imitate as bringing the pathos of the subject more home to the beholder.

The umbrella which the husband holds to shield his wife from flying spray, together with the oval composition, stresses the couple's isolation from the passengers roistering in the background. Their firmly clasped hands denote the devotion and fortitude with which they face the rigours of exile; yet their faces, on which Brown concentrates attention, express divergent responses to the ordeal in store. Wide-eyed and wistful, the wife seems to linger over fond memories of the homeland which the baby sheltered beneath her cape will never share, while her husband's visage is marked with brooding melancholy over disappointed hopes. An element of bitter irony is contributed by the name of the ship inscribed on the lifeboat behind, *Eldorado*.[32]

Scenes representing the kind of hardship which drove people to emigrate are relatively rare in Victorian painting, doubtless because the public would have found their subject-matter too painful to contemplate. This makes all the more remarkable the stark commentary of *The Irish Vagrants* (1853–4, *fig. 164*) by Walter Howell Deverell (1827–54), a close associate of the Pre-Raphaelites whose promising career was cut short by his early death. With regard to this unfinished painting Holman Hunt wrote of him: 'He was an eager reader, and had contracted the prevailing taste among the young of that day, which Carlyle had inaugurated and Charles Kingsley had accentuated, of dwelling on the miseries of the poor, the friendless, and the fallen . . .' The subject, which Rossetti thought 'so good & important' that he urged Deverell to 'paint it on a larger scale', was inspired by the plight of the Irish labouring poor driven into exile by the potato famine. The vagrants' faces and postures declare with disturbing realism the brutalizing effects of hunger, exhaustion and despair; and their hopeless state is brought into cruel relief by the harvesting activities of native-born workers in the background and by the haughty disdain of the lady riding by.[33]

Realism tempered with deep compassion provides the informing spirit of *The Stonebreaker* (1857, *fig. 165*) by Henry Wallis (1830–1916), another artist greatly influenced by Pre-Raphaelite theory and practice. No form of phsyical labour in the Victorian age was harder or more degrading than stonebreaking, part of the

Fig. 164
Walter Howell Deverell
The Irish Vagrants
1853–4

Fig. 165
Henry Wallis
The Stonebreaker
1857

established procedure for building improved roads throughout the British Isles, following the prescriptions of McAdam and Telford. Under the Poor Law this form of livelihood was commonly assigned to the able-bodied poor, and the spectacle of them at work formed the subject of a whole category of pictures. As early as 1830 Landseer had painted *The Stonebreaker's Daughter*; and among other artists the theme was treated with varying degrees of seriousness by John Brett (1830–1902), George William Mote (1832–1909), George Henry Boughton (1833–1905) and Sir James Guthrie (1859–1930).[34] No version, however, approaches the sombre power of Wallis' conception. Like both Brown and Deverell, he was a disciple of Thomas Carlyle's radical humanitarianism; and when exhibited the painting carried the following indignant quotation from that writer's *Sartor Resartus*: 'Hardly entreated Brother! For us was thy back so bent, for us were thy straight limbs and fingers so deformed; thou wert our Conscript, on whom the lot fell, and fighting our battles wert so marred. For in thee too lay a god-created Form, but it was not to be unfolded;

Fig. 166
Augustus Edwin Mulready
Remembering Joys that have passed away
1873

Fig. 167
Emily Mary Osborn
*Home Thoughts: 'One heart heavy,
one heart light'*
1856

encrusted must it stand with the thick adhesions and defacements of Labour: and thy body, like thy soul, was not to know freedom.' The afterglow, rendered with Pre-Raphaelite vibrancy, provides an eerie requiem for the worn-out labourer who has died beside the pile of rocks he was crushing. A stoat has ventured out by his right foot, emphasizing the immobility of the bowed figure, which in the dignity conferred by death merges so harmoniously with the quiet beauty of the natural setting.

Despite the legislative reforms of Lord Shaftesbury and the charitable work of such organizations as the Foundling Hospital and Dr Barnardo's Home, Victorian children continued to suffer terribly from neglect or maltreatment, as the novels of Dickens bear witness. This state of affairs, however, was too shocking to receive much recognition from artists reluctant to offend public sensibilities. One painter, Augustus Edwin Mulready (?1843–after 1903), a late associate of the Cranbrook colony, did make it his special province to portray the lot of London waifs and strays. Although his children often seem too sweetly appealing, there is no mistaking the authenticity of Mulready's pictures of life in the city streets, or his tender regard for those condemned to struggle for survival there. Posters advertising every sort of popular entertainment were a prominent feature of the city's thoroughfares; and Mulready frequently employed them for purposes of ironic contrast, to stress the pathos of the dispossessed among so many inducements to pleasure. Thus, in a picture entitled *Remembering Joys that have passed away* (1873, *fig. 166*), the little match-seller and the crossing-sweeper, all oblivious of their isolation and the snow swirling about, stand spellbound before the notice of a Christmas pantomime whose run has already closed.

Nor were the pangs of neglect confined to the poor. In *Home Thoughts* (1856,

Fig. 170
Arthur Hughes
The Long Engagement
c1854–9

Fig. 168
Richard Redgrave
The Poor Teacher
1844

Fig. 169
Richard Redgrave
The Sempstress
1846

fig. 167), which bears the subtitle, 'One heart heavy, one heart light', Emily Mary Osborn (1834–1908) illustrated the breaking up of a school for young ladies at holiday time. The pampered darling in the centre is being readied for departure, while her mother waits, a coachman in the hallway collects her luggage, and the carriage, possibly occupied by the grandmother, waits outside. Meanwhile, in the window corner, concealed by a curtain, another girl listens sadly to these preparations. Her black dress suggests that she may recently have been orphaned. From her hat on the chair it is not clear whether she is waiting to be called for by strangers, or whether she is doomed to pass the holidays in loneliness at the school. In either event, the prospect is clearly a miserable one, made the more so by the stony bearing of the headmistress at the right.

It was, however, the misfortunes of women that elicited the strongest sympathies of Victorian genre artists. For gently born young women who were without means and who remained unmarried, there were really only two solutions to the problem of self-support: to become teachers or governesses, or to sink into the ranks of the working class. Richard Redgrave (1804–88) depicted the unhappiness of either path several years before the Pre-Raphaelites. His picture, *The Poor Teacher (fig. 168)*, may have been inspired by the case of his sister Jane, who, we are told by his son, 'pined over the duties of a governess away from home, caught typhoid fever, and was brought back only to die amongst us'. Yet the situation shown here was all too common in Victorian society, as anyone familiar with the life of Charlotte Brontë and her novels, *Jane Eyre* and *Villette*, well knows. Redgrave painted four versions of the subject during the 1840s, calling the later ones *The Governess*. In the original (1843) the girl was shown as a solitary figure; but Sheepshanks, who commissioned the first replica (1844), found her forlorn state in the empty schoolroom so heart-rending that he had the artist add the three pupils by the door at the right. It may seem, however, that their blithe disregard of their teacher only emphasizes her isolation. The black-bordered letter which she holds implies the death of a near relation; and the score of 'Home, sweet Home' on the piano behind further suggests the direction in which her sad thoughts have turned.

Perhaps no single piece of Victorian writing had so many artistic repercussions as Thomas Hood's poem, 'The Song of the Shirt', exposing the intolerable conditions of servitude to which women who did piece-work in the garment industry were subjected. It appeared in *Punch* in 1843, and is said to have tripled the magazine's circulation. The subject attracted artists as different as Anna Elizabeth Blunden (1830–1915), Claude Andrew Calthrop (1845–93), Charles Rossiter, Frank Holl (1845–88), Millais and Watts, down to Albert Rutherston (1881–1953). But Redgrave was first in the field with *The Sempstress* (1844, untraced; later version 1846, *fig. 169*). The poor girl has stitched throughout the night in her lonely garret room; now, exhausted, with dawn breaking through the window, she looks up, hopelessly disconsolate, as her thoughts go back to happier times. The *Art Union*, precursor of the *Art Journal*, defined the picture's wide appeal as follows: 'The story is told in such a way as to approach the best feelings of the human heart: she is not a low-born drudge to proclaim her patient endurance to the vulgar world; her suffering is read only in the shrunken cheek, and the eye feverish and dim with watching.' Redgrave, who was to go on to a distinguished career as art director of the South Kensington (now the

Victoria and Albert) Museum and Surveyor of the Queen's Pictures, during the 1840s painted other works exhibiting sympathy with young women in distressed circumstances, such as *Fashion's Slaves* (1847). He thus took a leading role in dedicating art to supporting the movement for social reform eloquently voiced in the literature of the time. 'It is', he wrote, 'one of my most gratifying feelings, that many of my best efforts in art have aimed at calling attention to the trials and struggles of the poor and oppressed.'[35]

Artists called attention to another source of acute suffering for young Victorian women: the barrier to matrimony imposed by financial need or inequality of station in a convention-shackled society. *The Long Engagement* (c1854–9, *fig. 170*) by Arthur Hughes (1832–1915), who was much influenced by Millais, poignantly evokes the frustration implied by the picture's title. Hughes originally conceived the picture as a work of literary genre deriving from Shakespeare and entitled *Orlando in the Forest of Arden*, but repainted it in modern guise, showing the meeting in a woodland setting of a poor curate and his fiancée, kept apart by his poverty. That their waiting has been interminable is indicated by the ivy now obscuring her name, Amy, which he had long ago carved on the tree trunk. Their faces are as charged with intense emotion as those of the couple in Brown's *The Last of England (fig. 163)*, his uplifted eyes expressing agonized protest against the circumstances of their lives, in contrast to the steadfast devotion of her gaze. The glowing colours in which the setting is rendered, with wild roses in riotous bloom and every detail of foliage bearing witness to nature's fecundity, are a mordant comment on the couple's sexual frustration.

Still more pathetic in its dramatic implications is the picture entitled *Too Late* (1857–8, *fig. 171*) by William Lindsay Windus (1822–1907), a Liverpool associate of the Pre-Raphaelites during his brief active career. A tardy suitor has at last returned only to find his intended marked for death in the last stages of consumption. Her cold gaze of repudiation causes him to throw up his arms in guilty recognition of love betrayed, a guilt that may be the more burning if the accusing eyes of the young girl intimate, as they seem to do, that she is the illegitimate child of their former passion. The lines from Tennyson's lyric, 'Come not, when I am dead', which Windus' picture was designed to illustrate, intensify the bleak finality of the encounter:

> . . . if it were thine error or thy crime
> I care no longer, being all unblest:
> Wed whom thou wilt, but I am sick of Time,
> And I desire to rest.

Death itself has intervened to account for the destitution of the bereaved woman and her son in Emily Mary Osborn's *Nameless and Friendless* (1857, *fig. 172*). Having offered a painting by her late lover to a dealer, she timidly awaits the verdict, which, judging by his supercilious scrutiny, is unlikely to be favourable. The sense shared by the pair of being at the mercy of an alien and probably hostile world is further accentuated by the presence of the two top-hatted connoisseurs to the left, who seem to suspect that the woman is the original for the sketch of a ballerina that one of them is holding up. The picture's title provides a necessary clue to its meaning; for the woman does not wear a wedding-ring. A happier solution to the plight of a fatherless and impoverished family, and one which introduces the familiar theme of charity, is

OPPOSITE LEFT

Fig. 171
William Lindsay Windus
Too Late
1857–8

OPPOSITE RIGHT

Fig. 172
Emily Mary Osborn
Nameless and Friendless
1857

OPPOSITE

Fig. 173
Thomas Brooks
Relenting
1855

proposed by Thomas Brooks in *Relenting* (1855, *fig. 173*). The pleas of the widowed mother as she points to her four children have evidently softened the heart of the landlord, who is reconsidering his decision to evict them for failure to pay rent. The cavalry sabre hanging by the portrait above the mantel, taken with the date of the picture, indicates that the father has died fighting for his country in the Crimea.

For the impoverished young Victorian woman, unable or unwilling to support herself by conventionally acceptable means, the only remaining solution, short of suicide,[36] was either to go on the streets as a prostitute or to accept male protection outside marriage. The former path provided the subject for *Found (fig. 174)*, the only picture with social content which Dante Gabriel Rossetti (1828–82) ever undertook. This 'town subject' was to be the 'great modern work' which the artist had declared the intention of painting as early as 1853, and to which he devoted himself on and off for many years without ever being able to complete it to his satisfaction. The theme, common enough in the eighteenth century, as we have seen, opposes the innocence of rustic life to the corruption of the city. A young drover, bringing his calf to the slaughterhouse, has encountered his former love at dawn near London Bridge. Her tawdry finery and the shame with which she shrinks from his grasp against the wall of the graveyard indicate the profession which she has taken up. The unsuspecting calf tangled in the net exemplifies the Pre-Raphaelite fondness for symbolic commentary.

The full extent to which the Pre-Raphaelites took over Hogarth's practice of endowing realistic details with emblematic significance is seen in the most famous of all Victorian depictions of the fallen woman, *The Awakening Conscience* (1853–4, *fig. 175*) by William Holman Hunt. The situation was originally inspired by Dickens' account in *David Copperfield* of the seduction of Little Em'ly by Steerforth. The girl's face eloquently expresses the awareness of lost innocence and happiness to which she has been aroused by her lover's careless fingering on the piano of Tom Moore's lyric, 'Oft in the stilly night'. As has been often pointed out, every feature of the setting is emblematic of the situation which it helps to dramatize: the mangled bird in the cat's clutches beneath the table, the unravelling tapestry on the frame, the soiled and discarded glove. What has been less noticed is the telling contrast between the harsh brightness of the carpet and polished furniture, which impart to the room the infernal atmosphere of a *chambre damnée*,[37] and the paradisal freshness of the garden outside reflected in the mirror on the rear wall. The room is lit by an unseen window, which is also the viewer's point of vantage; and it not only illuminates the girl's face with its trace of newborn hope, but also, since she faces the window, paradoxically shows her reflection in the mirror as if she has turned her back on the garden in symbolic re-enactment of Eve's transgression and expulsion from Eden.

The girl's features were originally more guilt-ridden. According to Hunt, he repainted it in its present more hopeful guise at the request of the owner, Sir Thomas Fairbairn, who found the initial expression too painful. Some notion of Hunt's original conception of the conscience-stricken girl may be gathered from Ruskin's response to the painting when first exhibited: 'I suppose that no one possessing the slightest knowledge of expression could remain untouched by the countenance of the lost girl, rent from its beauty into sudden horror; the lips half open, indistinct in their purple quivering, the teeth set hard, the eyes filled with the fearful light of futurity and with tears of ancient days.' The girl's face now clearly reflects the hope of redemption, a state of mind supported by Hunt's habitual designation of his work as *The Awakened Conscience*. The title, *The Awakening Conscience*, thus preserves his initial intent, which was to emphasize the psychological agony attendant on conversion, as the girl confronts her lost innocence, metaphorically represented by the garden.

No such implications of spiritual regeneration are present in *Thoughts of the Past* (1858–9, *fig. 176*) by John Roddam Spencer-Stanhope (1829–1908), who was affiliated with the Pre-Raphaelites during the 1850s. In contrast to the highly charged emotional expression of Hunt's girl, the face and attitude of Spencer-Stanhope's prostitute register the stony passivity of hopeless despair, in a setting where every detail tells with stark realism of her abandoned state. The view from the window overlooking Thames shipping at Blackfriars locates her lodging in the meanest quarter of London; and the squalid room itself, with its plants gone to seed and dying and the cheap finery strewn about the dressing-table, further emphasizes the depths of degradation to which its occupant has sunk.

In illustration of the sway which the dilemma of the fallen woman exercised over the imagination of Victorian artists, two additional variations may be cited for their originality and evocative power: *On the Brink* (1865, *fig. 177*) by Alfred Elmore (1815–80) and *'Take your Son, Sir'* (1851–7, *fig. 178*) by Ford Madox Brown.[38] The former, set outside the gambling casino at Homburg, the scene of Frith's *Salon d'Or*, brings to mind Hogarth's *The Lady's Last Stake* in the ambiguity of its intention. Is it the woman's virtue which is in question? or her fortune? or both? The contrast between the garishly illuminated interior and the cold moonlight outside, connected by the shadowy Mephistophelian figure leaning between (his cloak back-lit with splashes of lurid red), projects in a masterly way the torment of indecision expressed in the woman's features and posture. The juxtaposition of lily and passion flower on the terrace beside her provides an objective correlative to the conflict within her mind.

With his customary bold disregard for popular sentiment, Brown made his unfinished drama of illegitimacy into a parody of the madonna and child. In a gesture of defiance the mother, a portrait of his wife, thrusts out her newborn child as if challenging the viewer to accept paternity. Through the arresting use of a device loved by the Pre-Raphaelite Brotherhood, and in this case undoubtedly borrowed from Van Eyck's *Arnolfini Wedding*, the designated father only appears as a reflection in the mirror that surrounds the woman's head like a halo. The fact that in this mirror-image Brown has presented a grotesquely mocking self-portrait adds yet another incongruous element to a picture manifold in its moral implications.

To the Victorian mind no domestic tragedy could be so grave as that which undermined the institution of the home and jeopardized the sanctity of family life. The ruination of a family through addiction to betting, which Frith portrayed in the five pictures of *The Road to Ruin*, was condensed into a single canvas by Robert Braithwaite Martineau (1826–69) in *The Last Day in the Old Home* (1862, *fig. 179*), over which he is said to have laboured for ten years. The Christie's catalogue on the floor gives the name of the owner and his house as Sir Charles Pulleyne, Bart., of Hardham Court. All of the objects in the room have been numbered for sale; and the owner's mother by the window is exchanging a bank note for the keys surrendered by the elderly retainer. In the father's hand draped over his son's shoulder is a racing notebook, the token of his fatal weakness. Clearly unrepentant over the folly which has

OPPOSITE RIGHT

Fig. 178
Ford Madox Brown
'Take your Son, Sir'
1851–7 (unfinished)

OPPOSITE LEFT

Fig. 177
Alfred Elmore
On the Brink
1865

OPPOSITE

Fig. 179
Robert Braithwaite Martineau
The Last Day in the Old Home
1862

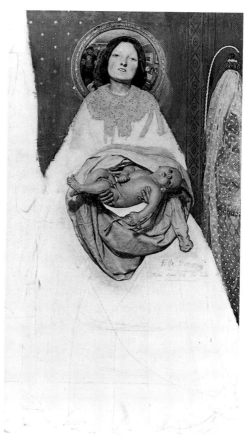

sacrificed his hereditary estate and brought misery on the members of his family, the man lightheartedly raises his glass to the future in a spirit of bravado which he has communicated to his son, despite the mother's gesture of protest. The pieces of armour and other heraldic devices about the walls silently proclaim the demise of a proud line.

A still graver threat to domestic happiness is posed in *Waiting for the Verdict* (1857, *fig. 180*) by Abraham Solomon, who during his short life showed adeptness matching that of Redgrave in exploiting topical issues. This finely composed painting suggests the strain that the members of a closely knit family are undergoing as they await the issue of a legal action against the father of the family. In a pendant entitled *The Acquittal* (1859) the artist provided a happy ending to his story, but one in which sentimental effusiveness replaces the genuine dramatic suspense of the initial scene of waiting outside the court room. In both pictures, which enjoyed enormous popularity as engravings, the room where the family is gathered opens on an outer chamber, in one case leading inward to the court where the trial is taking place, in the other opening on the exterior world of freedom.

Augustus Leopold Egg (1816–63), whose manner, like that of Martineau, mediates between the narrative dexterity of Frith and the tonal brilliance of the Pre-Raphaelites, painted in imitation of the Hogarthian 'moral progress' a series of three pictures portraying the break-up of a Victorian middle-class family, now known by the title *Past and Present* (1858, *figs 181–3*). When originally shown at the Royal Academy the sequence was unnamed, but bore the suggestive caption: 'August the

OPPOSITE

Fig. 181
Augustus Leopold Egg
Past and Present – I
1858

OPPOSITE BELOW LEFT

Fig. 182
Augustus Leopold Egg
Past and Present – II
1858

OPPOSITE BELOW RIGHT

Fig. 183
Augustus Leopold Egg
Past and Present – III
1858

Fig. 180
Abraham Solomon
Waiting for the Verdict
1857

4$\underline{th}$. Have just heard that B— has been dead more than a fortnight, so her poor children have now lost both their parents. I hear she was seen on Friday last near the Strand, evidently without a place to lay her head – What a fall her's has been!' The first picture is entirely Hogarthian in conception. The unfaithful wife lies crumpled on the floor beside her husband, who has just read the incriminating letter and who grinds the portrait of the betrayer underfoot. Emblematic details expound every implication of the scene. An apple, divided between table and floor, exposes a rotten core. One of the pictures on the rear wall shows Adam and Eve being driven from Paradise; the other is a copy of Clarkson Stanfield's recent canvas of a derelict hulk wallowing in the waves, entitled *The Abandoned*. The children's play with a tumbling house of cards rehearses the traditional motif of fortune's instability. Close inspection reveals that the cards are based on a novel by Balzac, the acknowledged master of stories of adultery.

The second picture discovers the two daughters, after the lapse of a few years, in a moonlit garret, the sparse decorations of which include portraits of both father and mother. The former has recently died according to the information of the caption; and the posture of the pair, the younger kneeling with her head in the lap of the elder who sadly gazes out over the roof-tops, denotes their forsaken state. The position of the moon, again the only source of illumination, makes it clear that the third picture occurs at precisely the same time as its predecessor. Its light reveals the outcast mother crouched beneath the Adelphi arches, a refuge of social outcasts in Victorian London. The child in her arms is evidently the issue of her illicit passion, now a thing of the past. The posters on the wall, advertising theatrical entertainments, entitled *Victims* and *A Cure for Love*, as well as pleasure excursions to Paris, comment ironically on the situation. It is perhaps indicative of the Victorians' reluctance to confront calamities which impugned their most dearly cherished domestic ideals that, while Egg's sequence attracted a good deal of shocked attention when exhibited at the Royal Academy, it remained unsold during his lifetime.[39]

That the issues raised by serious genre painting in the Victorian period involved problems of interpretation not only for the public at large but also among critics is apparent from written comments. As if in anticipation of these difficulties, painters not only strewed clues throughout their compositions and gave them informative titles, but also spelled out their meanings through additional captions and catalogue descriptions, as we have seen. Nevertheless, the problems remained, perhaps because the pictures increasingly involved themes of a kind more suitable to novels, plays or poems. An example of the misreadings which these paintings often invited was a blunder occurring in *La Peinture Anglaise* (1882) by Ernest Chesneau, one of the best informed and most perceptive French critics of British art. According to the author, Martineau's *The Last Day in the Old Home (fig. 179)* portrayed the sale of the house by the mother seated in the window to a new breed of callous speculators, represented by the auctioneer's agent drinking champagne with his son. Although Chesneau acknowledged his error in the footnote to a later edition, he left the original text unchanged, with the following explanation: 'Rien ne prouve mieux le danger des intentions trop subtiles, trop littéraires en peinture que la méprise que j'ai commise en analysant ce tableau, méprise que je maintiens intentionellement dans ce texte.'[41]

In the case of many of the pictures which have been cited, however, the ambiguity

Fig. 185
William Holman Hunt
The Hireling Shepherd
1851–2

Fig. 184
William Dyce
Pegwell Bay – A Recollection of October 5th 1858
?1858–60

in meaning was a deliberate artifice on the painter's part. For one of the noteworthy innovations in Victorian painting was the development of the problem picture as a recognizable category of genre, especially among the Pre-Raphaelites and their successors. The term 'problem picture' carries a dual significance. In the first place it signifies the artist's intent to associate his scene with crucial social concerns of the age. The problem, however, is not presented primarily in its external implications for society at large, but rather through its impact on the lives of the individuals affected. Overshadowing the overt action are its psychological implications, conveyed by all the expressive devices at the artist's disposal. The success of the problem picture depends on the artist's skill in selecting the precise climactic moment which will awaken the viewer to the full range of behavioural responses inherent in this twofold perspective. Furthermore, since by the very limitations of the medium the action in these paintings is arrested short of resolution, the viewer is invited not only to reconstruct the events leading up to the scene before him, but also to project its future consequences. In calling for this complexity of response, the best examples of Victorian genre thus transcend the purely anecdotal content of run-of-the-mill subject painting in the age.

ABOVE LEFT

Fig. 186
Sir John Everett Millais
The Blind Girl
1854–6

ABOVE RIGHT

Fig. 187
Sir John Everett Millais
Autumn Leaves
1855–6

The treatment of setting was an essential aspect of Pre-Raphaelite painting, since its details provided a principal means through which nuances of meaning were communicated. Among the most memorable achievements of the school were works which effected a unique fusion between landscape and genre. Although he was never a member of the Brotherhood, William Dyce (1806–64) shared its approach to the natural world in what has been called the 'daguerreotype vision' of *Pegwell Bay – A Recollection of October 5th 1858* (?1858–60, *fig. 184*). Pegwell Bay lies next along the coast to Ramsgate Sands; but this picture of a few late holiday-makers collecting seashells could hardly be more different from Frith's ebullient throng at the height of the season. The prominent figures were portraits of (from the right) the artist's wife, her two sisters, and one of his sons. They wander in a setting haunted by the immensities of time and space. As readers of Sir Charles Lyell's *Principles of Geology* (1830–3) would have known, the chalk cliffs in the background were the burial ground of prehistoric fossils, while in the zenith appears the comet named after Giovanni Battista Donati, first sighted on 2 June 1858, and at its most brilliant on 5 October. Amidst these desolate surroundings the human element seems spectre-like, an alien intrusion on a world from which the pallid light of the declining day has drained all colour and vitality.

The full originality of Holman Hunt's *The Hireling Shepherd* (1851–2, *fig. 185*) emerges when it is viewed in the context of the pastoral idyll. The artist had this in mind in a sardonic comment made in 1897 when the work was acquired by the City Art Gallery, Manchester: '. . . my first object as an artist was to paint, not dresden china bergers, but – a real Shepherd, and a real Shepherdess, and a landscape in full sunlight, with all the colour of luscious summer without the faintest fear of the precedents of any landscape painters who had rendered Nature before.' For once the contemporary press was not slow to recognize the success with which the artist's purpose had been accomplished. A writer in the *British Quarterly Review*, for example, declared: 'There is certainly no attempt at poetry here; for a fellow more capable than the shepherd of drinking a great quantity of beer, or a more sunburnt slut than the shepherdess, we never saw in a picture.'[42] Explaining why he called his shepherd a hireling, Hunt wrote that the word 'in its proper suggestion represents a man neglecting his duties for selfish and idle fancies.' But since it was apparent that the artist had on a secondary level conceived his work in allegorical terms as a commentary on religious abuses of the age, he admitted that the shepherd was to be taken as 'a type . . . of other muddle-headed pastors who instead of performing their services to their flock – which is in constant peril – discuss vain questions of no value to any human soul.'

Theological interpretations, of which there have been many, should not be allowed to deflect appreciation of the sparkling beauty of the landscape, painted in the open at Ewell in Surrey. Yet, it is a sinister beauty, fraught with implications of disaster. For the sheep, having been allowed through neglect to stray among the ripe wheat, not only threaten the crop, but after feeding on the grain will swell with gas and die, as has already been the fate of three 'blown' animals at the left. Furthermore, the sickly lamb in the girl's lap is also being allowed to destroy itself through eating green apples. The boldness of her admirer's addresses is received with brazen effrontery that leaves little doubt of the issue of their dalliance; but this again is of ill omen. For the insect he holds up for her inspection is a death's-head moth. Thus, while retaining all the properties of the rustic pastoral with exquisite fidelity, the artist has yet converted his picture into an ironic parody of the tradition of which it is a product.

In 1856 Millais exhibited two canvases, *The Blind Girl* (1854–6) and *Autumn Leaves* (1855–6), which show how deeply and with what lyric intensity the Pre-Raphaelite artist explored the affinities between the human and natural worlds. The background of the former (*fig. 186*) was painted on the spot near Winchelsea, Sussex, which is shown on the hill; and the figures and other portions of the setting in Perth. It is a measure of the artist's regard for accuracy that he repainted the rainbow on being informed that the spectrum of colours in the two arcs should be reversed. The rapt expression of the blind girl's face suggests that she is experiencing some sort of epiphany born of intuitive harmony with the beauty of the surrounding scene. A Wordsworthian communion with nature is expressed in the tenderness with which she fingers the harebell in her right hand and by the trustful way the butterfly, a red admiral, perches on her shawl. Her tranquil countenance, which seems to be enthralled by an inner vision still lovelier than the spectacle presented by the surrounding world, forms a contrast to the wondering fear with which the younger girl gazes at the stormy sky in the distance. In his *Diary* Ford Madox Brown called *The Blind Girl* 'the finest subject a glorious one a religious picture', an opinion substantiated by the symbolic force of several details. For in Christian iconography the rainbow and the butterfly signify respectively hope of spiritual rebirth and the human soul. Furthermore, the way in which the younger draws the scarf of her sister over her head as if for protection confers on the pose of the blind girl a secular likeness to traditional artistic representations of the Virgin of Pity.

The inception of *Autumn Leaves (fig. 187)* can be traced to a nostalgic remark which Hunt attributed to Millais: 'Is there any sensation more delicious than that awakened by the odour of burning leaves? To me nothing brings back sweeter memories of the days that are gone; it is the incense offered by departing summer to the sky, and it brings one a happy conviction that Time puts a peaceful seal on all that has gone.' Testimonies differ as to the artist's intent in this painting. Lady Millais wrote that he meant 'to paint a picture full of beauty and without subject'; but the artist told the critic, F.G.Stephens, that he 'always felt insulted when people have regarded the picture as a simple little domestic episode, chosen for effect and colour', since it was designed to 'awaken by its solemnity the deepest religious reflection.'

The picture was painted during the autumn of 1855 at Millais' residence in Scotland, Annat Lodge, Perth. The models for the four figures were all under thirteen years of age. The girls holding the basket and letting fall the leaves were the artist's sisters-in-law, Alice and Sophie Gray; and the other two were local girls, Matilda Proudfoot and Isabella Nicol, who also posed for *The Blind Girl*. The afterglow in the western sky and the autumnal hues in the foreground, deepened by the shadows of evening, accentuate the haunting sadness imprinted on the girls' faces. Millais, a great admirer of the lyrics in Tennyson's *The Princess*, can hardly have failed to have had in mind the most memorable one, beginning 'Tears, idle tears...' As they gather the leaves of the dying year for burning, the girls are like hierophants presiding over some sorrowful ritual that remains a mystery to which they can give only emotional assent.[43]

Chapter Six

VICTORIAN
PERSPECTIVES
(II)

THE VICTORIAN SOCIAL WORLD is reflected with considerably greater breadth and vividness in the genre painting of the first half of the Queen's reign, the period covered in the preceding chapter, than during the closing decades of the nineteenth century. As if surfeited with the banalities of life about them, leading artists from about 1870 turned to the remote past for their subjects. George Frederick Watts immersed himself more and more in allegorical fantasies. Following the example of Dante Gabriel Rossetti, who was never more than half-hearted in his support of the original goals of Pre-Raphaelitism, Sir Edward Coley Burne-Jones (1838–98) and a host of lesser disciples evoked a visionary dream world of myth and fable. Lord Leighton (1830–96) initiated a neo-classical revival; and his search to recover the legendary splendour of ancient Greece was joined by artists as diverse as Sir Edward John Poynter (1836–1919), Albert Joseph Moore (1841–93) and Walter Crane (1845–1915). Sir Lawrence Alma-Tadema (1836–1912) painted the Romans in their daily lives, and Edwin Long (1829–91) attempted to do the same for the older civilizations of the eastern Mediterranean.

While domestic genre retained its popularity throughout the later nineteenth century, it became increasingly frivolous, as is indicated by the titles given to paintings in a transparent effort to solicit a public that turned to art solely for diversion. Sometimes they declared the unabashed sentimentality of the subjects: *Granny's Spectacles* or *The Sick Violet*; sometimes they coyly resorted to punning: *Sea Urchins* or *Catching a Crab*; sometimes the names evoked 'high-falutin' associations: *Our Coastal Defences* (children playing in the dunes) or *War of the Roses* (a young woman's indecision between white and red roses to adorn her ball-gown). As they became more apparent, the tendencies corrupting the artistic performances even of established painters gave rise to a chorus of critical protest. Henry James recorded his impression of the Royal Academy exhibition of 1878 as follows:

> There is a great deal of vulgarity, of triviality and crudity, and of that singular 'goodiness', as one may say for want of a better word, with a certain dose of which

the average English painter appears to have discovered it to be needful to flavour his picture in order to make it palatable to the average English purchaser.

Writing nearly a decade later, Harry Quilter, art critic for the *Spectator* and *The Times*, was considerably more scathing in his denunciation of the forces corrupting contemporary taste:

> It is not our painters who are to blame, or, at least, not chiefly; the painters are but tradesmen of a certain kind, who supply the wants of their customers. It is the fashionable, enlightened patrons of art who have produced this puling-woman and playing-baby sort of picture, who won't buy anything unless it is pleasant, trivial, and pretty, as if their galleries were but big sweetmeat boxes. ... And the dealers who minister to them are even more reprehensible, since they do all in their power to foster this foolish taste.

Quilter's reference to dealers is highly significant, since there can be no doubt that from the 1860s their influence, for good or bad, was the single most cogent force in the Victorian art market. As middlemen between the painters and their public, their influence was exerted in two directions. On the one hand, they had to a large extent replaced the collector-patrons of an earlier day. They were the ones who now commissioned paintings, as in the case of Flatow with Frith's *The Railway Station*, or, failing this, acquired them from the artist's studio or on varnishing day at the Royal Academy prior to public exhibition.[1] Indeed, the popular landscape artist, John Linnell, had during many years an agreement with the firm of Agnew whereby it received a regular consignment of his canvases. Since the dealers were also among the leading buyers at auctions, they were able to exercise firm control over the market value of works by artists in whom they had a special interest.

On the other hand, the earlier generation of collectors, who showed independent judgement in their acquisitions, made from a genuine love of painting, had increasingly been replaced by individuals with no pretensions to knowledge or taste, who regarded works of art either as investments or as a bid for social recognition, and who therefore bought largely on the advice of dealers.[2] Agnew's, for example, played an instrumental role in the formation of the majority of important collections made in Great Britain during the latter part of the nineteenth century. As early as 1859 Millais was writing, with Gambart in mind: 'There is no chance of my selling pictures *to gentlemen* – the dealers are too strong. Picture-buyers can barter with them when they cannot with the artists ...' Nevertheless, since it was to their own interest to do so, dealers such as Agnew's and Gambart asked consistently high prices for the living artists whom they represented; and this was equally the case with the established artists of earlier periods. For by now the presence of leading British genre painters had become as obligatory in art collections of any standing as the Old Masters had once been; and as a result the competition for prizes at auctions ensured a continuing demand for such artists as Morland, Wilkie, Mulready, Collins, Webster and Landseer. The phenomenal rise in the value of pictures of the native school became apparent, as has been said, at the great Gillot sale of 1872, at which Agnew's was a leading buyer. For example, this firm bid 3,550 guineas for Webster's scene of a family feast, *Roast Pig*, which Gillot had commissioned ten years earlier for 700 guineas.

The control of the copyright of pictures which they had acquired contributed not only to the wealth of dealers, but also to their power in furthering the reputations of the artists concerned. In particular, there was a lucrative traffic in the sale of proofs, which were offered in a variety of categories to avid collectors.[3] On the other hand, when photographic methods of reproduction began to replace engravings during the 1870s, cheap prints were circulated more widely than ever before. Whereas a steel engraving might cost two pounds, photogravures of pictures could be sold for a shilling each, and there was no limit to the size of editions which could be printed.

The cause of British art was perhaps best served, however, by the public galleries which were coming into existence at this period. Among the most important were the City of Birmingham Museum and Art Gallery (1867), the Walker Art Gallery, Liverpool (1877), Manchester City Art Galleries (1882), the Guildhall Art Gallery, London (1886), the Mappin Art Gallery, Sheffield (1887), and the Leeds City Art Gallery (1888). Of the function of these institutions Charles Kingsley wrote: 'Picture galleries should be the townsman's paradise of refreshment', transporting him from 'the grim city world of stone and iron, smokey chimneys, and roaring wheels, into the world of beautiful things.' In 1899 the Walker Art Gallery described the principles governing its acquisitions in terms that applied to other municipal museums:

> When purchasing pictures the Committee has borne in mind that the collection is intended to foster a taste for art amongst the people, and with this in view they have frequently chosen subjects of popular character, such as appeal to our common sympathies and delineating domestic scenes and every day incidents of life. By this means very large numbers of the working classes have been attracted to the Gallery and it is gratifying to know that they carry with them to their homes vivid impressions of a refining and elevating character.

Such a policy was clearly in accordance with the tastes of potential benefactors, who were largely drawn from the industrial middle class in the surrounding area; and as a result these galleries from the first became important repositories of contemporary genre art. Of the 130 pictures listed in the first catalogue of the Leeds Art Gallery in 1898, virtually all were by nineteenth-century British painters. Some of these institutions were fortunate enough to receive at the outset large founding gifts from discriminating collectors, such as the bequests of the Mappins at Sheffield, of Charles Gassiott at the Guildhall, of John Burton at York, of Sidney Cartwright at Wolverhampton, and of Alfred Ashton at Tunbridge Wells, each of which consisted largely of representative subject pictures by leading British artists of the time.

Millais is often cited as the prime example of a Victorian artist of indisputable genius whose pliability to tides of popular taste sapped the brilliant promise of his early career. Whether he was the victim of his own virtuosity through too great a readiness to please, or whether he deliberately exploited opportunities for the material reward they brought, his career offers many instances of the corrupting pressures with which the succcessful artist had to contend in late Victorian times.[4] The inducements to conform to current fashions are illustrated by Millais' portraits of young girls, latter-day versions of the 'fancy piece' in the manner of Reynolds. Indeed, one of his first ventures in this vein, *Cherry Ripe* (1879, *fig. 188*), was painted in direct imitation of the master. The sitter was Edie Ramage, niece of the editor of *Graphic*. Millais had

Fig. 190
Sir John Everett Millais
Bubbles
1886

TOP

Fig. 188

Sir John Everett Millais

Cherry Ripe

1881, engraving by Samuel Cousins

ABOVE

Fig. 189

Sir Joshua Reynolds

Penelope Boothby

1874, engraving by Samuel Cousins

been struck by her appearance at a fancy dress ball, dressed as Reynolds' portrait of *Penelope Boothby* (1789, *fig. 189*), and for a fee of a thousand guineas had accepted the commission to paint her in her costume. A comparison between the two portraits is instructive. Millais', ingratiating as it is, lacks the disarming candour, the fugitive grace and wistfulness that characterize Reynolds' child portraits. The Victorian miss seems a little too aware of her charms, too self-conscious in her desire to win the viewer. In James' phrase there is an element of sentimental 'goodiness' that strikes an artificial note. Yet, the contemporary public had no such reservations. The Christmas supplement of *Graphic* in which *Cherry Ripe* appeared as a wood engraving sold out of 600,000 copies, and it is said the figure could have reached a million if the supply had been available. Samuel Cousins then made a mezzotint which, in the words of the artist's son, 'found its way into the remotest parts of the English-speaking world, and everywhere that sweet presentment of English childhood won the hearts of the people. From Australian miners, Canadian backwoodsmen, South African trekkers, and all sorts and conditions of colonial residents, came to the artist letters of warmest congratulation, some of which stirred his heart by the deep emotion they expressed.'[5]

In 1886 Millais exhibited his best-known child picture, *Bubbles (fig. 190)*, a portrait of his four-year-old grandson Willie (later to become Admiral Sir William James). The broken flowerpot by the seated boy, which is inexplicable except as a *memento mori*, indicates that the artist was also aware of the traditional meaning of bubble-blowing as an emblem for the fleeting nature of illusions; but there is no evidence that popular appreciation of the picture penetrated deeper than acclaim for the artist's success in capturing a child's wondering delight in a familiar pastime. The work was promptly purchased along with the copyright by Sir William Ingram, who published it as a coloured supplement to the Christmas number of the *Illustrated London News* (1887). Prior to its appearance, *Bubbles* was again sold with copyright, for £2,200, to the firm that manufactured Pears Soap, and subsequently achieved world-wide fame as an advertisement. Since the print included a bar of soap, Pears' manager had to secure the artist's permission to make this change in the original, and Millais' initial expressions of displeasure over the commercial end to which his picture had been put were probably motivated less by personal disapproval than by the hostile comments which greeted this apparent abdication of artistic principle. It should be said, however, that the artist had clearly painted the subject in the first instance with no suspicion that it would become the forerunner of a new type of patronage.[6]

Offsetting the frivolity of pictures designed primarily to catch the popular fancy in the 1870s and 1880s were two significant developments from serious genre painting of the preceding generation. One of these was concerned with pressing economic issues of the age, and displayed a deepening social awareness fostered by the press. Up until this time painters had tended to ignore life among the very poor. For such scenes one must turn to illustrations of a sensational kind appearing in the cheap tabloids, the *Illustrated Times* and *Penny Illustrated Paper*, or to the documentary evidence supplied by the engravings based on photographs used to illustrate Henry Mayhew's great sociological treatise, *London Labour and the London Poor* (1861–2).[7] During the 1860s a tragically short-lived trio, Arthur Boyd Houghton, George John Pinwell (1842–75) and Frederick Walker (1840–75), shared a deeply felt concern for the lot of the underprivileged. Their best work was in black-and-white and watercolour, though with occasional oils worked up from these media, and is distinguished by a clear-eyed yet compassionate confrontation of facts usually ignored in contemporary art. Of the three, Walker had the most influence on subsequent artists. His portrayal of a gipsy family in *The Vagrants* (1868, *fig. 191*) shows the statuesque dignity which he attributed to the poor in enduring their hard lot.

A more burning sense of social neglect entered British journalism with the appearance in 1869 of *Graphic*, an illustrated weekly edited by William Luson Thomas, a wood-engraver with a strong faith in the power of illustrations to influence public opinion.[8] Among the gifted group of artists whom Thomas enlisted in his campaign against poverty and injustice, and whose reputations *Graphic* helped establish, three were outstanding: Sir Luke Fildes (1843–1927), Sir Hubert von Herkomer (1849–1914) and Frank Holl (1845–88).

In the first issue of *Graphic*, 4 December 1869, was a wood-engraving by Fildes, entitled *Houseless and Hungry*. Millais showed it to Dickens, who was so enthusiastic that he promptly commissioned Fildes to illustrate *The Mystery of Edwin Drood*, unfinished at the time of Dickens' death in 1870. Of the origin of this scene, set in St Martin's-in-the-Fields on a wintry night, Fildes wrote: 'I had been to a dinner party, I think, and happened to return by a police-station, when I saw an awful crowd of poor wretches applying for permits to lodge in the Casual Ward. I made a note of the scene and after that often went again, making friends with the policeman and talking with the people themselves.' In the years immediately afterwards the engraving evolved through many changes into the very large oil painting entitled *Applicants for Admission to a Casual Ward* (1874, *fig. 192*). At precisely this time naturalism was becoming an influential concept in literature and the arts; and Fildes showed a Zola-like regard for fidelity to the evidence of his eyes in building up his study of the 'poor wretches' who were applying for tickets which entitled them, under the Houseless Poor Act, to a night's free shelter and food in the casual ward of a workhouse. The twenty-one figures in the composition were actual portraits of vagrants whom Fildes had encountered in his nightly wanderings and persuaded to sit for him.

Despite its melancholy subject, *Applicants for Admission* achieved immediate popularity when exhibited at the Royal Academy, a barricade being erected to protect it from the admiring crowds, and the artist being hailed as 'Hogarth's successor'.[9] Perhaps the most original aspect of Fildes' conception is that it does not isolate individual cases for the viewer's sympathy, but rather projects a corporate image of an entire stratum of the social order condemned to deprivation and suffering. To lend weight to the picture's implicit criticism of a society in which such conditions were allowed to exist, it was accompanied when placed on view by the following ominous quotation from a letter by Dickens: 'Dumb, wet, silent horrors! Sphinxes set up against that dead wall, and none likely to be at the pains of solving them until the *general overthrow*.' The placards on the wall at the back inject an additional element of satire into the scene. One reads: 'Child Deserted £2 Reward'; another advertises: 'Lost, a Pug Dog, £20 Reward'.

Herkomer, the son of a Bavarian wood-engraver, was himself trained as an illustrator, studying for a time under Fildes. His first great artistic success was *The Last Muster* (1875), which portrayed the death of an old pensioner among his fellows at Sunday morning chapel in the Royal Hospital, Chelsea. The subject had originally appeared as an illustration in *Graphic* in 1871. It was followed by a second painting, *Eventide – A Scene in the Westminster Union* (1878), a pathetic study of elderly female inmates in a London workhouse, which exhibits the same sympathetic grasp of group identity observed in Fildes' *Applicants for Admission*. 'These poor old bodies', the artist wrote in a letter, 'formed a most touching picture. Work they would, for industry was still in them, but it was of the most childish work – still, it *was* work. The agony of threading their needles was affecting indeed.' Herkomer, in the words of his biographer, J. Saxon Mills, 'was always impressed with the historical aspect of the artist's calling. One of the most important functions of the artist, he believed, was to reproduce and interpret the spirit of his own age in characteristic scenes for the benefit of generations to come.' The regard for documentary accuracy of Herkomer and his associates who worked for *Graphic* was, of course, in accord with their goal. 'The more reality I could put into the painting,' Herkomer once said, 'the more it became true history painting.'

The period from the mid-1870s, a time of severe hardship among the working class, was commemorated by two of Herkomer's most powerful works: *Pressing to the West* (1884), dealing with the theme of emigration, and *Hard Times* (1885, *fig. 193*). The setting of the latter was a country road near the painter's home at Bushey Heath in Hertfordshire, which became known as 'Hard Times Lane'. It depicts a migrant farm worker, accompanied by his wife and two small children, momentarily resting by the wayside, exhausted by his search for work. Although the empty road winding into the distance seems to symbolize the bleakness of his prospects, the man's pose conveys a sense of heroic fortitude modelled on Fred Walker's treatment of similar subjects; and the grouping of the family members, with the weary mother cradling her baby, suggests the rest on the flight into Egypt in secular guise.

Frank Holl was a finer painter than either Fildes or Herkomer, and his reputation was already established before the founding of *Graphic*, for which he worked extensively during the 1870s. Holl's self-appointed mission was in his own words 'to illustrate modern society', but by temperament he was inclined to view its darker side. The titles of his paintings reflect this attraction to sombre subjects, especially ones shadowed by death: *The Lord gave and the Lord hath taken away* (1869), *No Tidings from the Sea* (1871), *Deserted – A Foundling* (1874), *The Village Funeral* (1874), *The Funeral of the First Born* (1876), *Widowed* (1879). Many of Holl's pictures were transcriptions from scenes which he had actually witnessed, as was the case with his masterpiece, *Newgate – Committed for Trial* (1878, *fig. 194*), which concerned a bank clerk who had embezzled funds and was shortly to be sentenced to five years' imprisonment. The setting was the so-called 'cage' at Newgate, where the family and friends of the prisoners were allowed brief conversations with them through two sets of bars, separated by a walkway for the warder in charge. In the interests of verisimilitude the artist dressed the women and children in ragged garments collected from second-hand shops in East London. Writing in *The Magazine of Art* (1891), Walter Shaw Sparrow remarked on the narrative implications of the scene: 'The characters are so real in this fine work that one feels there is a story to be told of ruined ambitions, of broken home ties, of devotion scorned and trampled underfoot.' The guilt-stricken appearance of the two culprits, seen full face but in shadow, is dramatically played off against the highlighted groupings of the two wives with their

OVERLEAF LEFT ABOVE

Fig. 191
Frederick Walker
The Vagrants
1868

OVERLEAF LEFT BELOW

Fig. 192
Sir Luke Fildes
Applicants for Admission to a Casual Ward
1874

OVERLEAF RIGHT ABOVE

Fig. 193
Sir Hubert von Herkomer
Hard Times
1885

OVERLEAF RIGHT BELOW

Fig. 194
Frank Holl
Newgate – Committed for Trial
1878

children, whose attitudes express, along with lasting devotion, incredulity at their betrayal by loved ones and fear of what the future may hold in store.

The naturalistic vein of genre painting encouraged by *Graphic* was a short-lived phenomenon. The works which it produced, with a few exceptions, never achieved a popularity as great as their notoriety among a public which did not like its art to confront the harsher realities of life. Quite apart from the distastefulness of the subject-matter, furthermore, social realism called for a kind of reportage more appropriate to its journalistic origins, and which was beginning to be better served by the medium of photography.[10] The last important examples of the mode were two pictures exhibited in 1891: Herkomer's *On Strike*, occasioned by the Great Dock Strike of that year; and Fildes' perennially popular *The Doctor*, commissioned by Sir Henry Tate at a cost of £3,000 for presentation to the nation. Ironically enough, Holl, Herkomer and Fildes all turned away from the contemporary scene to pursue lucrative careers as portrait painters of the rich and famous.

Meanwhile, problem pictures of a very different kind enjoyed a continuing vogue. These were concerned not with issues affecting society at large, but rather with the

Fig. 195
James Abbott McNeill Whistler
Wapping on Thames
1860–4

Fig. 196
James Abbott McNeill Whistler
The White Girl (Symphony in White, No. 1)
1861–2

drama of private lives. They dealt with the manners and morals of the economically stable middle and upper classes rather than with living conditions among the depressed orders of society; and the appeal was directed rather to viewers' psychological acuity than to their capacity for humanitarian sympathy. Furthermore, the overt appeal for emotional response in the work of the social realists was replaced by a quality of reticence in the portrayal of scenes so intimate in nature as to convert the viewer into an eavesdropper on secrets not meant for sharing.

It is not uncommon for artists trained in foreign traditions to be more sensitive to the emergence of new aesthetic tendencies in their adopted countries than those who are native-born. Such was the case with James Abbott McNeill Whistler (1834–1903), American by birth and schooled in Paris when the influence of Courbet's realism was still dominant. On arriving in London in 1859, Whistler fell under the spell of the Thames; and for a period he lived below London Bridge in Rotherhithe, where he recorded the teeming marine activity of the Pool of London. When his Thames series of etchings was exhibited in Paris in 1862, Baudelaire immediately recognized the magic with which they evoked the 'poésie profonde et compliquée d'une vaste capitale'. Related to these plates is an oil, entitled *Wapping on Thames (fig. 195)*, begun as early as 1860 but carried on until 1864 through a series of alterations which tended to diminish its original narrative content. The setting was the Angel Inn in Rotherhithe looking across through dense and meticulously rendered shipping activity to the north side of the river. The artist's red-haired Irish mistress, Joanna Hiffernan, the French expatriate artist Alphonse Legros, who resided in London from 1863, and an unnamed sailor were the models for the three figures. The portraits of actual individuals intimately grouped within an identifiable setting gives the picture something of the semblance of a conversation piece. But an atmosphere of ambiguity, even of submerged tension in the relationship of the trio, is produced by the oblique, Degas-like perspective in which the figures, cut off and in shadow, occupy only a fraction of the canvas.

While Whistler was occupied with *Wapping*, he also produced one of the earliest of his important figural studies, *The White Girl*, painted in Paris in 1861–2 *(fig. 196)*. Rejected by the Royal Academy and by the French Salon, it became the sensation of the Salon des Refusés in 1863, along with Manet's *Déjeuner sur l'Herbe*. The model was again Jo Hiffernan; and the artist was to insist – in repudiating the suggestion that he had been inspired by the heroine of Wilkie Collins' novel, *The Woman in White* – that the picture had been conceived in purely painterly terms to exploit patterns of colour.[11] Yet, on his first arrival in England Whistler had been drawn to the elements of mystery and strangeness inherent in Millais' *Apple Blossoms* and *The Vale of Rest* (1858); and one can hardly fail to recognize the kinship of *The White Girl* with the Pre-Raphaelite vision of distraught femininity. To the French critic, Jules Antoine Castagnary, the model's pose suggested '*le lendemain de l'épousée, cette minute troublante où la jeune femme s'interroge et s'étonne de ne plus reconnaître en elle sa virginité de la veille.*'[12] And certainly the contrast between the virginal whiteness of the girl's gown and her flushed and overstrained countenance in its burning aureole of dishevelled hair projects disturbing sexual implications, intensified by such emblematic details as the lily drooping from listless fingers, the blossoms wilting on the bearskin rug, and the virile threat of the animal's expressive muzzle.

As he moved through successive stages of experimentation to the final manner of the *Nocturnes*, Whistler was to eliminate all grounds for literal interpretation from his work;[13] but the native influences to which he was subject during his early years in England were transmitted to a French artist who took up residence in London following the fall of the Commune in 1871. Born in Nantes, Jacques-Joseph Tissot (1836–1902), who later took the name of James, shared Whistler's love of marine activities. Among the canvases painted soon after his arrival from France, which reveal his intimate knowledge of shipping, is *The Last Evening* (1873, *fig. 197*).[14] While the narrative content is considerably more explicit than in Whistler's *Wapping*, it is no less ambiguous. On the eve of the ship's departure, the owner has come on board to give last-minute instructions to the captain. These are of sufficient interest to hold the attention of the young girl eavesdropping in the rear. The couple in the foreground curiously duplicates the colloquy of the pair on the bench, in the anxiety with which the young officer regards his companion and in the pensive air with which she submits to his scrutiny. Her languorous posture, reclining beneath a travelling rug in a chair surely provided just for her, suggests that she is an invalid, perhaps so ill that

Fig. 197

James Jacques Joseph Tissot
The Last Evening
1873

Fig. 198
James Jacques Joseph Tissot
The Convalescent
*c*1875–6

this is quite literally their 'last evening' together. Is she a widow, as her dress might indicate, the daughter of the ship-owner and mother of the girl, or the intended of the officer? The artist provides no answers. It is for the viewer to imagine a story adequate to account for the air of finality that so poignantly shrouds the scene.

Tissot's portrait by Degas shows him in his affected role of dandy; and his almost exclusive concern with scenes of high life in his English paintings won him an unmerited reputation for frivolity. Ruskin said of his paintings that they were 'mere coloured photographs of vulgar society': and for the Goncourts he was 'cet ingénieux exploiteur de la bêtise anglaise'. Such comments do less than justice to Tissot's brilliance as a historian of manners; nor do they recognize the brooding note of mutability that infuses these sparkling scenes with a mood of Proustian nostalgia. This note became increasingly perceptible in Tissot's work from 1876, the year in which he formed a secret liaison with a mysterious divorcee, Kathleen Newton. During the following six years, until her death from tuberculosis at the age of twenty-eight, her sad-eyed beauty dominates the artist's canvases.

Mrs Newton is the central figure in the picture *The Convalescent* (*c*1875–6, *fig. 198*), shown in a posture similar to that of the reclining woman in *The Last Evening*. Her indolence is in marked contrast to the alert manner of the older woman behind, who has looked up from her book as if in alarm. Although there are only two cups on the tea-tray, the man's hat and walking-stick on the empty chair indicate that a male visitor is inexplicably absent. The setting for this picture was the garden of Tissot's house at 17 Grove End Road, St John's Wood. Despite the title,[15] the woman's white gown and shawl stand out with pall-like vividness against the dark waters of the pool, imparting a sense of foreboding that is intensified by the autumn colours of the chestnut leaves hanging over her.

On Mrs Newton's death in November 1882, Tissot returned to France, heartbroken, henceforth to devote himself largely to religious subjects. Among his last pictures painted in England was a Hogarthian 'progress', entitled *The Prodigal Son in Modern Life* (1882).[16] In such works he might well have been responding, like his contemporary, Constantin Guys, to the challenge of Baudelaire in his comment on the Salon of 1845: '... l'héroisme de la vie moderne nous entoure et nous presse ... Celui-là sera le peintre, le vrai peintre, qui saura arracher à la vie actuelle son côté épique, et nous faire voir et comprendre, avec de la couleur ou du dessin, combien nous sommes grands et poétiques dans nos cravates et nos bottes vernies.'[17]

Tissot's sensitivity to nuances of polite social behaviour was shared by Sir William Quiller Orchardson (1832–1910). Senior among the group of brilliant pupils who studied under Robert Scott Lauder in Edinburgh in the middle of the century, Orchardson, who came to London from Scotland in 1862, built his early reputation on costume pieces of historical and literary genre. He once told his daughter 'that what appealed to him personally' in choosing subject-matter 'was the dramatic moment'; and his instinct for the precise instant which lays bare the heart of a situation is especially apparent in the episodes from contemporary life to which he turned in his later career.

Orchardson's masterpieces are the pair entitled *Mariage de Convenance* (1883, fig. 199) and *Mariage de Convenance – After!* (1886, fig. 200),[18] which present in truncated form a Victorian version of Hogarth's *Marriage A-la-Mode (figs 10–12)*. The artist was a master of tell-tale facial expressions and gestures, in the Scottish tradition of characterization descending from Wilkie; and in *Mariage de Convenance* the postures of husband and wife project a marriage at breaking point. She sits in bored and sullen introspection before her untasted meal, pondering over the happiness which she has forfeited through contracting marriage with a wealthy older man. Her husband's puzzled glance expresses a blend of resentment and in-comprehension, along with a pretence of male authority fortified by the butler's obsequious presence at his end of the table. Orchardson was particularly adept at placing figures within the picture area; and here the empty space surrounding the pair contributes to the sense of apartness created by the length of table separating them, and at the same time provides a visual analogy to the pall of silence which has replaced any effort at communication between the pair. It is sometimes said that Orchardson's pictured stories are conceived in theatrical terms; but they are equally akin to the scenes of a novelist such as Henry James, the impact of which lies below the verbal surface in the realm of inference and suggestion.

Orchardson had originally planned to call the pendant to the preceding picture *Ichabod*, with its Biblical connotation, 'the glory that is departed from Israel'; but the utter desolation emanating from *Mariage de Convenance – After!* needs no gloss. The figure slumped in the chair is unwarmed by the fire in the grate. Nor does the splendour of the familiar surroundings now bolster the broken pride of the deserted husband, to whose state of mind the untouched wine glass beside the full decanter on the table bears witness. The spiritless droop of head and shoulders, the helpless hands and splayed feet make up an image of solitude without reprieve.

Fig. 199
Sir William Quiller Orchardson
Mariage de Convenance
1883

Fig. 200
Sir William Quiller Orchardson
Mariage de Convenance – After!
1886

Fig. 201
Sir Frank (Francis Bernard)
Dicksee
The Confession
1896

Orchardson's daughter narrates a revealing anecdote about a picture showing 'a young man and a young woman sitting on a sofa together'. She inquired: 'But whatever is it? Are they quarrelling? Or has he proposed or been refused? Or does he want to propose but feels afraid?' 'I don't know,' her father replied, 'it might be any of these things, it is an enigma.'[19] The sophisticated vogue for a type of problem picture which involved the viewer in its interpretation persisted to the end of the century. In 1896 Sir Frank (Francis Bernard) Dicksee (1853–1928), future President of the Royal Academy, painted an intentionally ambiguous work, entitled *The Confession (fig. 201)*. The deep shadow into which the male figure has been cast and the strained tendons of the hand which he presses to his head suggest that he is the confessor, and that the nature of his revelation is intensely painful. From the fact that she wears a wedding-ring, we may assume that the listener is his wife, while the stark lighting, which by contrast throws her expression and posture into such strong relief, symbolically conveys the flood-tide of awareness sweeping over her. In arresting the situation at its climactic moment, the artist thus challenges the viewer to draw his own conclusions about its implications for future relations between the couple.

Equally evocative of sexual conflict and indeterminate in its outcome is *The Doll's House* (1899, *fig. 202*), by Sir William Rothenstein (1872–1945). The artist had seen and greatly admired Ibsen's play with Janet Achurch in the role of the emancipated wife, Nora, and had subsequently met the actress through Bernard Shaw. The picture was painted at Vattetot in Normandy, where Rothenstein and his wife Alice were spending their honeymoon in the summer of 1896. Alice was the original of the woman in the scene, and the painter, Augustus John, posed for her companion. It is said that the episode represents the moment in the play when Mrs Linden and Krogstad are listening for the end of the dance on the floor above; but in retrospect

Fig. 202
Sir William Rothenstein
The Doll's House
1899

John recalled no literary reference for the emotional crisis shown in the picture. In his introduction to the catalogue of Rothenstein's Memorial Exhibition (1950) he wrote:

> This is a regular problem picture. I am portrayed standing at the foot of a staircase upon which Alice has unaccountably seated herself. I appear to be ready for the road, for I am carrying a mackintosh on my arm and am shod and hatted. But Alice seems to hesitate. Can she have changed her mind at the last moment? But what could have been her intention? Perhaps the weather has changed for the worse and made a promenade inadvisable: but we shall never know. The picture will remain a perpetual enigma, to disturb, fascinate or repel.

The last two decades of the nineteenth century marked the noticeable decline of a tradition of British genre painting which had survived with undiminished vigour for a century and a half. As all that has gone before shows, it was an indigenous tradition, sustained through its inherent vitality and responsiveness to social change. Even in the rare cases when it derived stimulus from Continental artistic trends, these were so thoroughly assimilated that there can never be any hesitation in identifying an eighteenth- or nineteenth-century British painting as belonging to the native school. The transmission from one generation to the next of generic characteristics in the choice and handling of subject was largely due to the fact that the great majority of artists specializing in genre had been schooled on home ground, and painted for a popular audience with whose tastes they were fully in accord.

By the 1870s, however, young painters were finding the discipline of the Royal Academy schools so stultifying that in increasing numbers they crossed the Channel to study under Continental masters, whose methods of instruction were more liberal. And what they brought home with them was a concept of realism based largely on execution, in which the making of a picture became an end in itself, its success, quite irrespective of subject, conditioned by the artist's skill in manipulating such purely formal properties as design, tone, and texture. Meanwhile, in England art for art's sake had found its champion in Whistler, whose 'Ten O'Clock Lecture' delivered in 1885 preached that art has no ulterior purpose but is 'occupied with her own perfection only'. Commenting on the effect of Continental training on British painters towards the end of the nineteenth century, George Moore declared: '. . . one thing really comes home to the careful observer, and that is, the steady obliteration of all English feeling and mode of thought. The younger men practise an art purged of all nationality.'

Yet few English artists were prepared to follow Whistler's example in sacrificing content to abstract compositional harmonies. While they admired Corot and the Barbizon painters, they drew the line at Impressionism. Thus, they continued to turn to the world about them for subject-matter, although moralistic bias was increasingly frowned on, the emphasis on narrative content was greatly reduced, and types tended to take the place of individual characterization. At one time or another most of the artists schooled in the new artistic theories from France and the Low Countries exhibited their work at the New English Art Club some time after its establishment in 1886. Of these paintings Sickert was to write in 1910: 'The New English Art Club picture has tended to be a composite product in which an educated colour vision has been applied to themes already long approved and accepted in this country.'

The most convenient blanket term to describe the new mode of painting is *pleinairisme*, since whatever their individual differences, all artists caught up in the movement subscribed to the creed, already proclaimed by the Pre-Raphaelites, that the colours and atmospheric effects of the natural world could only be captured in pictures painted on the spot. Among the first painters who endeavoured to put this principle into practice was a group which gathered at the fishing village of Newlyn in Cornwall from about 1882. The mild climate and predominance of grey days with their suffused light provided ideal conditions for painting out-of-doors the year round. The circle took as its mentor the French painter Jules Bastien-Lepage (1848–84), whose early death at the age of thirty-six ended a career more remarkable for its influence than for its actual achievement. Lepage's portraits of French peasants owe much to the example of Millet, and it was perhaps as much the humanity underlying his vision as the impartial realism of the methods by which he sought to translate it into paint that endeared him to the Newlyn school.

The Newlyn painters felt deep sympathy with the Cornish fishermen and their families, whose existence they shared; and the *plein-air* techniques learned from Lepage could not in their opinion be better employed than in rendering the lives of these people in their natural environment. In 1901 Stanhope Alexander Forbes (1857–1947), the leading member of the group, was to say that more and more he had come 'to see his past work as a visual record documenting changing scenes and customs'. In this statement Forbes aligned himself with such artists as Wilkie and Frith, for whom genre was a form of history painting.

Forbes took up residence in Newlyn in 1884, after studying at Bonnat's studio in Paris and spending several summers painting in Brittany. Of his first important oil, the large canvas entitled *A Fish Sale on a Cornish Beach (fig. 203)* exhibited at the Royal Academy in 1885, Wilfrid Meynell wrote in 1892: 'It was a picture which, besides being delightful in itself, awakened expectations, and those expectations have since been realised. If it did not make an era in English Art, it began to make one.' For his subject the artist chose a scene made familiar by generations of genre painters, but here presented with a new immediacy through its handling of tonal harmonies. A luminous pearly glow suffuses the entire scene, its subtle gradations carrying the eye from the substantial figures in the foreground to the groupings in the middle distance reflected in the wet sands, and ultimately over the waters gently lapping the beach to the sails of the fishing fleet silhouetted against the high horizon. Absorbed in the enveloping atmosphere, individual details blend in a totality of impression in which the viewer fairly smells and feels the salt dampness of the beach, with its fish laid out for sale.

Plein-air methods were equally applicable to interior scenes; and three of Forbes' finest achievements, *The Village Philharmonic* (1888), *The Health of the Bride* (1889) and *By Order of the Court* (1890), all traditionally popular genre subjects, were of that type. Another memorable example by a Newlyn painter, Frank Bramley (1857–1915), is *A Hopeless Dawn* (1888, *fig. 204*). In a dawn-lit cottage room looking out on a stormy sea two women keep vigil for the son and husband who has not returned from the fishing grounds. The bowed head of the older woman and the limp hand of the wife collapsed across her knees express loss of hope. This is eloquently confirmed by such details as the candle placed as a beacon in the window and which has guttered out, the

Fig. 203
Stanhope Alexander Forbes
A Fish Sale on a Cornish Beach
1885

supper laid out and turned cold, and the open Bible beneath the window. That there might be no mistaking its message the catalogue entry for the picture when exhibited at the Royal Academy bore a quotation from Ruskin, beginning: 'Human effort and sorrow going on perpetually from age to age; waves rolling for ever and winds moaning, and faithful hearts wasting and sickening for ever, and brave lives dashed away about the rattling beach like weeds for ever . . .'

Alice Meynell, in her pioneer article on Newlyn in the *Art Journal* (1889), recognized that Bramley's painting invited a more aesthetic response as well: 'The picture is complete, whether as a study of sorrow, or as that of a little grey window letting in cold daylight into a room where the candles are dying . . .' The presence of windows as the principal source of illumination is, of course, a commonplace feature of genre pictures with indoor settings; but in previous periods this device had been employed primarily to lead the viewer's eye to salient narrative aspects of the scene without regard for truthfulness in the dispersion of light. In *A Hopeless Dawn* the illumination is so handled as to become the chief medium not only for elucidating the story, but also for organizing its compositional features and establishing the tonal values from which the work's emotional appeal in large part derives.

A second artistic movement exactly contemporary with that at Newlyn grew up in the west of Scotland, where a loosely associated coterie of painters acquired the name of the 'Glasgow boys'. While in its later phase this school developed a more decorative manner, it shared at the outset the Newlyn affinities with French theory and practice, especially the *plein-air* teaching of Bastien-Lepage. A further important source of influence, transmitted through the example of Scott Lauder's pupils, George Paul Chalmers (1833–78) and Hugh Cameron (1835–1918), was the low-key realism of members of the Hague School (in turn influenced by Millet and Barbizon), whose members included Bosboom, the brothers Maris, Mauve and, above all, Jozef Israëls.

The Scottish painters found from the outset a ready audience among collectors in Glasgow, which had become an industrial centre of international importance. Such enlightened picture-dealers as the Aberdonian Daniel Cottier, his agent Craibe Angus, who opened a gallery in Glasgow in 1874, and Alex Reid who followed soon after, cultivated a taste for contemporary French and Dutch painting, while patronizing their Scottish counterparts. And the Glasgow Institute of the Fine Arts, founded in 1861, held throughout the 1870s and 1880s a series of exhibitions of contemporary paintings in which works by Continental and native artists were hung together. The Glasgow school received its ultimate cachet in the number of examples shown at the great international exhibitions of 1886 and 1888 in Edinburgh and Glasgow, while an equally strong representation at the Grosvenor Gallery in London helped spread their reputation first to Munich, and then to cities throughout Europe and the United States during the following decade.

Like the Newlyn painters, their Glasgow contemporaries sought to give elevation to subject-matter chosen from the humblest walks of life. The fishing population of the former was replaced by Scottish peasantry, shown among the cabbage patches, chicken runs and duck ponds which circumscribed its daily existence. But, again like the Newlynites, the Glasgow boys were anything but provincial in their treatment of this banal material. Although the majority had received training in Continental studios, two who were largely self-taught, Sir James Guthrie (1859–1930) and

Fig. 204
Frank Bramley
A Hopeless Dawn
1888

Edward Arthur Walton (1860–1922), defined the approaches to realistic genre painting followed by their group of fellow artists. After his early success, *Funeral Service in the Highlands* (1882) in the muted style of Israëls, and after a visit to Paris, in *A Hind's Daughter* (1883, *fig. 205*) Guthrie turned to the *plein-air* manner of Lepage. Painted at Cockburnspath in Berwickshire, and devoid of narrative content or any expressive demand on the viewer's sympathies, the picture makes its appeal through the play of colour harmonies which, in uniting the girl with her rustic surroundings, imparts a grave beauty to her menial task of picking cabbages. *The Daydream* (1885, *fig. 206*) by Walton transmutes the reveries of two peasant children into an idyll of young love. The wistful, wide-eyed girl and her brooding companion are held in the embrace of the landscape of which they seem a part, and yet are lost in incomprehension of the natural forces impelling them towards each other.

A far more original artist was William McTaggart (1835–1910), who was held in high esteem by the Glasgow boys, although he was never closely affiliated with them. His career is a paradigm of the transition from traditional narrative genre to the kind of painting in which subject survived only in its pictorial aspect. *The Past and the Present* (1860, *fig. 207*), originally called *The Builders*, typifies McTaggart's manner at the beginning of his career. It represents five children making a structure of bricks by the chapel ruins of Kilchousland, overlooking Kilbrannan Sound. The figures within this romanticized setting are rendered with Pre-Raphaelite clarity; and this realism of treatment, combined with the philosophic reflections the scene has been designed to inspire, ally the work with the more typical examples of Victorian genre painting. McTaggart, however, went on rapidly to develop his own brand of vividly impressionistic painting, totally independent of French influence, but equally concerned with appearances as they are revealed by light. In a style characterized by great breadth of conception, prismatically sparkling colour, and exultantly free brushwork, he registered the outer world, drenched in sunlight or darkened by storm, but always alive and in motion. The play of the wind and the waves especially fascinated him, whether over open water or in commotion along coastal stretches. Figures continue to people these great seascapes, but were treated now as hardly more than animated specks in the whole vast panoramic drama unleashed by the elements. In the words of P. Mc'Omish Dott: 'The eye and the heart feel the presence of his figures without dwelling on them.' Painted in the same place as *The Past and the Present* but more than twenty years later, *North Wind, Kilbrannan Sound* (1883, *fig. 208*) illustrates the striking modernity of McTaggart's mature manner. The three children are barely discernible on the headland which shelters them. Yet in their excited response to the brisk gale that is blowing they are an essential part of the scene, caught up in the rhythmic dance of the waves sweeping across the dark blue sea.

As is apparent from these examples, children retained their popularity with later nineteenth-century painters of the contemporary scene, even though they filled new and very different pictorial roles. Indeed, the various ways in which they were depicted is an index to the conflicting styles competing for dominance. Representative of the later decorative phase of the Glasgow school was Edward Atkinson Hornel (1864–1933). He was a product of Verlat's studio in Antwerp, where he was encouraged to develop such breadth of handling that, as he said, 'one was painting and drawing at the same time'; and he further adopted from Adolphe Monticelli

OPPOSITE LEFT

Fig. 205
Sir James Guthrie
A Hind's Daughter
1883

OPPOSITE RIGHT

Fig. 206
Edward Arthur Walton
The Daydream
1885

LEFT

Fig. 207
William McTaggart
The Past and the Present
1860

BELOW

Fig. 208
William McTaggart
North Wind, Kilbrannan Sound
1883

(1824–86), an artist much admired in Scotland at that time, the use of a thick impasto which imparted to the bright colours of his canvases a mosaic-like glow. Painted in 1891, on the eve of his departure for Japan with George Henry (1858/60–1943), Hornel's *Summer* (1891, *fig. 209*) makes use of traditional motifs in its portrayal of two girls, one chasing butterflies and the other in the background tending cattle. Yet, as with McTaggart's *North Wind, Kilbrannan Sound*, the impersonality of the title indicates where the artist wished the emphasis to fall in viewing his work. The expressionistic fervour of handling and the rich tonality of the resulting surface pattern rhapsodically evoke the pageantry of high summer, into which the figures blend in exultant abandon.

Children paddling, Walberswick (*c*1889–94, *fig. 210*) by Philip Wilson Steer (1860–1942) is contemporary with Hornel's picture and similar in mood, yet exhibits very different technical resources. To the time-honoured subject of children playing by the seaside, exploited by such artists as William Collins and James Clarke Hook, Steer (after a brief period of study under Bouguereau and Cabanel in Paris) brought a full awareness of the methods of the Impressionists – especially Monet – and even in modified form of *pointilliste* procedures of rendering colour. The girls disporting themselves in the foreground are devoid of individuality; like every other detail in the beautifully harmonized composition, their forms and bright dresses are defined only by the blazing sunlight against the shimmering background of sand and sea. Yet, so ingrained was the inherited habit of attaching extraneous associations to paintings that George Moore, the inveterate enemy of pictorial narrative, could write of Steer's work:

> Paddling in the warm sea-water gives oblivion to those children. They forget their little worries in the sensation of sea and sand, as I forget mine in that dreamy blue which fades and deepens imperceptibly, like a flower from the intense heart to the delicate edge of the petals. . . . Happy sensation of daylight; a flower-like afternoon; little children paddling; the world is behind them; they are as flowers, and are conscious only of the benedictive influences of sand and sea and sky.

Another delightfully original vision of children at play is *Carnation, Lily, Lily, Rose* (1885–6, *fig. 211*), painted by the American artist John Singer Sargent (1856–1925) at about the time that he took up permanent residence in England. The picture, which derived its title from a popular song of the day, was painted out-of-doors at Broadway in Worcestershire. The models for the two girls lighting Chinese lanterns were the daughters of an artist friend, Frederick Barnard. In its notalgic mood, composed, as one writer has said, 'of transient light and evanescent youth', Sargent's picture is reminiscent of Millais' *Autumn Leaves (fig. 187)*, though with debts to Whistler and the current *japonisme*. In the mingled light of dusk and the lanterns, the lilies and rose trees, along with the girls' white dresses and the warm flesh tones of their faces, make up a symphony of delicately glowing colours.[20]

The British *pleinairistes*, like their Continental counterparts but unlike Whistler and the Impressionists, generally ignored the challenge of the city in their obsession with landscape. Their work was in this respect a continuation of the pastoral tradition going back to the preceding century. However, whereas country people had earlier been represented resting from their daily toil, there was now an insistence on the hard

OPPOSITE LEFT

Fig. 209

Edward Atkinson Hornel
Summer
1891

OPPOSITE RIGHT

Fig. 211

John Singer Sargent
Carnation, Lily, Lily, Rose
1885–6

OPPOSITE

Fig. 210

Philip Wilson Steer
Children paddling – Walberswick
*c*1889–94

Fig. 212
Sir George Clausen
Garden Allotments
1899

– and ennobling – realities of agricultural labour. The heroic stature accorded farm workers in the pictures of Jean François Millet was reflected in contemporary British painting; but the French artist's implacable portrayal of the peasant's bondage to the soil was replaced by the traditionally more idyllic English view. This tendency to idealize was related in turn to an increasingly nostalgic awareness of the passing of the ways of life being depicted, a sense far keener in industrialized Britain than in France with its more deep-rooted agricultural economy. Writing of the landscapist's art in 1882, Alice Meynell declared that a true artist

> would not wish to separate humanity from nature, and he knows that the sights and sounds and scents of labour – the husbandman at toil, the sound of a pickaxe in some distant quarry of the hills, the odour of smouldering weeds and leaves – should add to a landscape almost all its meaning and pathos. He would not banish the peasant from the land. . . . Man's rural labour does not disfigure the land, but man himself – English man, at least – undoubtedly requires idealising . . .

As has been stated, it was the short-lived Fred Walker, an early disciple of Millet, whose youthful study of classical sculpture in the British Museum helped to invest his sympathetic portraits of country types with an aura of nobility that established a pattern for treating such subjects. Herkomer, who was much influenced by Walker, wrote in 1893:

> In Walker we have the creator of the English Renaissance, for it was he who saw the possibility of combining the grace of the antique with the realism of our everyday life in England. His navvies are Greek gods, and yet not a bit less true to nature. . . . The dirty nails of a peasant, such as I have seen painted by a modern realist, were invisible to him. Nor did he leave out the faces of the peasants, in order to produce grandeur, as the French Millet did.

Walker's example led to the rustic idylls of such artists as George Heming Mason (1818–72) and Edward Stott (1859–1918), in which the pastoral vein of Samuel Palmer and Edward Calvert (1799–1883) re-emerged in a more atmospheric handling.

A greater degree of realism, with no loss of the subject's inherent dignity, appeared in the pictures of country people at their work by Sir George Clausen (1852–1944). An early trip through Belgium and Holland left the artist with a lasting regard for the genre style of those countries, and he was to come under the spell of Bastien-Lepage as well as Millet, while Peter Henry Emerson's (1856–1936) photographs of life in rural East Anglia were an additional formative influence.[21] Clausen has been called the Thomas Hardy of painting; and *Garden Allotments* (1899, *fig. 212*) shows how appropriate this was, as well as the painter's debt to Millet. The light of sunset throws into relief the timeless dignity of the two figures digging potatoes, while at the same time instilling sympathy with their hard lot.

The Man with the Scythe (*c*1896, *fig. 213*) by Henry Herbert La Thangue (1859–1929) illustrates the extent to which the naturalistic methods of the *pleinairistes* could accommodate more imaginative elements of genre painting. The mother's manner, a blend of incredulity and anxiety, indicates that she is just awakening to the fact that her invalid daughter has died while she was cutting cabbages. La Thangue was another leading follower of Bastien-Lepage and close friend of Stanhope Forbes,

Fig. 213
Henry Herbert La Thangue
The Man with the Scythe
*c*1896

although he was never a member of the Newlyn School; and the treatment of the rustic setting in this painting shows the matter-of-fact presentation of reality at which he and his fellows aimed, including the peasant with scythe pausing at the gate. This figure is also, of course, immediately identifiable as the traditional effigy of death, the grim reaper. This symbolic dimension startlingly enhances the pathos of the scene, while at the same time being quite consistent with the simple factual reference of all other details.

Whistler was one of the very few artists in Great Britain during the nineteenth century to derive inspiration from the modern metropolis;[22] and no one could pretend that his *Nocturnes* are anything other than a subjective response to the spectacle of night-time London.[23] For Walter Richard Sickert (1860–1942) London exercised an equally strong fascination. In his Introduction to the catalogue of 'London Impressionists' at the Goupil Gallery in 1889 he wrote that Impressionism 'does not admit the narrow interpretation of the word "Nature" which would stop short outside the four-mile radius. It is, on the contrary, strong in the belief that for those who live in the most wonderful and complex city in the world, the most fruitful course of study lies in a persistent effort to render the magic and the poetry which they daily see around them . . .' But while the urban scene stirred the same 'lyric impulse' in Sickert as in Whistler, Sickert was far more susceptible to the diverse forms of magic behind the façades of buildings and to the beauty lurking within the commonplace lives of their inhabitants. Stressing his rejection of the fashionably genteel in art, he declared in a piece in *Art News* (1910): 'The more art is serious, the more it will tend to avoid the drawing-room and stick to the kitchen. The plastic arts are gross arts, dealing joyously with gross material facts . . . and while they flourish in the scullery, or on the dunghill, they fade at a breath from the drawing-room.'

Although he was as much at home in France as in England and his manner was shaped under Impressionist influences, Sickert steadfastly upheld the British tradition of genre painting.[24] Virginia Woolf remembered a letter by Sickert in which he said that he had 'always been a literary painter, thank goodness, like all decent painters'; and writing in the *English Review* in 1912, he stated:

> It is just about a quarter of a century ago since I ranged myself . . . definitely against the Whistlerian anti-literary theory of drawing. All the greater draughtsmen tell a story. When people, who care about art, criticise the anecdotic 'Picture of the Year', the essence of our criticism is that the story is a poor one, poor in structure or poor as drama, poor as psychology. . . . A painter may tell his story like Balzac, or like Mr Hichens. He may tell it with relentless impartiality, he may pack it tight, until it is dense with suggestion and refreshment, or his dilute stream may trickle to its appointed crisis of adultery sown thick with deprecating and extenuating generalisations about 'sweet women'.[25]

The literary titles which Sickert was fond of attaching to his pictures call attention to their content, though they were certainly not originally conceived to illustrate ideas, and the naming of them was in no sense meant to distract attention from their artistic merits. For Sickert there could be no question as to the relative importance of subject and expression, since they were inseparable and mutually supporting aspects of the creative act.

Sickert, following in the footsteps of his maternal grandmother, had at the outset entered on an acting career; and it is not surprising, therefore, that he shared Hogarth's passion for the stage and that, also like Hogarth, his first important pictures, painted during the 1880s, were theatrical pieces. At the heart of the world of entertainment in late Victorian London was the music hall, and Sickert was its unrivalled artist-laureate. The most evocative of his paintings of the subject is perhaps *Little Dot Hetherington at the Bedford Music Hall* (c1888–9, *fig. 214*). Only on careful inspection does the viewer become aware that the entire scene is conveyed through its reflection in a mirror.[26] By this means the artist was able to encompass in a single focus the spotlit performance in its stage setting (which includes a second actor waiting in the wings) and the spectators in the theatre proper, thus capturing in graphic terms that close intimacy between entertainer and audience which constituted the major attraction of the music hall. Indeed, the organization of the picture knits this bond still tighter through Dot Hetherington's extended arm pointing at the box above the stage, as she sings (according to the picture's extended title) 'The Boy I love is up in the Gallery'. Sickert's treatment of the interaction in play-acting between make-believe and reality may bring to mind Hogarth's portrayal of *The Beggar's Opera (fig. 6)*, with its charged exchange of glances between the leading actress and her noble protector in the audience. Whereas Hogarth invites a serial reading of the details of his picture, however, the restricted focus and compositional density of Sickert's canvas formidably gathers its wealth of meaning within a single instantaneous impression. That Sickert was aiming at this immediacy of impact is apparent from a written comment of 1915, made with Hogarth specifically in mind: 'One of the things in which it seems to me that we have a right to speak of progress is the intensity of dramatic truth in the modern conversation-piece or *genre* picture.'

Sickert thought of the two-figure compositions, which he produced in great numbers during his Camden Town period, 1905–14, as conversation pieces. These, including the so-called Camden Town Murder series, generally represent a man and woman locked in some intensely dramatic but ambiguous situation. The culminating example is *Ennui* (1914, *fig. 215*), which exists in five oil versions as well as many drawings. The models were the artist's servants, Hubby and Marie Hayes. As with Orchardson's *Mariage de Convenance (fig. 199)*, the theme is a present-day handling of Hogarth's *Marriage A-la-Mode* (especially the second picture of the Viscount and his wife at home, *fig. 11*), although Sickert's middle-aged couple, typically, belong to the lower middle class. Here also setting is an essential agent in the definition of mood. For within the shabbily genteel confines of their parlour, with its imprisoning vertical and horizontal lines, the man and wife convey through their apathetic postures the very image of that ennui to which, under the name of *accidie*, Aldous Huxley attributed the spiritual emptiness of modern society.

The supremely expressive quality of Sickert's painting cannot be better illustrated than in Virginia Woolf's reading of it, given in an imaginary exchange among dinner guests discussing an exhibition of the artist's work in 1924.[27] 'But to me,' proposes one speaker,

Sickert always seems more of a novelist than a biographer. ... He likes to set his characters in motion, to watch them in action. As I remember it, his show was full of pictures that might be stories, as indeed their names suggest. . . . The figures are motionless, of course, but each has been seized in a moment of crisis; it is difficult to look at them and not invent a plot, to hear what they are saying. You remember the picture of the old publican, with his glass on the table before him and a cigar gone cold at his lips, looking out of his shrewd little pig's eyes at the intolerable wastes of desolation in front of him? A fat woman lounges, her arm on a cheap yellow chest of drawers, behind him. It is all over with them, one feels. The accumulated weariness of innumerable days has discharged its burden on them. They are buried under an avalanche of rubbish. In the streets beneath, the trams are squeaking, children are shrieking. Even now somebody is tapping his glass impatiently on the bar counter. She will have to bestir herself; to pull her heavy, indolent body together and go and serve him. The grimness of that situation lies in the fact that there is no crisis; dull minutes are mounting, old matches are accumulating, and dirty glasses and dead cigars; still on they must go, up they must get.

To this someone responds:

And yet it is beautiful . . . satisfactory; complete in some way. Perhaps it is the flash of the stuffed birds in the glass case, or the relation of the chest of drawers to the woman's body; anyhow, there is a quality in that picture which makes me feel that though the publican is done for, and his disillusion complete, still in the other world, of which he is mysteriously a part, without knowing it, beauty and order prevail . . .

In a new and playful departure Sickert produced from the late 1920s and well into the following decade a series of *jeux d'esprit*, named *English Echoes*. The first of these, *c*1927, was derived from the lid of a pomade pot and showed a Highland soldier taking leave of his family on the eve of battle. Henceforth Sickert quarried the wood engravings of the black-and-white illustrators of the 1860s and 1870s for which he had always had a fondness – such figures as Kenny Meadows (1790–1874), Georgie Bowers (1836–1912), Francesco Sargent (active 1840–60), and especially Sir John Gilbert (1817–97). The subject-matter which he appropriated was trivial enough, for the most part humorous or sentimental anecdotes of the kind dear to the Victorian audience for cheap fiction; but with imaginative amplifications in its treatment and transcribed with extreme boldness into glowing colour, it came to new life under his hand. Like the recurrent vogue for the songs of Victorian music halls, these pictures express Sickert's nostalgia for a world to which he had always felt emotionally drawn. More than this, they may be seen as his parting salute to a tradition of painting which had prevailed in Great Britain for two centuries, through an unbroken succession of distinguished genre artists of whom he was the last survivor.

Fig. 214
Walter Richard Sickert
Little Dot Hetherington at the Bedford Music Hall
*c*1888–9

Fig. 215
Walter Richard Sickert
Ennui
1914

NOTES

CHAPTER ONE

1 An even more isolated example, because painted a century earlier, is Joris Hoefnagel's *Wedding at Horsleydown in Bermondsey* (*c*1568–9).

2 The *Autobiographical Notes* refer to the system of 'visual mnemonics' through which the artist trained his memory to retain 'lineally' the sights to which he would later give graphic expression. He 'never', he says, 'accustomed himself to coppy but took the short way of getting objects by heart,' and 'by this means ... was apt [to] catch momentary actions and expressions ...'

3 The closest literary analogue to *The Four Times of the Day* is John Gay's *Trivia: or, the Art of Walking the Streets of London* (1716), with which the artist was certainly familiar and from which he may have taken some slight hints.

4 Details of the activity in this picture have generally been assumed to refer to 29 May, the day commemorating the restoration of Charles II to the throne, annually marked by Jacobite disturbances. The September date, however, as has been plausibly suggested, is more consonant with the ordering of the four scenes to coincide with the successive seasons of the year.

5 Sean Shesgreen, however, in *Hogarth and the Times-of-Day Tradition* presents convincing evidence that in conception and handling Hogarth's series makes satiric play with conventionalized allegorical and Arcadian motifs in Netherlandish versions of the *points-du-jour* theme.

6 It is insufficiently recognized that Hogarth's repeated attacks on received artistic theory were motivated not by disrespect for the acknowledged Old Masters, but by animus against the traffic in fakes, conducted, as he wrote, by '*Picture-Jobbers from abroad*' who imported 'Ship Loads of dead *Christs, Holy Families, Madona's*, and other dismal Dark Subjects, neither entertaining nor Ornamental; on which they scrawl the terrible cramp Names

of some Italian Masters, and fix on us poor *Englishmen*, the character of *Universal Dupes*.' In fact, at periodic intervals throughout his career Hogarth produced pictures which he hoped would gain him acclaim as a history painter. The most ambitious of these were: *The Pool of Bethesda* (*c*1735) and *The Good Samaritan* (1737), which hang on the staircase of St Bartholomew's Hospital; *Moses brought to Pharaoh's Daughter* (1746), presented to the Foundling Hospital; *Paul before Felix* (1748), commissioned by Lincoln's Inn in the hall of which it hangs; and the altarpiece of the Ascension, a triptych painted for St Mary Redcliffe, Bristol (1756).

7 The sign above, labelled *The Stage Mutiny*, is a recondite reference to the threatened demise of Drury Lane Theatre at that time under the management of John Highmore. Note how the figure diving from the church tower and the performer on the slack-rope connect the realm of dramatic illusion with the actual happenings in the square below.

8 Among Hogarth's most important early productions were the two sets of plates which he made for Samuel Butler's burlesque poem, *Hudibras*.

9 Indeed, Betterton had recommended that actors should study the history paintings of such artists as Le Brun and Coypel in developing their own repertoires of gesture and facial expression.

10 Hogarth found support for Le Brun's doctrines in the writing of one of his friends, Dr James Parsons, who in 1747 published a treatise entitled *Human Physiognomy Explain'd*. On the other hand, it is unlikely that he was acquainted with the *Discours prononcés dans les Conférences de l'Académie Royale* (1721) by Antoine Coypel (1661–1722), which provided the fullest and most eloquent discussion of the expressive possibilities of figurative painting, although without accompanying drawings. Coypel's son, Charles Antoine (1694–1752), however, shared his father's physiognomic theories, which he translated into graphic

terms, notably in his illustrations for *Don Quixote*. In his own early illustrations, such as the *Hudibras* plates, Hogarth was indebted to the example of the younger Coypel.

11 His early training as an engraver would also, of course, have made him familiar with the use of heraldic emblems in coats of arms.

12 Hogarth had already employed this allusion in his *Beggar's Opera* pictures, which show Macheath subjected to the rival claims of Lucy and Polly.

CHAPTER TWO

1 One is reminded of Thackeray's admittedly biased comment in *The History of Henry Esmond*: 'Such a man as Charles [II] should have had an Ostade or Mieris to paint him. Your Knellers and Le Bruns only deal in clumsy and impossible allegories; and it hath always seemed to me blasphemy to claim Olympus for such a wine-drabbled divinity as that.'

2 Hogarth satirized this stilted mode of portrait painting in the figure of the Earl in the first picture of *Marriage A-la-Mode*, whose pose comes close to parodying that of Captain Coram.

3 A further telling detail is the hat by Coram's right foot. He had been instrumental in securing more advantageous tariff regulations for London hatters in their colonial trade, and refusing a more substantial reward in gratitude for his services, received the gift of a new hat whenever he needed one.

4 Watteau's fame in England was spread by prints of his pictures. The two folio albums, known as the *Recueil Jullienne*, published in 1735, contained 271 engravings; and it has been estimated that by 1738 there were more than 700 graphic reproductions of his work.

5 Vertue describes him as having 'imploy'd himself in painting conversations Drolls &c ... his thoughts in his pictures shew him to be a Man of *levity*. (of

loose conversation & *morals* suteable to his birth & education. being *low* & *spurious*).'

6 Slightly later, Hayman, Highmore and Gainsborough were to make similar use of lay figures in their compositions, a practice learned from Gravelot.

7 In a letter of 1744 John Russell, a young artist, urged his recently married brother to have a numerous family, giving the following reason: '... it may yield me the opportunity of displaying the utmost of my art in a conversation-piece. In which my Sister [-in-law] and you must be the principal figures, with a groupe of my nephews and nieces, on each side, represented at employments or diversions proper to their age and sex.'

8 Highmore's description of the advantages which the painter enjoys over the writer as story-teller, appearing in *The Gentleman's Magazine*, August 1766, is equally applicable to Hogarth's practice: '... where the principal incidents are crowded into a moment, and are, as it were, instantaneous, there is room for the display of the painter's skill ... Such a story is better and more emphatically told in pictures than in words, because the circumstances that happen at the same time, must, in narration, be successive.'

9 One such manual which may have supplied Hogarth, Highmore and Gainsborough, as well as Devis, with poses was François Nivelon's *Rudiments of Genteel Behaviour* (1737). For this work Dandridge produced twelve designs, which were engraved by Louis-Philippe Boitard instead of Gravelot, who had originally accepted the commission.

10 *The Farmer's Return* was dedicated to Hogarth, who made a drawing engraved by James Basire (1730–1802) as frontispiece to the published version, of which Zoffany's painting is reminiscent in many respects.

11 The *Discobolus* in the left foreground was a later addition to the painting, since it was not discovered until 1791.

12 Returning to England in 1779, he found that his practice had so fallen off that he went to India. During his years there, 1783–9, he painted a number of remarkable conversation pieces of resident English and native dignitaries in local settings.

13 Sometimes the painting of the scenic background was delegated to a landscape artist.

14 In the life-size portraits of his later London period, such as *The Duke and Duchess of Cumberland* (c1783–5) and *William Hallett and his Wife, Elizabeth* known as *The Morning Walk* (1785), Gainsborough achieved an even more integral relationship between scene and subject. In these pictures, however, the landscapes, of which the living figures often seem a subtle emanation, are largely imaginary.

15 An anecdote attaching to the painting indicates what store patrons set by the images created in portraits which they commissioned. On discovering that his wife had been unfaithful to him, Musters instructed another artist to paint out the figures of himself and his wife and to replace them with a pair of grooms leading the horses, whose portraits he was unwilling to sacrifice. Not until 1938 was the work restored to its original appearance.

16 The originality and power of Wright's conception become apparent if his picture is compared with one of a similar experiment by the French artist, C.-A.-P. Vanloo (1719–95), exhibited at the Salon in 1771. Diderot was the first to point out that the spectators in the French work manifest no vestige of interest in the demonstration.

CHAPTER THREE

1 During the 1760s public interest in painting was further encouraged by the establishment of annual exhibitions. The first of these was held in 1760 by a group which two years later took on the name of the Free Society of Artists. In 1761 a more influential group, the Society of Artists in Great Britain (renamed in 1765 the Incorporated Society of Artists in Great Britain, on receiving a royal charter), began to hold exhibitions at its headquarters in Spring Gardens, continuing this practice until 1791. The majority of the leading painters of the time, however, joined the Royal Academy on its foundation in 1768; and from this date its yearly exhibitions were the high point of the season in the artistic realm. The example of the Royal Academy awakened corresponding activity in the provinces, where the Liverpool Society of Arts came into being as early as 1769.

2 Hogarth's fierce candour, although without its humanitarian complexion, survived towards the end of the century in the work of Gillray and Rowlandson. The latter's drawings, in particular, present a matchless panorama of the late eighteenth-century and Regency worlds in all their boisterous vitality; but the realism of Rowlandson's transcriptions of the social scene are too often flawed by the caricaturist's tendency to settle for easy effects through distortion.

3 In the concluding plate of the set he is shown removing a valuable ring from his expiring daughter's finger before *rigor mortis* sets in.

4 In a second series four years later, entitled *The Deserter*, Morland recounted in four pictures the story of a press-ganged recruit who, after deserting from the army and being recaptured, is in the end exonerated and reunited with his wife and children.

5 In 1783 Hogarth's example inspired a pathetic sporting version of the moral progress in Thomas Gooch's *The Life and Death of a Racehorse in Six Stages*. Nine years later the series appeared as prints, accompanied by an essay by Dr Hawksworth, 'tending to excite a benevolent conduct to the Brute Creation'. Other series following in the wake of Hogarth included the anonymous *Modern Harlot's Progress, or Adventures of Harriet Heedless* (1780), and a pair by Maria Cosway, wife of the miniaturist Richard Cosway, entitled *Progress of Female Virtue* and *Progress of Female Dissipation* (both 1800).

6 No subject derived from literature was more popular with artists of the late eighteenth century than the lovelorn Maria of *A Sentimental Journey*. Here is the author's account of Yorick's meeting with her: 'I sat down close by her; and Maria let me wipe them [her tears] away as they fell with my own handkerchief. – I then steep'd it in my own – and then in hers, and then in mine, – and then I wip'd hers again, – and as I did it, I felt such indescribable emotions within me, as I am sure could not be accounted for from any combination of matter and motion.'

7 A formative influence on Greuze's conceptions was Hogarth, engravings of whose works were widely known in France. In his response to Hogarth the French artist anticipated the moralistic bias of later English followers. About 1760 he projected, but never carried beyond some preliminary drawings, a pictorial narrative in twenty-six episodes, to be entitled *Bazile et Thibault, ou les Deux Educations*, closely modelled on *Industry and Idleness*. For the French, Hogarth's reputation as primarily a painter of sentimental genre in Greuze's manner seems to have persisted. Writing as late as 1862, Théophile Gautier could state of *A Rake's Progress*, doubtless with reference to the rake's cast-off mistress who keeps reappearing: 'A travers cette histoire, Hogarth a fait circular adroitement un interêt sentimental et bourgeois bien fait pour toucher les âmes tendres.' And André Malraux asserts in *Saturne: Essai sur Goya* (1950) that: 'L'ironie de la peinture de Hogarth, parce qu'elle est fondée sur un sentimentalisme protestant, retrouve ... un style sentimental.'

8 Hogarth was a pioneer in the production of such pendants with the two versions of his seduction episode, *Before* and *After* (1730–1), as well as in the pair *Beer Street* and *Gin Lane* (1750–1).

9 Fielding's Squire Allworthy is the literary embodiment of all the qualities going to make the man of good will; and a generation later in Dr Primrose, Vicar of Wakefield, Goldsmith showed how readily assimilable the type was to the cult of sensibility.

10 The theme of charity was evidently especially dear to Bigg's heart. Other paintings exhibited by him at the Royal Academy bore the titles: *Schoolboys giving Charity to a Blind Man* (1780), *A Lady and her Children relieving a Distressed Cottager* (1781); *Generous Schoolboys, or the Collection for a Soldier's Widow* (1798). The setting for the last named is a cricket ground.

11 Another painting in which Wheatley dealt with the theme of charity, *Rustic Benevolence* (1797), was derived from a similar work by Gainsborough, *Peasant Family receiving Charity* (1784–7).

12 Hogarth's *The Shrimp Girl* (c1745) might well seem the prototype of the fancy picture, save that it so far transcends the type through the timeless quality imparted by the matchless bravura of the artist's brushwork.

13 Faber engraved two of Chardin's paintings in 1740.

14 The fourteenth, *Pots and Pans to Mend*, was not issued until 1927.

15 The wrapper of the original sets of *Cries of London* bore the title *The Itinerant Trades of London*.

16 Similarly, John Hoppner (1759–1810) painted in 1782 an informal portrait of his wife, the engraving of which was entitled *The Salad Girl*.

17 In this connection it should be remembered that the presence of figures was expected in landscapes at this time, and substantially increased their market value. For scenes devoid of figures Richard Wilson (1713–83) received fifty guineas; when they were present, the price more than doubled.

18 Gainsborough's success in his fancy pictures inspired many imitators around the turn of the nineteenth century. These artists, most of whom worked in other styles as well, especially portrait painting, included James Northcote (1746–1831), John Opie (1761–1807), Richard Westall (1765–1836), William Owen (1769–1825) and Thomas Barker of Bath (1769–1847). Of these Opie, who was largely self-taught, is in many ways the most interesting. The exhibition of his first important genre work at the Royal Academy in 1784, entitled *A School* and derived from Shenstone's poem, *The Schoolmistress*, elicited the following comment from the *Morning Post*: 'Could people in vulgar life afford to pay for pictures, Opie would be their man.'

19 Noteworthy in this connection is another canvas, entitled *Landscape with Farmworkers*, which Lambert painted in collaboration with Hogarth.

20 In the version reproduced the landscape in the right background was extensively repainted by Amos Green (1735–1807).

21 There are remarkably few graphic representations of the cottage industries which accompanied agricultural labour. One example is *Industrious Cottagers* (engraved in 1801) by James Ward, which presents an idealized picture of a group of women and children spinning and lacemaking.

CHAPTER FOUR

1 The affinity between these poems and Dutch genre painting was often remarked upon. Hazlitt, for example, wrote: '... the adept in Dutch interiors, hovels, and pig-styes must find in such a writer as Crabbe a man after his own heart. He is the very thing itself; he paints in words, instead of colours; that's all the difference ...'

2 Girtin and Turner were employed to colour some of these. In 1792 Daniel Orme, who owned approximately one hundred paintings by Morland, opened a second Morland Gallery in Brook Street.

3 A splendid caricature by Gillray of 1807 shows a posthumous exhibition of the dregs of Morland's studio being admired by the connoisseurs for whose critical pretensions the artist had as much contempt as Hogarth.

4 Recent research, however, has shown the extent to which Morland was victimized by his engravers, such as his brother-in-law, William Ward, who did not hesitate to take liberties with the original paintings, giving the figures a more genteel appearance and otherwise toning down the artist's realism to accord with the uninformed tastes of the print-buying public.

5 It is almost impossible to keep track of Morland's incessant flittings from one place to another to escape his creditors. His coastal scenes, for example, were the product of a period of exile on the Isle of Wight.

6 The title of the mezzotint after this painting is *Sun-set: A View in Leicestershire*.

7 Francis William Blagdon wrote of Morland's pictures in the introduction to *Authentic Memoirs of the late George Morland* (1806): '... to the mind of an Englishman they cannot fail to be peculiarly gratifying, as he may contemplate in them the genuine simplicity of his rustic brethren; while the foreigner will, from their inspection, acquire a better knowledge of the manners, appearance, and costume of the great mass of the British people, than he could obtain from the perusal of all the volumes that ever issued from the press.'

8 The catalogue likewise dwelt on the fact that Gainsborough's paintings 'were drawn entirely from English nature'. He was represented by sixty-eight landscapes and fancy pictures, as against only twelve portraits.

9 Boydell's sponsorship of a native tradition was abetted by Thomas Macklin in his two projects, the Poet's Gallery (1787) and an illustrated Bible (1800), and by Robert Bowyer in his illustrated edition of Hume's *History of England* (1792).

10 The rise of art centres in provincial cities, a phenomenon of the early nineteenth century, was usually promoted by the support of local magnates of the middle class. At Bristol, for example, a centre of lively artistic activity from an early date, the principal patrons were three industrialists: John Gibbons, ironmaster; D.W. Acraman, iron founder; and Charles Hare, manufacturer of floor coverings.

11 The artist John Calcott Horsley (1817–1903), remarked somewhat ungratefully of Vernon, who had bought his canvas *The Pride of the Village*, that his 'apparent interest in art was really used simply as a means of lifting him out of obscurity into some sort of *locus standi* in the world.'

12 Wilkie's portrait of *Sir Walter Scott and his Family* (1818), which the novelist described as having 'something in it of a domestic character', represents the great writer, members of his family, and friends, and retainers 'in the garb of south-country peasants ... concocting a merry-making.' Scott himself is dressed as a miller, and his two daughters as ewe-milkers, bare-footed and carrying wooden tubs.

13 Cunningham gave the following vivacious account of the custom: 'The Penny Wedding, of which Allan gives us such a lively image, was in his time common in Scotland, and was one of the many ways which the peasantry had of awakening mirth and giving a "day's discharge to care". As soon as a couple of rustics were proclaimed in the kirk, some nimble-footed friend was employed to summon the country round to the bridal. A large barn was cleared of its grain; split sticks were stuck in the walls to hold candles; a table was placed at the upper end for the graver guests, and all that remained of

space was surrendered freely to those who paid a shilling and desired to dance or be social. The bride was queen of the night till the hour of stocking-throwing came. People of condition mingled with the peasantry; the high-born damsel "set, and reeled, and crossed, and cleeket", with the plough-man – while a shepherd girl went down her two dozen couple of a country dance with the lord or a laird, just as it happened. The money raised went to discharge the cost of music and refreshments; and, according as the young pair were liked, they found a larger or smaller surplus to enable them to begin housekeeping.'

14 Wilkie wrote to Raimbach in December 1835, after learning that they had both been elected Corresponding Members of the Institute of France: 'This is a distinction to which my art could never have arrived – confined in nature to one place – were it not that it has been fortunately combined with yours, the excellence and beauty of which are wafted forth on a thousand wings, and speak simultaneously to all countries, and in all languages.'

15 'We must learn to read pictures and nature as others read books', the artist once remarked to John Burnet. The primary importance which Wilkie attached to the narrative aspect of art comes out in his criticism of David's *Rape of the Sabines*, which he saw during a visit to Paris in 1814: 'Some parts of this picture, particularly the hands, and some parts of the figures and horses, were well drawn; but the composition seemed confused, and without an object to arrest the attention, while the story, whether well adapted for a picture or not, lost its interest entirely from its not being well told.'

16 Sir William Allan, a fellow student in Edinburgh, remarked: 'He seemed to have, even at that early period, an innate feeling for character and expression, as the best of many of his drawings whilst at the Academy can testify ...' This aspect of Wilkie's technique seems particularly to have impressed other artists. Géricault, who during his time in England visited Wilkie while he was at work on the *Chelsea Pensioners* in 1821, wrote of this picture in a letter to Horace Vernet: 'Combien seraient utiles à voir les expressions touchantes de Wilkie! ... Il a varié tous ses caractères avec bien de sentiment ...'

17 According to Haydon, he and Wilkie were responsible for assembling the class at which these lectures were first delivered to help the impoverished young Scottish scientist get a start on his arrival in London. Haydon also asserts that Wilkie made several of the drawings that Bell used as illustrations.

18 For example, in *The Refusal*, taken from Burns' poem 'A Song of Duncan Gray' (1814), a picture which rivals *The Letter of Introduction* in liveliness of implication, Wilkie's sister was the model for Meg, his friend, the painter Mulready, for her suitor, Duncan Gray, and the artist's mother and Mulready's father for the girl's parents.

19 Just how daring West's innovation was may be inferred from the scandalized comment attributed to George III that it was 'very very ridiculous to exhibit heroes in coats, breeches and cock'd hats'. In fact, West had been anticipated by both George Romney and Edward Penny; the former exhibited a painting of Wolfe's death in modern dress in 1763, and Penny followed suit with two versions in 1763 and 1764. These works, however, sacrificed the historical aspect of the event in playing up its sentimental appeal.

20 Wellington told Lord Lyndhurst, Copley's son, that 'It was the only picture of a battle that ever satisfied him or displayed the reality of the scene, inasmuch as the artist had only attempted to represent *one* incident and but a small portion of the field – the rest being necessarily concealed by smoke and dust.' The pictures by West and Copley were the prelude to a number of panoramic battle scenes produced around the turn of the century and attesting a growing sense of national pride in England's military prowess, as demonstrated in the Napoleonic Wars. Painted by such artists as de Loutherbourg, they aimed at realism of effect, but dwelt primarily on the spectacular aspects of the scenes depicted.

21 At an earlier period Wilkie also worked from clay models, which he coloured and arranged in an enclosed box duplicating the picture's setting to help solve problems of composition and lighting. This practice may account for the fact that his subjects, such as *The Rent Day* (1807) and *Distraining for Rent* (1815), were found suitable for presentation as *tableaux-vivants*.

22 The central role of this soldier may convey, it has been suggested, a flattering allusion to West's painting of *The Death of General Wolfe*.

23 In his later historical paintings, such as *The Defence of Saragossa* (1828), *The Peep o' Day Boy's Cabin* (1836), and *The Empress Josephine and the Fortune Teller* (1837), Wilkie continued to emphasize the anecdotal aspects of his subjects. Despite their other artistic merits (and they have been unduly neglected), the breadth of conception and freer methods of handling paint which the artist brought back from his long stay in Italy and Spain (1825–8) did not lend themselves to the intimacy of the genre manner on which his fame had been established.

24 Haydon states that Benjamin West asked Wilkie to withdraw his painting, *The Wardrobe Ransacked*, from the Academy exhibition of 1811 for fear that it would not stand competition with Bird's submission in that year, *The Reading of the Will Concluded*.

25 'This little drama is rendered with that exquisite sense of expression and of pantomime which seems to have been the prerogative of English painters since Hogarth. ... they bring to their work a subtlety of analysis, care in composition and a study of facial expressions which are all their own.'

26 At the Victoria and Albert Museum is a series of drawings by Mulready entitled *Twelve Heads: with regard to the Influence of Zodiacal Signs*, exhibited in 1864 (the year after the artist's death), though they clearly date from much earlier.

27 One recalls in this connection Hogarth's visit to the death-cell of the condemned murderess, Sarah Malcolm, in order to paint her portrait.

28 Wilkie's patrons were equally prone to read patriotic meanings into his pictures. Allan Cunningham recounts the following anecdote with regard to *The Cut Finger* (1809), which depicts a boy holding out a finger which he has hurt while putting the mast into a toy boat: 'This picture was, when it appeared first, called The Young Navigator by the purchaser Mr Whitbread, who desired to see in its story the maritime glory of England in the dawn; but a boy who cried at the sight of his own blood was not considered a true representative of our conquering tars, and the picture soon took the humbler name which the great painter at first bestowed upon it.'

29 Tacit acknowledgment that popular art might encourage the competitive mood of the times occurs in a description in the *Art Union* for 1839 of Thomas Webster's *Foot Ball*, exhibited in that year: 'The whole scene is capital – the eager urchins rush forward in the very spirit of rivalry; each ardently struggles to get "the ball at his foot", as he will do for more important purposes in after life.'

30 Mulready's technical mastery did not compensate for his mundane subject-matter in the view of some critics. Ruskin, for example, wrote that 'having obtained a consummate method of execution, he has thrown it away on subjects either altogether uninteresting, or above his powers, or unfit for pictorial representation.'

31 As has been pointed out, the bather in the foreground was modelled on Titian's *Venus Anadyomene*, while the background contains borrowings from Michelangelo's *Battle of Cascina*.

32 Although they contained a sampling of fugitive poetry and prose, which began to appear in the mid-1820s and enjoyed their heyday during the following decade, existed primarily for their illustrations. They bore such titles as *Friendship's Offering* (1825), *The Amulet* (1827), *The Forget-Me-Not* (1828), *The Keepsake* (the longest lived of all those publications, which ran from 1828 to 1857 under the editorship of Lady Emmeline Stuart Wortley) and *The Book of Beauty* (1833–49), edited by the Countess of Blessington. The exquisitely finished steel engravings generally took the form of portraits of pretty women, exotically garbed and posed in romanticized settings. One of the publishers' favourite artists was Edmund Thomas Parris (1793–1873), whose contributions included feminine portraits deriving their titles from flowers and gems; but the trade in these publications was sufficiently lucrative to attract the services of many of the leading artists of the time, including Turner, Landseer, and Frith. Thackeray lost no opportunity to pour contempt on them as tending 'to encourage bad taste in the public, bad engraving, and worse painting'. Nevertheless, the Keepsake illustrations in turn inspired a number of artists, such as Charles Baxter (1809–79), to produce original oils in the same manner. The 'Baxter girls', as they came to be known, were mawkish versions of the eighteenth-century fancy piece, and their appearance gave a foretaste of the cloying sweetness characteristic of so much Victorian subject painting.

33 Woolner, however, found grounds in this painting for an entertaining allegorical interpretation: 'In "Happy as a King", our artist, to carry out the fancy of his title, has judiciously placed his little rustic king swinging on the top rail of the gate, with his arms spread aloft in delight. Also riding, but on lower rails, are a boy and girl, who, supporting his state, look up to him for countenance, and do duty as grace and strength: labour is embodied in the sturdy boy running the gate to and fro, and who is using his utmost energies for the others' enjoyment. While unnoticed by either, on the ground lies a small weakling, who has fallen; hinting at the feeble and neglected classes.'

34 Constable got his wish, but only posthumously when *The Cornfield* was acquired by private subscription for presentation to the National Gallery as a memorial to him. The selection committee may well have thought that its unusually specific detail would appeal to the public.

35 The fact that Collins, although twelve years younger, was made a full member of the Royal Academy in 1820, nine years before Constable, doubtless accounts in part for the latter's animosity. With regard to Boucher's *pastorales* he stated in his second lecture on landscape painting, delivered on 2 June 1836: 'His landscape, of which he was evidently fond, is pastoral; and such pastorality! The pastoral of the opera-house. ... His scenery is a bewildered dream of the picturesque. From cottages adorned with festoons of ivy, sparrow pots, etc., are seen issuing opera dancers with mops, brooms, milk pails, and guitars; children with cocked hats, queues, bag wigs, and swords, – and cats, poultry, and pigs. The scenery is diversified with winding streams, broken bridges, and water wheels; hedge stakes dancing minuets – and groves bowing and curtsying to each other; the whole leaving the mind in a state of bewilderment and confusion, from which laughter alone can relieve it.'

36 The Arcadian dream haunting eighteenth-century painting achieved visionary intensity in the work of Samuel Palmer (1805–81), especially during his Shoreham period of the late 1820s and early 1830s. His long-lived father-in-law John Linnell (1792–1882) continued to work this vein, with progressively declining conviction, in the popular landscapes he painted far into the Victorian period. The novelist George Eliot might have had Linnell's pastorals in mind when she stated that English painters display 'a total absence of acquaintance and sympathy with our peasantry ... even those among our painters who aim at giving the rustic type of features, who are far above the effeminate feebleness of the "Keepsake" style, treat their subjects under the influence of traditions and prepossessions rather than of direct observation. ... The painter is still under the influence of idyllic literature, which has always expressed the imagination of the cultivated and town-bred, rather than the truth of rustic life.'

37 As early as 1831, *Fraser's Magazine*, always caustic in its derision of current fads, stated: 'We have had enough, and more than enough, of the familiar in the humours of the dog-kennel ... and the waggeries of mischievous schoolboys.'

38 A society for the prevention of cruelty to animals was established in England in 1824.

39 Cosmo Monkhouse elaborated on this distinction in an article in the *Art Journal* (1879) about the two artists: 'The moral as well as the physical resemblances between man and brute were caught and utilised by both artists: the one [Landseer] mainly for the exaltation of the brute, the other mainly for the depreciation of man.'

CHAPTER FIVE

1 Of this exhibition Redgrave wrote: 'To pass from the grand salons appropriated in the Palais des Beaux Arts to French and Continental works, into the long gallery of British pictures, was to pass at once from the midst of warfare and its incidents, from passion, strife and bloodshed, from martyrdoms and suffering, to the peaceful scenes of home.'

2 Of the general impression created by this exhibition the *Art Journal* declared with patriotic fervour: '... the pictures in the "British Division" are truthful to nature, honest in sentiment, simple and heartfelt in subject, thoroughly earnest and independent in treatment, and as such are worthy of our people, thus serving as an index of our character, and therefore rising to the dignity and worth of a national and representative Art.'

3 The eventual disposal of some of these collections by auction not only vindicated the good judgement of the original owners, but helped establish the reputations of the artists represented through the prices which their pictures commanded. This was the case with the sale in 1863 of the collection assembled by Elhanan Bicknell, a dealer in whale-oil, which realized nearly £60,000. An even more notable example was the Gillott sale of 1872, including 365 oils, of which all but sixty were English. For these bidders paid a total of £130,547 4s, individual pictures bringing as much as ten times the price paid by Gillott when he commissioned them.

4 To cite only one example, Flatow, who paid Frith the handsome price of £5,250 for his painting of *The Railway Station*, sold it to the print dealer Henry Graves for £16,300.

5 Yet another factor in the growth of the print trade was the abolition in 1845 of the duty on glass imported from the Continent, as a result of which the cost of framing prints was brought within the reach of the humblest art-lover.

6 In Thackeray's view the Art-Unions exercised a corrupting influence on young painters. 'As one looks round the rooms of the Royal Academy,' he wrote, 'one cannot but deplore the fate of the poor fellows who have been speculating upon the Art-Unions; and yet in the act of grief there is a lurking satisfaction. The poor fellows can't sell their pictures; that is a pity. But why did the poor fellows paint such fiddle-faddle pictures? They catered for the *bourgeois*, the sly rogues! ... they are flinging themselves under the wheels of that great golden Juggernaut of an Art-Union. Alas! it is not for art they paint, but for the Art-Union!' Thackeray's

scorn for this enterprise was shared by Samuel Rogers, the venerable poet and art collector, who once remarked: 'The Art-Union is a perfect curse: it buys and engraves very inferior pictures, and consequently encourages mediocrity of talent; it makes young men, who have no genius, abandon the desk and counter, and set up for painters.'

7 In 1842 there were about twenty printsellers in London; by the 1860s 126 were registered with the Association. Between 1847 and 1894, the organization listed 4,823 plates.

8 The art criticism appearing in British periodicals was at a low ebb throughout the greater part of the nineteenth century. The fact that most notices of pictures in the *Art Journal* were devoted to detailed description of their narrative or anecdotal content speaks volumes with regard to how they were supposed to be viewed.

9 'Frith', wrote William Bell Scott, 'will be much thought of in some future day because he has illustrated the age in which we live.' In *Architectural Review* (September 1956) Sir Nikolaus Pevsner has verified the topographical fidelity of the parade of architecture along the cliffs in the background of this painting, in support of his contention that Frith was 'considerably more than a meticulous recorder'.

10 To the original, at the Tate Gallery, Frith actually preferred the slightly smaller replica now at Manchester, feeling that in the latter he had been more successful in handling the effects of light and shade.

11 This episode had autobiographical bearings. During his visit to the races Frith was on the verge of being similarly taken in when saved by the intervention of his companion, Augustus Egg.

12 Indeed, many of the figures in the throng have been identified as actual portraits. The buyer of the picture, Flatow, is shown in conversation with the engine-driver; Frith, along with his wife and children, posed for the family group; and the original of the foreigner disputing with the cab-driver was a Venetian nobleman employed to give Italian lessons to the artist's daughters.

13 For the sake of accuracy in depicting Paddington Station, Frith called in the services of W. Scott Morton, an architectural draughtsman, as well as a professional photographer, Samuel Fry.

14 The artist thus evened the score with Wilde, who once remarked of Frith that he had 'done so much to elevate painting to the dignity of photography.'

15 In her catalogue for the exhibition of Hicks at the Geffrye Museum in 1982–3, Rosamond Allwood suggests two other possible sources for the artist's treatment of the scene, in Charles Manby Smith's *Curiosities of London Life* (1854) and George Augustus Sala's *Twice round the Clock* (1859). In particular, she calls attention to compositional similarities between Hicks' picture and William M'Connell's illustration for Sala's work, 'The Newspaper Window at the General Post Office'.

16 Ritchie painted a pendant, *A Winter's Day in St James's Park* (1858), as well as a lively scene on *Hampstead Heath* (1859).

17 Indeed, according to the artist, the Prince of Wales was perplexed by the fact that Hunt's picture did not include portraits of the royal couple, until the artist pointed out to him that the picture 'dealt only with *London Bridge by Night on the Occasion of the Marriage*, crowded by the mob viewing the illuminations.'

18 The care with which Gregory built up his composition was indicated by the exhibition at the Maas Gallery in 1970 of nearly fifty pencil, crayon, and watercolour studies for *Boulter's Lock*.

19 The *Illustrated London News* recognized the originality of the painter's conception: 'Bravo! Mr. Brown, we would at once exclaim for the boldness of representing as your principal hero that potent agent in the work of British civilization, the excavator or "navvy".... We applaud, also, the variously suggestive, and by no means squeamish, way in which the theme "Work" is illustrated, positively and negatively. ... We applaud, we repeat, the honest effort to represent the actualities of workaday life.' In the opinion of Francis Taylor Palgrave, Brown's achievement entitled him to 'one of the leading places among our very small but honoured company of genuine historical painters. ... His "Work" is simply the most truthfully pathetic, and yet least sentimental, rendering of the dominant aspect of English life that any of our painters have given us.'

20 A slightly smaller version, similar in most respects, was made for James Leathart of Newcastle, and is now in Birmingham.

21 The monthly instalments of Dickens' *Bleak House* were appearing when Brown began to paint his picture; and it seems probable that the model for this reformer was the prohibitionist, Mrs Pardiggle, whose 'rapacious benevolence' Dickens ridicules.

22 For discussion of other evidence of Brown's debt to Hogarth, see the author's 'The making of Ford Madox Brown's *Work*', in *Victorian Artists and the City: A Collection of Critical Essays*, ed. I. B. Nadal and F. S. Schwarzbach, Pergamon Press, 1980. Brown was a founding member of the short-lived Hogarth Club, which between 1858 and 1861 provided the Pre-Raphaelite painters and their associates with an opportunity to exhibit their works elsewhere than at the Royal Academy. According to William Michael Rossetti, Brown suggested that the club be named after 'a painter whom he deeply reverenced as the originator of moral invention and drama in modern art.'

23 A comparison of this figure with Wheatley's 'Seller of Primroses' from the *Cries of London* is instructive, as it suggests how far social awareness had developed in two generations.

24 During the mid-1860s Sharples painted a companion piece to *The Forge*, entitled *The Smithy*.

25 A notable exception to this is the pair of enormous frescoes, *The Meeting of Blücher and Wellington after the Battle of Waterloo* (1861) and *The Death of Nelson* (1865), which Daniel Maclise (1806–70) painted for the Royal Gallery of the new Palace of Westminster, and of which Dante Gabriel Rossetti wrote that they united 'the value of almost

contemporary record with that wild legendary fire and contagious heart-pulse of hero-worship which are essential for the transmission of epic events through art.'

26 Such was the popularity of *Eastward Ho!* that in the following year O'Neil painted a pendant, *Home Again*, showing the return of the forces, including several figures appearing in the preceding picture.

27 Arthur Boyd Houghton was almost alone among contemporary painters in his iconoclastic attitude towards manifestations of patriotic fervour. In such small oils as *Recruiting Party* (1859), praised by the *Athenaeum* for 'its Hogarthian fullness and variety', *Volunteers marching out* (1860), and *Volunteers* (1860) he wittily satirized the recruiting of raw youths for the colonial army and, especially, the manning of the Rifle Volunteers, the company formed to repel a fancied French invasion in 1859–60. Later in 1870–2 as special artist and illustrator for *Graphic* he recorded with uncompromising realism the excesses of the Franco-Prussian War and the Paris Commune. Van Gogh, who greatly admired Houghton's work, wrote that 'he had something ghostly, or rather mysterious, like Goya'.

28 The Pre-Raphaelite concentration on facial expression particularly impressed Walter Sickert, who said of Millais that his 'interest was in faces'; and of Rossetti that his 'dramas were conceived firstly and chiefly in an attempt at facial expression.... They fall under the heading of the art of grimace.'

29 For example, *First Letter from the Emigrants* (1849) by Thomas Faed; *Answering the Emigrant's Letter* (1850) by James Collinson (1825–81); *A Letter from the Colonies* (1852) by Thomas Webster; and *The Emigrant's Last Sight of Home* (1859) by Richard Redgrave.

30 The two versions of *First Class: The Meeting* are often cited to illustrate the Victorian artist's subservience to contemporary mores. As originally presented, the young man is paying court to the girl seated opposite him, while her father dozes in the corner. Taken to task for the impropriety of this situation, Solomon radically revised its conception, moving the girl to coy retirement in the corner seat and converting her admirer into a very proper naval officer, whose attention is now monopolized by the father.

31 In addition to the original at Birmingham, there is another version at the Fitzwilliam Museum, Cambridge, and one in watercolour at the Tate Gallery.

32 Henry James called Brown's *Farewell to England*: '... an example of his queer, hard, ugly, but rich and full sincerity.... It would take more time than I command to give an idea of the curious "middle-class" poetry and prose of this work and say over all that it adds up, as it were, to hand you, on a total made grimly distinct and without an attenuating flourish, as straight as an unpaid bill. The intensity is extraordinary; marvellous the truth, the flatness, the directness of the "British" note, and the wealth of drama in the faces; the force, above all, of the discrimination between the emotion of the woman and the emotion of the man. These things and fifty others make the picture surely one of the most expressive in the world.'

33 An untypical work by George Frederick Watts (1817–1904), entitled *The Irish Famine* (1849), is similar in its representation of economic degradation, although Watts lent to his outcasts a greater measure of dignity. (The composition of Watts' painting evokes traditional representations of the rest on the flight into Egypt.) Their fellows also appear as the migrant workers asleep below the railing in Brown's *Work*.

34 The best-known painting of the subject was French, Gustave Courbet's *Casseurs de Pierre* (1849), which no longer exists.

35 The success of Redgrave's efforts to arouse public feeling was attested by a fellow artist, Paul Falconer Poole (1807–79), who wrote to him with regard to *The Sempstress*: 'Believe me, I think it the most powerful for truth and touching from its pathos of any picture I have ever seen. Who can help exclaiming, "Poor soul! God help her"? If any circumstance could make me wage war against present social arrangements, and make us go down shirtless to our graves, it is the contemplation of this truthful and wonderful picture.' Others, however, voiced reservations over the artist's treatment of his source. The critic of the *Literary Gazette* stated that 'the real picture for the lyric would be too saddening if painted, and our artist has only reached a sort of theatrical and elegant sorrow'; while in Thackeray's opinion Redgrave had 'illustrated every thing except the humour, the manliness, and the bitterness of the song. He has only depicted the tender, good-natured part of it.'

36 Watts' grim painting, *Found Drowned* (1848–50), illustrates one such case which the artist had witnessed.

37 The actual setting of the painting, on the evidence of Hunt's daughter, was a *maison de convenance* at Woodbine Villa, 7 Alpha Place, St John's Wood.

38 Still other examples are Richard Redgrave's *The Outcast* (1851) and Henry O'Neil's *Return of the Wanderer* (1855).

39 In its exhibition notice the *Art Journal* observed of Egg's paintings: 'Although the domestic wreck exhibited in these pictures ... may be in real life of daily occurrence, it is a subject too poignant for a series of paintings. We are saturated by the public prints with the details of such incidents, and would rather fall back upon the consoling influences of Art.'

40 In this connection the continuing prevalence in Victorian subject painting of situations gleaned from popular novels, plays, and historical works should be noted.

41 'Nothing is better proof of the danger of too subtle or too literary intentions in painting than the error that I committed in analysing this picture, and which I stand by intentionally here.'

42 Not everyone, however, endorsed this opinion. The novelist George Eliot wrote of Hunt's picture in the *Westminster Review* (1856): '... he gave us a landscape of marvellous truthfulness, [but] placed a pair of peasants in the foreground who were not much more real than the idyllic swains and damsels of our chimney ornaments.'

43 The partially eaten apple in the hands of the youngest girl, emblematic of the passing of youth and innocence, is analogous in its symbolic impact to the scythe-blade that so disturbingly protrudes into Millais' idyll of youth in a flowering orchard, *Apple Blossoms (Spring)* (1856–9).

CHAPTER SIX

1 Members of Agnew's staff were habitually present at the annual exhibition of the Royal Academy to arrange for the sale of pictures previously acquired in this way.

2 Writing in 1883 of contemporary painters and their patrons, William Archer Shee stated: 'The apathy, the neglect, and the ignorance that marked feeling in England regarding English painters have given place to a costly, indiscriminating and rackless patronage which, however calculated it may be to promote the interests of individual artists, is unlikely, from its origin, to be lasting, and is not of a nature to raise the character of the art of the professional. ... the movement is unsound and essentially commercial. ... it may be said that no picture, at the present day, by a comparatively unknown hand, creeps into the public interest by the simple force of its artistic merit.'

3 Gambart, who had paid Hunt 5,500 guineas for his painting, *The Finding of the Saviour in the Temple* (1854–60), including copyright and exhibition rights, wrote in November 1860 to a printseller of his plans for the engraving, which he estimated would cost an additional £3,000: 'I propose to Print from 1,000 to 2,000 artists' Proofs at 15 Gs, 1,000 Before letters Proofs at 12 Gs, 1,000 Proofs at 8 Gs, & I hope 10,000 Prints at 5 Gs – I have now already orders which I can Submit to you for verification amounting to 10,000 Gs, & I have no doubt these orders will reach 50,000 Gs in 4 years.'

4 Millais was not unaware that the panache of his later manner did not compensate for the emotional intensity infusing paintings of his Pre-Raphaelite period during the 1850s. On visiting a retrospective exhibition at the Grosvenor Gallery in 1886, he is said to have remarked: 'I'm not ashamed of avowing that I have so far failed in my maturity to fulfil the full forecast of my youth.'

5 For example, *Cherry Ripe* inspired one correspondent, who called himself 'an humble Cannok', to send from Athole Bank, Hamilton, Ontario, a poem designed to express 'some little portion of the gratitude of Canadians towards one who had done so much to brighten the homes of the Anglo-Saxon race all over the world with his wonderful creations.' The fact that works of this sort, whatever the artist's intention, so readily lent themselves to such observations shows how little the ordinary viewer of the time was inclined to judge a picture on its own merits, or indeed was capable of doing so.

6 Soap manufacturers seem to have taken the lead in promoting the advertising potential of paintings.

To publicize its product Pears also used a painting by James Hayllar (1829–1920), entitled *Soap Suds*, showing two girls lathering their hands in a wash-basin. And in 1889, before he began to form his collection of paintings, Lord Leverhulme appropriated Frith's *New Frock* (1889) to recommend the soap which he manufactured. The artist was justifiably incensed to see his picture reproduced with the subtitle, 'So Clean' on one side of the garment and 'Sunlight Soap' above the sitter's head.

7 No English artist dared to match the horrifying glimpses into the London underworld revealed by two French artists: Sulpice-Guillaume Chevalier, known as Gavarni (1804–66), whose wood-engravings of derelict city dwellers appeared in *L'Illustration* in 1850–1, and in a subsequent series of lithographs entitled *Les Anglais chez eux*; and Gustave Doré (1832–83), whose illustrations for *London: A Pilgrimage* (1872), with text by William Blanchard Jerrold, remain the supreme graphic indictment of slum life in the Victorian metropolis.

8 Frequent references in Vincent van Gogh's correspondence during the years 1873–6, when he lived in England, attest to his admiration for the engravings in *Graphic* (as well as in the more conservative *Illustrated London News*). In the years immediately following he formed a large collection of them.

9 The general acclaim was not, however, unanimous. The critic in the *Art Journal*, while admitting the stern actuality of Fildes' representation of 'human misery', went on to say: 'These deformed and wretched creatures who wait for admission to a wretched resting-place, are only admissible into art that is indifferent to beauty.... But looking now, as we are bound to do, only to considerations purely artistic, there is little in a theme of such grovelling misery to recommend it to a painter whose purpose is beauty. ... The state of things he [Fildes] represents to us ought rather to be removed than to be perpetuated, and its introduction into art which should be permanent is rather matter for regret.'

10 John Thomson, who with Adolphe Smith published in monthly parts *Street Life in London* (1877–8), a photographic record of the city's underworld, wrote: 'The precision and accuracy of photography enables us to present true types of the London poor and shields us from the accusation of either under-rating or exaggerating individual peculiarities of appearance.'

11 'My painting simply represents a girl dressed in white standing in front of a white curtain.' In an important notice the French critic, Paul Mantz, referred to Whistler's picture as a *Symphonie du blanc*. The artist took over the musical analogy as descriptive of his intent, and in 1872 renamed the composition *Symphony in White, No. 1*.

12 '*The bride on the day after her wedding*, the disturbing moment when a young woman questions herself, and is astonished no longer to find in herself the virgin of the day before.'

13 *Variations in Flesh Colour and Green: The Balcony* (1867–8) preserves the format of the conversation piece, much as *Wapping* does, in the grouping of the figures on a balcony and the use of the Thames at Battersea as a backdrop; but the models, derived from an eighteenth-century woodcut by Kiyonaga, lack any individuality, and with their colourful oriental garments are arranged simply as elements in a design. Whistler's fondness for double titles, however, one abstract and one substantive, indicates that he continued to derive his compositions from observation of the phenomenal world.

14 After scrupulous inspection of the intricate network of masts, spars, and halyards, a nautical contemporary declared of this picture, 'Blast if I can see a single thing wrong with the rigging.' The figures in the painting were modelled on seafaring friends whom the artist had met in his early London days, the bearded man being Captain John Freebody, and the pair at the right being his wife, Margaret Kennedy, and her brother, Captain Lumley Kennedy. They appear in other shipboard pictures by Tissot, notably *Boarding the Yacht* and *The Captain and the Mate* (both 1873). Captain Freebody was master of the *Warwick Castle*, 1870–2, and of the *Arundel Castle*, 1872–3; so the setting of *The Last Evening* is presumably the deck of one or the other.

15 The uncertainty of response which Tissot's paintings invite is matched by their titles, which often exist in various forms.

16 There is further evidence of the traditional roots of Tissot's art in four portraits of Mrs Newton, dressed to represent the seasons of the year, painted 1878–80.

17 'The heroism of modern life surrounds us and presses in on us ... The true painter will be he who can wrest the epic quality from real life; and make us see and understand, through colour or design, how great and poetic we are in our cravats and polished boots.'

18 A third picture, *The First Cloud* (1887), is often viewed as belonging to this sequence, although the husband is represented as a much younger man.

19 The painting, then given the title *An Enigma* (1891), is in the Kirkcaldy Museum and Art Gallery.

20 Sargent's virtuosity in adapting traditional modes to contemporary tastes is nowhere more apparent than in his rehabilitation of the conver-

sation piece, examples being the charmingly informal diploma work, *An Interior in Venice* (1889–1900), and the more posed *The Sitwell Family* (1900). In commissioning the latter as a pendant to Copley's *Sitwell Children* (1786), Sir George Sitwell stipulated that it should be a family portrait 'that will give information and tell its own story'.

21 A similar reciprocal relationship existed between the Newlyn painters and Emerson's contemporary, Frank Meadow Sutcliffe (1853–1941), whose photographs provide an intimate picture of life in the fishing town of Whitby.

22 The great line of black-and-white illustrators, Cruikshank, Leech, Keene, du Maurier and Phil May, who found most of their material in the city, is of course, an exception to this.

23 In his 'Ten O'Clock Lecture' Whistler sought to conjure up in words some of the magic which the city disclosed to the painter's eye: 'And when the evening mist clothes the riverside with poetry, as with a veil, and the poor buildings lose themselves in the dim sky, and the tall chimneys become campanili, and the warehouses are palaces in the night, and the whole city hangs in the heavens, and fairy-land is before us – then the wayfarer hastens home; the working man and the cultured one, the wise man and the one of pleasure, cease to understand, as they have ceased to see, and Nature, who for once, has sung in tune, sings her exquisite song to the artist alone, her son and her master – her son in that he loves her, her master in that he knows her.'

24 Sir Osbert Sitwell is authority for the fact that Sickert was a great admirer of Marcellus Laroon. Among his contemporaries he singled out for praise Orchardson and John Pettie, whom he regarded as 'descendants of Rubens, through Wilkie'.

25 An article by Sickert on Frith's *Derby Day* (*Burlington Magazine*, 1922) contains the following ironic passage: 'The great paintings of the world are got out of the way by the convenient anathema of "illustration". Mantegna, Michelangelo, Veronese, Canaletto, Ford Madox Brown, Hogarth, Leech, Keene, *e tutti quanti*, falling, certainly, under the heading of "illustration", must, I am afraid, go. Rubens, ... and a few other worms of that ilk, can still be mentioned in decent company, but only, if you please, as "the ancestors of Cézanne"!'

26 Indeed, there is a double reflection; for a second mirror at the left duplicates the crowded theatre box mirrored at the upper right.

27 This dialogue in which Sickert delighted was based on the smaller version of *Ennui* at the Ashmolean Museum, the composition of which departs in no important respect from the Tate version.

INDEX